INSIDE THE IRON WORKS

7/08

INSIDE THE IRON WORKS
How Grumman's Glory Days Faded

George M. Skurla

AND

William H. Gregory

Ingram 8/04

NAVAL INSTITUTE PRESS
Annapolis, Maryland

Naval Institute Press
291 Wood Road
Annapolis, MD 21402

© 2004 by George M. Skurla and William H. Gregory

All photos, unless otherwise noted, are courtesy of Northrop Grumman.

Library of Congress Cataloging-in-Publication Data
Gregory, William H.
        Inside the Iron Works : how Grumman's glory days faded /
William H. Gregory and George M. Skurla.
        p. cm.
        Includes index.
        ISBN 1-55750-329-X (alk. paper)
        1. Skurla, George M. 2. Aerospace engineers—Biography. 3. Grumman
Aerospace Corporation—History. 4. United States. Navy—Aviation—History.
I. Skurla, George M. II. Title.
        TL540.S5736G74 2004
        629.13'0092—dc22
                                                        2004003601

Printed in the United States of America on acid-free paper ∞

11 10 09 08 07 06 05 04   9 8 7 6 5 4 3 2
First printing

CONTENTS

This book is dedicated to the Grumman family.

The beginning was the spark from Leroy Grumman and the founding fathers, passed to management and on to the workers on the shop floor, and to the engineers who designed the great war birds for the Navy's war years and to the test pilots who first flew them.

Thomas J. Kelly's Lunar Excursion Module opened Cape Kennedy's door to us and made Grumman a partner with NASA to help the nation realize its dreams for space.

We may be part of an unfulfilled destiny for Grumman, but at least we are part of its destiny, and it lives today in Northrop Grumman.

We are the Grumman men, women, and kids who followed in their parents' footsteps.

This is our story.

—MRS. GEORGE SKURLA
from George's notes

PREFACE

N AVAL AVIATORS CHRISTENED GRUMMAN AIRCRAFT ENGINEERING as the Iron Works because of the habit its battle-damaged airplanes had of getting their pilots back to the carrier deck. That name stuck, even though dedicated Grummanites like George Skurla didn't savor the name later as the jet age and maneuverability made it sound pokey.

This is George Skurla's story from inside the Iron Works, his eye-witness account or recollections from associates, of how Grumman became the toast of the Navy in World War Two. Grumman carried on as a naval aviation pillar through the Korean War and Vietnam, through what seemed to be a perpetual Cold War, and then lost its navy cachet and finally its independence with an unwelcome merger when the Berlin Wall came down. George, a frustrated naval aviator himself, saw all of this happen, as a young apprentice engineer, as a mid-level engineering manager, as president and chief operating officer of Grumman Aerospace Company from 1974 to 1985, and finally as elected president of Grumman Corporation in 1985.

His story is personal history, not the footnoted kind that makes textbooks. Neither is it a memoir. Many of the recollections here are just that: recollections—with all their pitfalls. His perspective is that of "I was there," not that of a researcher. His opinions are salty in more ways than one, of a player in industrial achievement that liter-ally landed on the moon and later ended his career in frustration. Along the road he learned about managing people, managing tech-nology, and managing operations. How did George look at this process? To me, George was typical of the Grumman culture: make it practical, make it work, and rely on common sense, not airy theories.

Here are a few of his pungent ideas on management gleaned from conversations George and I had early in our collaboration.

- *On subordinates:* "Anyone could walk in," he said, "and tell me, 'You're all screwed up boss. This isn't going anywhere.' Then I wanted to be able to say, in so many words, 'baloney' and argue about it. Finally, with a decision, I could say, 'I hear you talking, but I have right to be wrong, too. I want to do this, and I want your full—not halfhearted—support. If it's going off the cliff you better pound me in the head. Your responsibility is to stop me from committing suicide.'"

- *On people:* Don't try to play the game alone was his bylaw. Good people meant people who are loyal, and, especially, emotionally involved in what they are doing, willing to sacrifice their personal lives to get something significant accomplished. He was never too keen on the smart academic types. More to his taste were the salts of the earth that had survived the factory floor and grown through the ranks, absorbing their hits and misses. Not just wisdom, but experience, too, was valued. Most important, to build airplanes, people have to be dedicated to them.

- *On going outside the company for talent:* A company has to augment its inside capability with outside talent. George plumped for that, although to his colleagues he often seemed to stand for the opposite. When Grumman's corporate leadership wanted to move him over to that aerie, he argued that it wasn't the right thing to do. Grumman's corporate future was hanging in balance, and he thought it needed someone from outside who understood and could make acquisitions or mergers. He didn't convince them.

- *On strategic planning:* McDonnell Douglas, Grumman's chief rival with the Navy, did a lot of "here's what we ought to be doing" planning. George's espousal for Grumman to do the same never went anywhere in the company. Too bad, for with a good plan comes understanding of where the organization is, how it got there, and where it should be ten years in the future—a strong sense of where to go, but with big ears to the people you hold in high value around you.

Diversification as it played out later at Grumman dismayed George—and many of his coworkers at Grumman are even more caustic—though he was not an enemy of diversification per se. His story of diversification is enough to furnish business-school case study material for aerospace and defense companies. Can a defense business be managed strategically or is it like war, unpredictable and a matter of who makes the fewest mistakes—the luck of the draw? George held with the first proposition, and he agonized off and on as we worked on this book about whether he should have made a suicide charge against diversification. Grumman's story in a sense is of too little diversification by its founders much too late.

So much changed from the days when Grumman's imprint decorated more rudder pedals on a carrier's deck than any other. Yet Grumman never stopped building airplanes completely. Though it delivered its last new production F-14D to the Navy in 1993, the last new airplane from Long Island was an E-2C early-warning-radar aircraft for Taiwan delivered from Calverton in 1995, after the company was acquired by Northrop. New E-2Cs and refurbished ones still roll out of a plant in St. Augustine, Florida, and refurbished JointSTARS 707s are fitted out with ground target tracking electronics at a Grumman-built plant in Melbourne, Florida. George considered JointSTARS the wave of the future and, thinking so, he reiterated the phrase "unfulfilled destiny," sometimes in indignation, sometimes in frustration. That was a good summation of what follows.

George and I started working on this book in 1998 and the interviews and taping stretched over the next three years. He had a mission. Having spent his working life at Grumman, he was profoundly proud of the company's accomplishments but wounded at its final descent into an acquisition that he was convinced should have been Grumman's to make. Unfulfilled destiny is a constant phrase in this book, for that is what frustrated George about Grumman so much in the later days of his life.

As our work slogged on, I could detect a change in George's enthusiasm for putting his story of Grumman down on paper. Though he seemed to be bouncing back from a heart problem in the late summer of 2001, his weakened resistance left him prey to pneumonia, and he died on the second of September, exactly two months after his eightieth birthday. Sadly, he never had a chance to read this distillation of hours of conversations with him, his Grumman colleagues, and naval officers. So any missteps are mine.

Twenty-six years before, I met George on the shop floor at Grumman's Calverton final assembly plant, where in unvarnished detail he laid out the production misery and recovery of the F-14. Writers are allergic to hype, and my first impression of George was of an engineer formed on the shop floor who shot straight with the facts. We bumped into each other later at places like the Paris Air Show. When he asked me to collaborate on this project I was eager to do it because I knew George's straightforward style. Engineers who knew how to build things as well as design them are disappearing. George was one, and Gerhard Neumann at General Electric was another—wise, forthright, and never glib. They could operate on the shop floor or in the boardroom. George felt he had to work harder than the corporate suits, who tended to disappear into the woodwork eventually.

Like those of us who grew up in the wake of the Lindbergh flight to Paris, George built airplane models. Unlike the rest of us, his models were exquisite and he built airplane models almost to his last days. A builder of model airplanes had a gold star after their name in George's book. Aero engineers had to live and breathe airplanes, and model building was their halo. He was right, and, sadly, those model builders like George are slowly leaving us.

ACKNOWLEDGMENTS

*B*OTH AUTHORS OWE A HUGE DEBT TO GEORGE SKURLA'S NUMEROUS coworkers at Grumman for the generous gifts of their time and their insights into the Grumman story. We also profited from the detailed oral history compiled by the Smithsonian Air & Space Museum of the late George Spangenberg, the Navy's Mr. Fighter. Similarly we owe thanks to the naval officers and civilians who also generously shared their experiences for this project. George, I know, would want to thank his wife, Marie, for her patience and support through three years of taping and interviewing. Similarly, the co-author would like to thank his wife, Virginia, for her critical reading of the manuscript, and to his daughter, Nancy Gregory Covault, for transcribing many of the interview tapes. Larry A. Feliu, manager of the Northrop Grumman History Center, searched with diligence through the files there for photographs to illustrate the book. At the Naval Institute, Paul Wilderson, executive editor, never lost interest in the book amid rewrites, and Kristin Wye-Rodney improved the final product with her careful editing.

INSIDE THE IRON WORKS

1

REQUIEM FOR PLANT TWO

S NOW WAS STARTING TO FALL LIGHTLY AS I PARKED OPPOSITE THE
main lobby of Plant Two early in the afternoon of a chilly
December day. Plant Two, Grumman's main production facility
during the Second World War, looked almost totally abandoned and
somber in the grayness of fading daylight. No peeling paint or broken
windows in front, it was true. The facade looked pretty much the way
it had, although smart defense contractors never made brick and
mortar look too architecturally sleek and well heeled. This was the
twilight of what had been a glorious twentieth century for Grumman,
a year or two after it all ended with Grumman's takeover by Northrop
in 1993.

As I sat in the car and looked at the main lobby memories drifted
down through my mind like the snowflakes slanting outside the car.
In that same building I had been introduced to a company where I
would spend more than half my life and my entire professional career.

My life at Grumman, forty-three years at what the Navy called
the Iron Works, began in that building in Bethpage, Long Island.
I reported to work at that lobby on a date I haven't forgotten: March
6, 1944. As an apprentice engineer, I was ready to go to work in the
Plant Two production shop, a place where I and other apprentices
were destined to spend a month or two rotating through various

departments. Each of us was given a small, green, wooden toolbox that was a far cry from today's high-powered computer workstation and monitor array. Inside was little more than screwdrivers, a pair of pliers, and a small steel rule. For a week or two at a time, a new engineer was supposed to absorb an appreciation for manufacturing before he was called up to the drafting table in the engineering department. The idea was a good one. Too many engineering departments over subsequent years lost touch with manufacturing, at a price in reliability and product cost. I liked the production shop enough to stave off reassignment for over six months. Even then I stayed as a liaison engineer in Plant Two before moving over to Plant Five as a stress analyst. Those months paid dividends in future years. Not only were they the start of camaraderie with the manufacturing crew, but they also were a foundation that I returned to when I had to straighten out the navy F-14 fighter program thirty years later.

World War Two was still unwon, and engineers were hard to find. As a graduate of the University of Michigan I had twelve offers to choose from and had picked Grumman because I had navy fever. Salaries then were laughable by today's standards: a big $1.05 an hour. But I was building navy airplanes.

Almost ten years before, in 1936, I had my picture taken at Newark Airport, standing beside one of Grumman's classic F3F fighters from the Anacostia Naval Air Station near Washington. My trajectory toward a career as a dirigible designer slowed as I savored that gray biplane, trimmed with a red NACA cowl and yellow wings, a pathfinder. A rugged, barrel-shaped fuselage in the F3F housed an unusual landing gear that folded on itself to retract into a distended fuselage belly. Its predecessor, the FF-1 two-seater, pioneered this design that became the first fighter retractable landing gear in the U.S. Navy. When the German dirigible *Hindenberg*'s fiery demise hit the newsreels my interest in airships fully died, too. So it was off to the University of Michigan to become an aeronautical engineer. In my sophomore year at Michigan, with visions of flying F3Fs, I was one of a dozen students picked for the Civilian Pilot Training program—CPT as it was called for short. The government paid for the flight instruction of college and university students as a way to build a pilot cadre in the kind of numbers the military flying schools couldn't, but which the obviously looming U.S. involvement in war would require. I soloed on Thanksgiving Day, 1940, in a fabric-covered yellow Piper Cub high-wing monoplane—they were all yellow, and very forgiving to the uninitiated. Then I went on to fly a bigger, sluggish but aerobatic Waco UPF open-cockpit biplane for another fifty hours in secondary CPT flight training. That was enough to send me to my navy recruiter to sign up for the V-5 aviation cadet program in the summer of 1942. Actually, I had been thrown out of school a couple of times because I was fooling around in the glider club, and the Civilian Pilot Training program helped me to negotiate a way back in. In fact, I was headed for the navy V-5 program to train as an aviator when I hurt my back at school hauling a heavy dolly upstairs. An operation to fuse a disk put an end to any military career and to learning how to fly in the Navy, which I had wanted so badly.

After losing a semester to recuperation from a resulting spinal fusion operation later that year, I was reclassified as 4F in the draft. Disappointed as I was, I have to concede I might never have wound up running a major navy aircraft manufacturer but for that accident. Paradoxically, I kept on flying—in Grumman airplanes. Ten years of my life were spent in flight test, including some time as structural flight research group leader. And I logged about sixteen hours in the backseat of an F-14, with two of those hours off the carrier *Kennedy* in the Mediterranean Sea, firing guns from the systems officer's cockpit.

So another way into naval aviation, after the disk disaster, came on a bright sunny day in March 1944, when I walked into Grumman Plant Two, went through the badging process, and was escorted into the shop—all within about fifty feet from the front door. When I came to work for Grumman, because I had some experience, I had had at least a dozen offers if not more. It was January or February 1944 and the recruiters came around looking: North American, later bought by Rockwell; NACA Lewis; General Motors at Linden, New Jersey, making Grumman airplanes; and Grumman itself were among them. I actually came to Grumman because they gave me $1.05 an hour because I had worked a summer job at the Ford Willow Run plant near Detroit, where B-24 bombers were built.

Aircraft plants thus were not a brand-new experience. To me, Willow Run was staggering to the senses. A mile-long cavern, its aisles were so wide that New York City street-cleaning machines had to be used to sweep up metal shavings. Chaotic cacophony from riveting machines made conversations with someone next to you a shouting match, or impossible. Madhouse that it was, Willow Run was a god-send for me. The doctors in my screening physical found in X-rays that my vertebrae were fused with metal pins, something I hadn't known until then. Ford refused to take me on at first and I was desperate. To get through school, I had to have a job, and I pleaded about helping the war effort, too. They made phone calls and relented so far as to let me carry drawings from one station to another as a liaison engineer. Not that I did much at Willow Run, except roam around the plant and learn a lot about building airplanes.

At the Willow Run plant they made airplanes, sure enough. But auto builders didn't know what the hell they were doing, what the B-24 was all about, what the weight of each airplane was going to be. The planes were not properly tracked and often subject to engineering changes. But they turned them out like cupcakes. It was a wartime environment and nobody was standing around trying to be letter perfect. More B-24 bombers were built collectively between Ford and the designer, Consolidated Vultee, than any other airplane in this country during the war. Obviously there were wasted man-hours. Quality control was not in the same league that we have today. There wasn't the manned flight safety awareness that we had in the space program. People would be trained to drill a hole and shoot a rivet and that was that. These airplanes were never expected to last ten or twenty or thirty years. They were expendable things, either shot down in combat or obsolete when the shooting stopped.

Grumman's shop was noisy, too, that first day, but Bethpage seemed like the middle of New York's Central Park at two AM after life next to a jackhammer at Willow Run. Furthermore, the attitude was far different from the automobile standards at Willow Run; there was far more attention to precision fit and survivability. Wartime meant Rosie the Riveter, which was not merely public relations spinning. Sophie, my first lead supervisor at a huge fifty-ton vertical hydraulic press looked tough and she was—a no-nonsense lady. She assigned me to a couple of husky young women working the criss-cross press tables. I spent two sixty-hour work weeks being teased and bossed by them, learning how the plant worked and a lot more about what went on after hours. I was young enough to blush at their earthy jokes. Yet, after a few days, they more or less adopted me and we got along just fine. Sophie was sorry to see me move on, and I wonder if she ever knew that she had bossed around a future president of the company.

Now, forty-odd years later, I walked that same stretch. Sophie and her muscled cohorts were gone. So was the banging of aluminum sheets and the clanging press. Anxiously, after a decade of retirement, I searched around for something familiar. All I saw was emptiness and all I heard was silence. Where that fifty-ton press once stood was nothing, other than a faded outline of its footprint on the floor. Northrop Corporation, which had taken over the company I spent forty-three years with, had stripped the plant. The press was sold to the Italian helicopter builder Agusta. I wondered, as I stared at the empty floor, if some green, young Italian engineer was getting his start at that machine, just as I had. I turned slowly away, shaking my head.

Beyond what had been the press area was final assembly. I walked unbelieving toward this section, at the south end of the plant. Scraps and desolation, not fuselage sections and riveting, were cloaked in an eerie silence that the shadowy high bays accented. A ghost town, with the lost voices of my youth in my head. The front posed a presentable facade of the past. The back of the plant was, to put it euphemistically, unsightly.

Twelve O'Clock High, the motion picture about the daylight bombing raids on Germany in World War Two, had an unforgettable opening. A survivor goes back after the war to the airfield once throbbing with crews and B-17s, now weed-covered and deserted but for a tumbledown metal hut and a lonesome wind hissing through the grass. Plant Two had that same haunted aura. When I went to work there, the plant was crawling with people, a dissonant symphony of metal and machines. Each day we were building twenty Hellcats, the navy F6F carrier-based fighter. That was six hundred a month. Two shifts, and there were airplanes wall-to-wall. Production rates like that were never to be achieved again once the war ended. Even in the postwar years, what now seem like halcyon years in the 1980s, when Grumman had the A-6, EA-6B, E-2C, and F-14 in production concurrently, intensity never matched that of World War Two. (Pound for pound, though, it was a different story, for navy airplane weights had soared.) As I stood there in the silence the ghosts of aircraft past materialized in the dim light. Machinery, jigs, fixtures, benches, tool bins, all part of a climactic war effort, had been carted away for sale or scrap. Other than me, the only life was an occasional sparrow fluttering among the steel rafters.

Time marches on—strangely. History had been made here. This plant had its first open house for employees by fitting coincidence on Sunday, December 7, 1941, the day the Japanese fleet attacked Pearl Harbor. As counterpoint to navy E awards for excellence came the nickname for Grumman, the "Iron Works." Adm. John S. McCain, Senator McCain's grandfather, put it this way: "Grumman is to the Navy what sterling is to silver." Those words came back to me, words faded with the memories of a past that was indeed sterling silver.

Still alone in the gray winter half-light, I walked slowly toward the south end of the plant, the final assembly area where I spent most of my six months in the shop. I tried to envision again all of those dark-blue Hellcats, in lines abreast, facing each other. With twenty a day coming out of the plant, their Pratt & Whitney R-2800 engines were constantly firing up, a double-row radial with a deep-throated rumble when it started. The noise was exhilarating, before they were towed across the runway to Plant Four, where Grumman production test pilots flew them for acceptance before delivery to the Navy. We all looked forward to taking our lunch outside the plant on sunny days after a stretch of Long Island foggy weather. Then navy ferry pilots flew our work away in formations of twenty or thirty airplanes at a time, often putting on a short air show as they buzzed the field.

For months I hung armor plate behind the pilot's seat. Torquing up the four attachment bolts, I was always conscious that my simple job would perhaps save a pilot's life in combat over the Pacific. My other task on the Hellcat line was to fasten a two-inch channel extrusion horizontally across the fuselage bulkhead over the tail wheel. Roy Grumman, I was told, had personally directed the incorporation of that beef-up to prevent structural failure during arrested landings aboard ship. Not only was it a tight fit, but it was also a dirty job because of the grease on the control cables that ran through the aft fuselage section. Nevertheless, the fact that the founder of this critically important enterprise himself was involved made me conscious that I was doing something extra special.

Roy Grumman was a shy, retiring guy, who mostly sat at his desk. When he walked through the shop he didn't talk much and he didn't try to inspire people in any obvious kind of way. He wore dark glasses and could seem eccentric. In his last years of life, he wasn't very visible. He was a kind-hearted man, good to his people, not interested in making a lot of money. Perhaps that is why he never wanted a big company. Four hundred people at most was what he would say; he wanted it to remain as "Grumman Aircraft Engineering Company." Even during the Apollo program, he maintained, "I never wanted to get involved in manufacturing." He was kind of a tinkerer who wound up backing away from the company with his name on it.

I had to think about Roy Grumman as I looked at the empty bays inside Plant Two and at the "X"s marking the now-closed runway at the plant. Weeds grew through cracks in the former 6,600-foot macadam landing strip. Plant Four once had five big hangars and a control tower on top of flight operations. That tower that directed countless flights in and out of Bethpage over so many years is gone, bulldozed to ground level. At the south end of the runway, near Plant Two, homes for senior citizens have sprung up.

Retiring he may have been, but for Roy Grumman and the company he and his associates started in the winter of the great depression, January 1930, sterling silver is not an overstatement. Neither is the identification with naval aviation. Though not solely his contributions, he was instrumental in developing the first mono-plane fighter for the Navy, the F4F Wildcat. Besides the first retractable landing gear on a navy production aircraft, there was the idea of a diagonal hinge for an easy, safe wing-folding system for carrier aircraft that, among other things, led to the World War Two workhorse, the TBF torpedo bomber. This now forlorn plant had supplied the bulk of all navy fighters and torpedo bombers in World War Two. Roy Grumman's talent as a designer underlay all this.

At the north end of the runway lies Plant Twenty-five, where the lunar module was built, the spacecraft that took the first men from earth to the surface of the moon. Grumman's role with the Navy or aviation had not ended with World War Two, as the fabulous lunar module showed, particularly as the lifeboat that brought back the Apollo 13 crew from the moon when a burst oxygen tank in the Rockwell service module nearly cost them their lives. That plant has been sold and two warehouses are being erected; one is for a popcorn factory and warehouse, the other a warehouse for Goya Foods to store canned products, such as its garbanzo beans. Plant Five is between Plants Two and Twenty-five, also on the west side of the runway. There Roy Grumman had his office and I had mine for ten years as president and chairman of what had become a division of the corporation, Grumman Aerospace. What had Roy Grumman's temperament to do with the deserted factory that I walked slowly through?

He was lukewarm about growing the company. One opportunity after another slipped by. Roy and the original founding fathers were not out to create empires. I asked Roy in one of our rare conversations why the company never got into the light plane business. "Young man," he responded, "which would you rather do, build a million mousetraps or one locomotive?"—that is, one Gulfstream or a bunch of sport airplanes. That position was not necessarily wrong, but it implied a more limited market. Roy Grumman liked amphibians because the first company he worked for, Loening, was an amphibian pioneer. The twin-engine Widgeon was his favorite airplane. Yet he never carried his small amphibians from small utility transports to anything more imaginative. James S. McDonnell founded McDonnell Aircraft ten years later, in 1939. He was always interested in business jets and helicopters. When his own ideas didn't work out, he bought the Douglas Company and acquired the DC-9 and the DC-10 jet transports and the essentials of Hughes Helicopter with its Apache attack machine. What did Grumman do? Nothing on that scale. Though, in balance, it should be pointed out that the DC-10 and the helicopter company brought a huge bundle of headaches for McDonnell along with new markets. World War Two demobilization was precipitate and painful, but Grumman got into the jet age fairly soon, the F9F-2 jet fighter flew for the first time in 1947. War erupted again, in Korea, then Vietnam. Grumman came alive again in the 1950s.

Spring was in the air and sunshine in the business when I sat down with an interviewer in May 1981. By then I had become chairman and president of Grumman Aerospace. The fact that there was a Grumman Aerospace says something about how Grumman had changed. Aerospace was formed to handle what today's buzzword language would call core competencies, our traditional aviation and space business. Elsewhere in the corporation there were excursions into technologies and businesses that Grumman didn't know a lot about when it started to throw money at them. Nevertheless, aerospace was looking much better then after the trials of the 1970s post-Vietnam retrenchment in defense and tribulations with experimental kinds of contracting methods that had more parallels than might appear on the surface with our dream ventures into the commercial world.

Ronald Reagan was our new president and defense budgets were rising in 1981. Jimmy Carter had departed, along with a threat of closure for three of Grumman's four navy production lines. Of our four aces, the F-14 was down from seventy-two-a-year to thirty-a-year production rates, but the latter rate looked stable for the next five years. An F-14D was in gestation, with the new engine-airframe combination the airplane needed ready for prototype flight testing. The E-2C Hawkeye early warning aircraft for aircraft carriers soldiered on at a six-a-year rate and had overseas sales possibilities. The A-6 Intruder attack aircraft was still in the budget after twenty years. The electronic warfare version, the EA-6B, was going out the door, also at six a year. Not World War Two rates by any means, but, considering the ballooning in aircraft costs since then, a valuable business. As I told the interviewer: "I see Grumman Aerospace's future brighter than it has been for a long time. Frankly, I'm quite bullish on our overall business outlook for at least the next five to seven years—and then some."

Prophetic words, if they had been capitalized on. They weren't and why they weren't is a complicated story to follow. In a few words, Grumman didn't pursue and win new aerospace programs to follow these four aces and carry it into the twenty-first century. Diversions into strange new businesses were one reason. Grumman had moved into space brilliantly with the lunar module, but didn't maintain the thrust there either. Then there was the Navy, where Grumman stood so high. Dependence on one customer jeopardized the future if the relationship began to unravel. Unlike McDonnell, which expanded from its original navy programs into acting as a prime supplier for air force fighters, into space as the original Mercury and Gemini spacecraft builder, and into the Army developing battlefield missiles, Grumman was grossly late to break the air force barrier. If anything happened to bread-and-butter navy business my optimistic prophecy was toast. Most galling to me was the fact that Grumman had the engineering and manufacturing skill and experience and the financial strength to preserve and broaden its base. Even late in the game it could have survived. But survival meant marriage. Grumman's top management decided a bachelor's life was better.

Thinking about that confident interview, here I was a decade later walking slowly back to the lobby from the deserted field at Bethpage, my heart sinking to the level of my socks at the gritty reality. Destiny lay there unfulfilled. Later, sitting in my parked car, gazing through the swishing windshield wipers at Plant Two through a thickening snowstorm, a fitting backdrop for the mood of the day, I thought that at least I had been there in the glory days. From World War Two to the Apollo landing on the moon and the rescue of the F-14 Tomcat program from a manufacturing and financial morass. I hear it will be only a matter of time before every vestige of Grumman in Bethpage will vanish. Even the name Grumman could have disappeared from the corporate world if the abortive merger of Lockheed Martin with Northrop Grumman had not foundered in the Pentagon. Why, I asked myself in the middle of a snowstorm at a deserted factory, did it end this way? Where did things go wrong?

2

LEADERSHIP FROM A SHY ENGINEER

ROY GRUMMAN WAS A MYTHICAL CHARACTER AT GRUMMAN WHEN I got there. Yes, I knew him but not intimately. Neither did most others, for people at Grumman were aware that he was a very shy guy. He didn't get around much. By nature he wasn't gregarious, even when he was well and going to Washington to talk about airplanes. Occasionally he'd fly an F6F, just to get out of the office. But he wasn't the kind who walked through the shop, stopping and talking to people, asking, "How's the kids?" Leon A. Swirbul, also one of the founding fathers and always called Jake, was more that kind. Jake was a very good athlete, a basketball player, also a golfer, liked by everybody, a man's man—and a shirt-sleeve operations man, running the company day-to-day through the formative years.

Roy Grumman's personality was mirrored in his company. My limited exposure to him gave me an instinct for the Grumman culture and an understanding of why the story played out the way it did at the end of the century. The same applies to Swirbul, whose no-frills shop floor character and his feel for people also put a permanent stamp on Grumman. The third of the founders, Bill Schwendler, gave the company its foundation of rugged airplanes. The fourth, Clint Towl, shaped a conservative financial agenda. All of them influenced Grumman's culture.

When Charles Lindbergh flew nonstop to Paris, Roy Grumman was working for Loening Aeronautical Engineering Corporation in Manhattan as a general manager. This was a company started by two other aviation pioneer brothers, not the Wrights but Grover and Albert P. Loening, who built flying boats and floats for Vought scout airplanes. Jake Swirbul worked there as an inspector. Hayden, Stone & Company, the one-time New York investment bankers, bought Loening on the eve of the stock market collapse and combined it with Keystone in the Curtiss Wright conglomerate, which decided to consolidate operations at its plant in Bristol, Pennsylvania. Roy Grumman and some of his colleagues did not want to leave their homes on Long Island. Thus the company they decided to form had its nativity in what had been a run-down automobile garage converted from the old Cox-Klemin aircraft plant over in Baldwin on Long Island. Just a very small and closely knit group of guys getting together with barely enough money and the great depression under way. There were six altogether, including four who became the top management nucleus. They started off on January 2, 1930, with no plant, no product, no contracts. Grumman put up $16,875 of his own funds, his associates and friends $15,000, and the Loenings $30,000, which was big, big money after the stock market crash. Without a lot of formality, it was where the family spirit, the family culture, was born. Roy was fortunate in having cofounders and associates who shared his feeling for the people.

It took three years before they could get an airplane designed and try to sell it. That was the FF-1, which had the first retractable landing gear on a navy airplane. Before that they were repairing Loening air yachts. Bill Schwendler graduated from New York University, which had the Guggenheim school, a damn good aero school, and worked with Roy at Loening before going to Grumman. Clint Towl was the man with the books. He was like old frosty, but I think he considered me his boy. An administrative and financial type, he used go around with a little green Eberhard pencil, cut down almost to a stub, eraser on top, stuck in his vest pocket. At board meetings he'd get it out and scribble notes. He was different from the other three.

What got the Navy's attention early was an amphibian float for scout planes. Monocoque structure, a term from the French, had been developed to make all-metal airplanes possible. Thin aluminum skin panels attached to a frame-and-stringer skeleton shared the loads and were stronger and more durable than the old metal tubing core, in effect, a central truss, with a fabric cover. "All previous floats," Roy Grumman wrote, "had been built with a central longitudinal truss from the keel up to the deck for the full length of the float. Our float had no such central truss. We carried the bottom loads over to the sides of the float with bulkheads and cross-floors, and the longitudinal strength of the float was in the two vertical sides." Monocoque construction was so new then that navy structures stress experts didn't know how to calculate its strength to clear the airplane on which it was fitted for its first catapult test. Roy Grumman told the Navy he had enough confidence in the structure to ride in the first test himself, and he did so crammed in the rear cockpit of one of the early navy Corsairs, a Vought O2U-3 biplane, catapulted from a battleship. From the float landing gear followed the full-up aircraft retractable landing gear that led to the FF-1, a concept which skeptics thought would make a fuselage cross section so large that performance could not compete with existing fighters.

Grumman's "Iron Works" nickname reflects Roy's engineering philosophy. But I have to say this, Bill Schwendler was really the chief engineer. Both were engineers with the same approach. Design it for abuse, rather than just use. Make it strong. Consider who's going to fly it—the user. Don't cut corners. Get the best. Bill Schwendler was a wonderful guy, easy to talk to, very compassionate, and he showed his concern for you. Roy Grumman, as I've stressed, was reserved. Jake was the outside guy, the fixer, the facilitator, but not an engineer. Schwendler was very congenial, like a favorite uncle. Always dressed very well, always pleasant, a nice smile, an engineer first and foremost, but I was told, much to my surprise, in his youth he used to be able to rip telephone books in half.

That had something of the Grumman engineering mode of ruggedness. Structurally Grumman wanted the airplane to be able to take what it had to take and then more. This meant something that engineers understand very well but outsiders don't necessarily: good stress analysis as well as good design. Larry Mead, one of the pioneers whose crowning achievement was as project engineer for the A-6 Intruder, was a great stress man. And Grant Hedrick was the stress guru at Grumman. I worked in the stress department so I know.

Times got awfully tough for the young Grumman company in the mid-thirties. That's when one of Roy's friends gave him a contract to build aluminum single-axle trailers. Always the innovator, Roy conceived his torselastic spring for them. One tube fit inside another tube with about half an inch of rubber bonding. All it did was twist. The spring never went anywhere, but he got a patent on it and we built some trailers. In fact, that was the genesis of Grumman in the truck body business, which grew much bigger after the war.

Now it's a corporate cliché, but Roy realized that people were any company's most important asset, and he had to protect that asset and nourish it. Not immediately, but as the business grew, he began to give out turkeys to everybody at Christmas. Bonuses came in the war years because we were making or exceeding production quotas. The government allowed Grumman to pass out bonuses—averaging 25 percent of wages and based on total plant output—every three months. I remember I was very impressed with that when I first came to work at Grumman for a tad more than forty dollars a week. Subsequently, and it's hard to say whether he personally did this or someone came to him, Grumman reserved two beds at the Mayo Clinic and sent people out to Minnesota when local doctors couldn't help. No waiting, four to five months or four to five weeks, whatever. Two beds were always there, and this lasted right through to the end of my career. Anyone could walk into Swirbul's office and talk, argue, or complain about anything or even hash over family problems most big companies avoid like disease. Nurseries were open for the mothers who poured into the defense work force. Cheap hot meals were subsidized by the company. All these things were not standard corporate practice in the 1930s or 1940s. Interface with employees rather than scientific personnel management was Grumman's approach toward motivating its people, and it worked. Turnover for all causes was 2.4 percent then, half that of other aircraft companies. Only 1.7 percent of Grumman workers left to look for other jobs, again compared to 5 percent at other aircraft plants. Labor leaders never made any progress in unionizing the old Grumman. Looking back, I remember the personal things they did, such as sending out little happy birthday cards. When someone got the twenty-fifth anniversary gold watch, the wife received a dozen roses.

Roy Grumman didn't look larger than life, although that's the way he was regarded around the company. Rather he was sort of bland looking, not very tall. He had reddish hair, soft spoken usually with a pipe in his hand, which he has in his portrait. Though he was known as Roy, his full name was Leroy. He came from humble circumstances in Huntington, Long Island. He graduated from Cornell in mechanical engineering—on a scholarship—joined the Navy in World War One and wound up in flight training, where he graduated as naval aviator No. 1216. He met the Loenings at the Naval Aircraft Factory in Philadelphia and resigned his commission to become a Loening test pilot. Naval aviators even today cultivate an attitude of "appropriate arrogance," but not Roy Grumman. He was ill at ease with people as a child and even with navy wings he still had a reputation for massive reticence.

Roy disliked socializing. That was Swirbul's forte in the early years, glad-handing employees and suppliers and especially making the Washington rounds with the Navy. He detested interviews but his picture was on the cover of *Time* magazine. Grumman had become the sweetheart of the Navy and won five E awards during the war. Secretary James Forrestal said at the time that Grumman won the Battle in the Pacific, especially in Guadalcanal, where the F4F Wildcat's ability to take punishment allowed navy fighter pilots like Jimmy Flatley and John (Jimmy) Thach to develop tactics to capitalize on its ruggedness and deal with the much greater maneuverability of the Japanese Zero fighter. They are often credited, amid dissent, with creating the so-called "Thach weave," where elements of two made continuous S-turns into each other, always with one airplane guarding the tail of another. With the F4F, Grumman acquired the Iron Works nickname. Iron Works did embody Roy Grumman's engineering philosophy. But sterling silver, quality as well as ruggedness, was vital, too.

Long visits with Roy Grumman in the office were rare, but I remember having one—though only after I had risen in the ranks later. Yet what he said then was revealing about his perspective on company strategy early on. I had asked to get my twenty-year pin from him personally, which took some doing. Fortunately I was friendly with one of the executive secretaries in the office. Normally a group was called into a conference room or office for the pin ceremony. Managers would say a few words about the company and where it was going. The twenty-five-year pin recipient would get a watch, a real good one, too, an eighteen-carat gold Bulova Accutron. Most of us at Grumman then were starry-eyed about the company, and the watch was overkill in that sense. We felt we had blue blood; we might as well have had Grumman tattooed on our chests. No other company could compete with us—Lockheed or Martin or McDonnell. They were all second-rate in the eyes of most Grumman people.

Anyway, in I went to see Mr. Grumman, as we always called him. He just sat at his desk, not very animated. "You been here twenty years?" he asked. "Yes, " I answered. "What do you do?" "Well right now Mr. Grumman I'm working on the Apollo lunar module." "You must be proud of that." But then he added: "I don't know too much about the space business. I guess we're doing the right thing." That was revealing, too, for it became evident later that his attitude toward space was the jaundiced one of an old-time airplane man. We talked a little bit about where the company was headed, and I asked him, "Why, Mr. Grumman, didn't we, after World War Two, go after the private airplane business?"

Grumman had built a couple of light plane prototypes, or had them built, as experimental airplanes. I flew one called the Tadpole, a two-seat amphibian like the Seabee that our neighbor on Long Island, Republic Aviation, had produced after the war. The other was a two-seat tricycle gear airplane, which looked something like the North American Navion, that its owners loved but didn't make money for the company. Roy turned to me and answered: "Young man, what would you rather do? Build a million mousetraps or one locomotive?" I was taken aback and answered: "I'm not quite sure what you're driving at. Republic built the Seabee. Certainly we can do that." Here a bit of the wisdom of Roy Grumman emerged. Inherently he was very conservative—don't go too fast or too far. "What do you think all of these young men coming out of the service are going to be doing after they get out?" he asked. I was too surprised to say anything for moment. "Get married. Right. Buy a home. Right. Have children. How are they going to afford an airplane? Besides, there are so many surplus military airplanes lying around, why should we compete with them?"

Only one other time in forty years with Grumman did I have another face-to-face with the company's legendary founder. Again it told me a great deal about his influence on the company. The encounter came in 1980, the year we celebrated the company's fiftieth anniversary, and the folks running the show wanted me to get Roy Grumman there. I went to his house to press the case, but he wouldn't come, irrespective of how important it was symbolically, as his wife, Rose, warned me. We were sitting on his patio in Port Washington and I brought my secretary along, Dolores, who was with me for years and a big thrill for her it was. Out of the blue and out of character, he asked: "You want a drink?" He was wearing dark glasses, smoking his pipe, with kind of a big chest apron on made out of asbestos. Hospitals do this for smokers who won't quit. In his state of declining health he would tamp his pipe and the ashes or hot coals would fall all over the place. Roy Grumman wasn't the kind of guy to offer people a drink, but he did that day as we sat overlooking Port Washington harbor. Roy took me down in his basement, which he had finished off in 1940; by today's standards it wasn't much, just some paneling around. Yet there were walls full of pictures of him with James Forrestal, secretary of the navy and later the first secretary of defense, and with Lord Beaverbrook when he went to England. I didn't know then just how far his health was deteriorating, and he would die a couple of years later.

Because he had eye trouble, Roy Grumman got out of the main-stream around 1960, as I recall, and became even less visible. He was going blind and becoming even more self-conscious. He took to wearing dark glasses, to a point where he couldn't see very well. Not that he was completely blind, but he was very limited in his mobility. He had diabetes, too, which eventually cost him the vestiges of his eyesight. So he just withdrew from the public scene at Grumman.

If it were up to me, George Skurla, to say who from top management had the most influence on how Grumman designed hardware, how we designed it as fail-safe and rugged, it would be Bill Schwendler. Not only was he the focus of all that engineering decision making, but he also was on the board of directors, where he acted as protector of the engineering staff. He was no fast-talking, slick corporate suit and neither was Roy.

Grumman employees ran in families, and Schwendler encouraged that. As Ed Markow reminded me when he turned up at one of our Grumman reunions in Florida for large-scale reminiscing: "My going to Grumman was predetermined," he said. Ed, a second-generation Grummanite, remembers his father's tenure there in the 1930s. "I can remember going to the plant on Saturdays, myself and quite a few other sons, and they'd let us play in the shop," Markow said. "Mothers would have a day off. Grumman was real family, not lip service. Years later Mr. Schwendler had us to his place in Great River. I took my kids down to the dock, and Mrs. Schwendler would put worms on the hooks for them. It was an amazing company in that way. During the tail end of the depression, the company wasn't paying Grumman employees good salaries. Instead they were paid in stock, half stock, half salary. My father came home with a piece of stock and I remember mother saying, 'I can't go to the grocery story with that.' Later on it turned out to be fine because everything changed with the war. He was foreman in one of the production plants, Plant Two, and I can vividly remember him sitting me down and saying, 'You do your best for Grumman, don't worry about what you're going to do for yourself.' The company would take care of that."

Jake Swirbul set the tone, Markow thinks, but Bill Schwendler— a great engineer as well as a great human being—was behind many good things that happened. Quietly, though, because no one knew it was happening, like the Mayo Clinic. That is how Ed remembered it anyway.

Richard C. Dunne, a veteran public relations man for Grumman who stayed on after the Northrop merger, points out there was another side to paternalism. Grumman did have a reputation as a high-cost producer, at least in some quarters, and he thinks that was really a product of the system. "It was a very paternalistic system," he told me the last time we met, "and whether it was getting your license plates or getting your eyes checked or getting a pair of crutches if you broke a leg or a wheelchair or whatever the hell it was, the company took care of it. All you had to do was call up what was known then as the Welfare Department. Now it's called human resources or something or other. All of that was overhead, though. No one ever got fired from here, not that I know of, so we had a lot of deadwood and that all contributed to costs." Grumman was a cradle to grave culture and everything was set up accordingly. Your salary was going to progress a nickel an hour until you died. Your pension program was set up so that you didn't get a hell of a lot in the beginning, but you did very well at the end. All that came to bite us later on in the Northrop acquisition when the pensioners sued over money due and won.

Dick Dunne and I agree that Grumman could be a very entre-preneurial place where an employee could move around and do the things he wanted to do, thus learning on the job. A mistake didn't mean getting canned or killed. It was a great place to work, but too many people came and never left, not knowing how good it was. Grumman, we agreed again, was ahead of everybody. Except, as I reminded Dick, in salaries, which were not very competitive.

Jake Swirbul was a wonderful alter ego to Roy. Extroverted and sociable, he also hung around with athletes. Once he came by my desk and said, "Shake hands with the champ." It was the boxing star Rocky Marciano. Jake had a staff that would respond to many requests. "Can you help my son get into West Point?" "Can you help my son get into medical school?" "My wife is sick and the doctor doesn't know what's wrong. Can you send her to Mayo?"

Jake was an old shoe. Instead of having a secretary of his own, he shared one with Roy Grumman. Jake sat in a very plain office, like government issue, with green paint on walls. We were a nonunion company, but the union world gave him a plaque that hung outside the boardroom, citing him for doing wonderful things for labor. He was charismatic. Even so, he was not a good manager by today's scientific management standards. He wasn't into that. He was one on one. He'd sit down, lean back, put his feet up on the desk, a toothpick in his mouth, and say, "Now—Bill or Joe or George—what's your problem?" Yet he was the president.

Unlike Roy Grumman, Jake was not an engineer. Neither was he a marketing whiz as we would think of today, even though he was Grumman's de facto marketing chief. He was a schmoozer. The Navy liked him. A wonderful thing is that he as president, starting in 1946, with Roy as chairman controlled the company. It was much simpler in those days. We had only a few officers, such as a vice president of administration and a treasurer and controller. Roy and Jake, just two people running everything, were a great match. No conflict of personalities there. No one tried to get in front of anyone. Roy set the overall policy and let Jake do his thing. Jake would run the people side, picking and choosing, and making sure everybody was happy. Jake was unstructured, not a slick talker on his feet. He never liked to say no or deliver bad news. Instead he much preferred to hand out good news. With beautiful blue eyes, he had a way with women as well as men, and he used to bring his girlfriends into the plant. Or he'd have a chauffeur take him to Manhattan, where he would carouse until three o'clock in the morning after a long day, for he had a playboy streak as well.

But Jake was known to break down and cry. My old associate, Jack Buxton, who was down at Houston with NASA, worked out of the Washington office before he went down there. Once he and Jake went to see an admiral who had lambasted the hell out of Jake. "Grumman isn't listening to us," was his thrust. The chief engineer at that time, Robert L. Hall, who was chief test pilot and an air racer before that, must have been getting a little bit hard-nosed. Arrogant was the standard government word when their engineers got into it with a contractor, and that theme would come back to haunt us later after I retired. When they left the office Jake began to cry. Back at the plant, he stopped George Titterton and Bill Schwendler from going to Washington. He even wanted to fire Schwendler, which is astounding to anyone who knew him. I heard that Schwendler was in tears over that, but gossip does get magnified around a big company.

One morning, around the turn of the century, in the Plant Five cafeteria I ran into Reno Nicoli, who had been around Grumman since 1940. He gave me a wonderful capsule contrast between the two men. Like most others at Grumman, he did not know Roy Grumman very well. Of the three occasions Nicoli had met him (and these were the days when the engineering department had at most thirty-two people), one was during the redesign of the hull of the G-44 Widgeon amphibian that first flew in 1944. Roy loved the amphibians, Reno reminded me, the G-44 and the earlier G-21 Goose. The Widgeon unfortunately had a shallow V hull, about twenty degrees dead rise. On landing, that shallow angle was not enough for the hull to bite into the water and consequently the airplane would skid on the surface.

One Widgeon was modified into a G-44A with a steeper V-hull, and Roy Grumman was aboard it when both the earlier and later versions went out for a test. "I was the project engineer, maybe twenty-three years old," Reno recalled. The G-44A landed first, and Reno was in the earlier version that landed about a quarter of a mile behind. "When we got back to the wharf," he said, "Mr. Grumman asked me what the water spray pattern looked like. 'Very nice,' I answered. And that was the end of that conversation." Though Reno didn't point this out, this kind of a technical review and buy off is a far place from today's, where dozens of committees, piles of paper, and weeks of meetings might ensue to get to the same modification accepted.

There was a small engineering room right across the hall from Roy Grumman's office in those early days. "I was walking there to my office," Reno recollected, "when I bumped into Roy Grumman going to his. When he came toward you, he kind of shied away, turned the other way, kept his head down—not that he didn't want to talk to you, but that was just his introverted, uncomfortable way with strangers or a group. When he talked to an individual, like the time he went out on the G-44, he spoke very nicely and professionally." Jake Swirbul was an entirely different brand of coffee. "One time," Reno said, "Jake made a speech over in Plant Two. Afterward, as I was going up the stairs here in Plant Five, I heard somebody walking up behind me. I looked around and it was Jake Swirbul. 'That was a wonderful speech you made, Mr. Swirbul,' I said. I was holding the door at the top of the stairs for him to go first and he just waved his hand and said, 'I want you to go through first,' and held the door for me. Then he cornered me, just kept talking to me, for about twenty minutes." Something untypical for a very busy man, and that's the kind of thing that made everybody his fan. Plus the fact that he knew what was going on down at the working level. Reno remembers Joe Gavin, later president of the corporation, as the same kind of engineer as Roy Grumman, often ill at ease around people. And Clint Towl, one of the four founders, could be pretty icy. "He wouldn't talk to people at my level," Reno remembered wryly. Even so, Grumman, the company, was far more characteristic of the Swirbul demeanor than the Towl mode. I used to do the people thing and later so did Carl Palladino, my financial vice president; that is, go out on the plant floor, see the people on the projects, and dipstick it from our own vantage point as to whether the stories coming to the head office were realistic and believable. "We had no pyramid," Palladino says, "no strata, no lines you couldn't cross over. I could go out and walk the floor and people would say, 'Hi Carl, how are you?' irrespective of my position or theirs."

Bill Zarkowsky, who later became president, remembers Jake Swirbul's trip to the Pacific during World War Two to talk with navy pilots. "He used to sit and eat with them, chat them up, drag out of them what was good with Grumman airplanes and what was not," Zarkowsky remembers. When he came back from the Pacific, the F6F prototype had been test flown with the Wright engine it started life with, an engine Zarkowsky described as torture. He was working then for Ralston Stalb, who would take him to meetings presided over by Swirbul to take notes. After the trip, Swirbul was pounding on the table, shouting that when the F4F went after a Zero, the nose of the airplane would block the pilot's view. (Grumman was then in the midst of trying to improve the F6F-1 because of that rotten Wright Aeronautical engine.) Swirbul demanded that pilots be able to see over the top of its cowl and that the F6F's nose be lowered. When all the logical reasons came back as to why it couldn't be done, Swirbul got up, pounded on the table some more, and demanded: "I want them to see over the top of the cowl. Drop that nose."

"So all of us technicians went back to our drafting boards," Zarkowsky went on. "They shut Ralston and me in a room and said, 'You guys redesign the F6F. Come up with your version.' To me, as a young engineer, that was like ascending Mount Olympus. Ralston sketched away, dropping the nose of the F6F from the firewall forward. Then he just looked at the sketches, but he made no calculations or anything. He had a peculiarity of whinnying when he spoke, and he squeaked to me: 'Willy, do you think the prop will hit the deck when she rotates on an arrestment?' Willy, me, with all the calculations, said, 'It sure as hell will.' 'I don't think so,' he whinnied back. All the calculations under the sun then said the prop would hit the deck. Ralston convinced the management that it wouldn't. So he gave me the redesign from the firewall forward, and I decided to change the engine."

One of Zarkowsky's professors at New York University, Perry Pratt, had gone back to Pratt & Whitney where he became an exalted name as head of research. Zarkowsky called Perry up and said that

Grumman wanted to use the engine from the F4U (which became the R-2800-10W in the F6F), but it didn't fit. The carburetor needed to be on the bottom and it was on the top. Silence followed that news for a while. "I think we ran one of those things down in the lab," Pratt said at last. So a couple days later he called back and said that it was still down there. At that time a production board in Washington, the WPB or War Production Board, run by Knudsen of General Motors, had to approve. Being in the design room, Zarkowsky didn't let any of that worry him. "That was Jake Swirbul's job," Zarkowsky said with a chuckle. "So Ralston and I got it to fit, though we had to redesign a lot. On the F6F cowl, the bottom mouth was for the intercoolers and the oil coolers, split inside. So we used a version of the engine with the carburetor on bottom and wrapped the intercoolers and oil coolers around it." Inside parts and the castings were different. Only about 20 percent were common.

A council of war followed between Pratt & Whitney and Grumman to see who wanted to tackle Washington. Bill Gwinn was president of Pratt at that time. "Those folks decided they had plenty of capacity to build the engine," Zarkowsky continued. "Although they knew they were going to have trouble with the board, Pratt decided to go ahead with it, cleaned up that lab engine and let us have it. That went into the first modified airplane, long before we had permission to build them. Larry Mead headed the team in engineering when Ralston released our drawings to engineering—sketches, whatever we called them then. Larry took a team of guys and designed the parts, did a fantastic job, and something like six weeks later they had the assembly on the floor. When we flew the airplane, it was terrific." So too thought a generation of navy pilots in the Pacific.

Jake, like Roy, probably would never make it in today's big corporation world. Again, that's my opinion. He would have if he had his own private business. He wouldn't have tolerated today's aerospace industry of giant companies, big government bureaucracies, and abundant regulations. When someone got to be president of a company of Grumman's size and capability, you'd expect him to get on his feet and talk with a golden tongue. Dealing with NASA or the DoD, he'd be expected to have a reasonable handle on some of the technology involved in the product. Jake wasn't the type, nor was he interested in management science. He preferred sports, and he was commissioner of horse racing. He was a wonderful man, though, all things said. He died in 1960 at sixty-two of cancer that went into pneumonia. His death made a lot of difference to Grumman later because we needed a people-oriented operations head when times got tough again.

* * *

What made employees walk around with Grumman tattooed on their chests? It was the same element that built up the Grumman culture, that family feeling that the company wasn't just trying to squeeze everything it could out of them. While it wasn't a big paying company, it had convinced its people that it was concerned about their day-by-day welfare, both on the job and at home with their families. During the war years, we had the famous little green trucks. When you had to go off to work at Grumman and there was a leaky pipe at home, it was easy to call in and ask, "Can somebody get over there to fix it?" There was a gang of fixers who would go over and do just that. It was wartime, of course, and they wanted the worker on the job. But it left an impression.

The green trucks were Swirbul's idea. He had them cruise the parking lots at the plant to change flat tires. Then, when Grumman took on eight thousand women, many with homes and families, he had the green trucks run errands for them, checking their homes to see whether windows were closed or irons turned off. He built baseball diamonds and organized a band to play for dancing at lunch. The bonus system I mentioned. Swirbul set that up so that it was based not on individual performance but on the plant's total output. From sweepers to executives, everybody shared, some as high as 30 percent of their salaries. Nothing could have fostered a common interest as well.

When Grumman merged with Northrop, the Grumman pin ceremonies stopped. So did the Grumman picnics every year at Calverton. One year we had thirty-two thousand people, but I have to add that many local neighbors came with Grumman families. I was president at that time, and there were F-14s and A-6s flathatting all over that place like crazy. It got so boisterous in the air that I had to call the tower and say, "Tell them to knock it off. They're getting too low."

Would Roy Grumman have been comfortable at that picnic, I wonder. Among Roy's complex discomfort zones were expansion and bigness and crowds, something not shared by me or by his other successors. A legend in the company was that he never wanted it to grow larger than 250 employees. According to Richard Thruelsen's book *The Grumman Story*, Roy said as much one day in 1934. "When it does," he said, "it's going to be too big and we're going to lose control of it. That's where we ought to stop." It fell to Clint Towl to break the bad news at that point: the company payroll had already climbed to 256. In a way Roy was right, but the loss of control he feared took about sixty years, until the post–Cold War aerospace consolidation brought the little-welcomed acquisition by Northrop.

At the peak in World War Two, Grumman had twenty-five thousand workers on the payroll and its sales in 1945 reached $236 million, a small company now but a giant prior to postwar inflation. Sales dropped to $38 million in 1946—though the company was profitable—and it fell to Swirbul to lay off the whole 25,000 work force, close all the plants for a time, and then hire back a nucleus of 5,400. Swirbul and Roy Grumman both worked in their shirtsleeves, and a picture from wartime shows Swirbul in the plant, in front of an F6F engine in its cowling, wearing an unbuttoned vest and no coat. Swirbul had the same feel for people but this translated far more into expressive backslapping around the plant. He was the boss who had to lay off the work force—though he didn't become president until 1946—but the one who also hired back the postwar nucleus.

Those layoffs may well have reinforced how Roy Grumman felt about expansionism. I don't think he was a great entrepreneurial guy. He wasn't that hungry to expand, to make a big company. He just didn't have the fire in his belly. Roy's caution and conservatism were the right mix for survival in the depression, the likes of which the country hasn't seen since. He could no more adapt to today's megamergers, stock hyping, and big debt loads than the go-go boys of today could have withstood more than a few weeks of operating in the depression. Swirbul, on the other hand, was the executor, at times a brusque operations boss. When the Navy thought it was dropping a bomb on Grumman when the war started, telling him the company had to expand, Swirbul pulled out the blueprints he had ready. When the Navy offered help to get a wartime priority for steel, Swirbul didn't need it. He had bought up the scrap from New York's Third Avenue elevated system when it was torn down. Swirbul had also noted what the British had done to disperse their aircraft plants for protection from German air raids during the war. When Swirbul did the same thing with Grumman, his rationale was different: to ease the way for plant expansion by having multiple core sites.

A contradictory character? That was Roy Grumman. On one hand, as I've said, a very reserved man and ill at ease with others. On other hand here was a man with very strong personal feelings for his people. His engineering philosophy set the original tone, the Grumman Iron Works. Roy was the archetypal engineer that too many people sneer at today and label as a nerd with a pocket protector. Design it for abuse, rather than just use. Make it strong. Consider who's going to fly it, the user. Don't cut corners. Get the best.

For all his solid, conservative engineering personality, Roy had another side. His salutatorian speech at his high school graduation said this: "The final perfection of the aeroplane will be one of the greatest triumphs that man has ever gained over matter." Quoting the Greek military genius Themistocles, who saw control of the sea as control over the land and forged a successful strategy for the victory over the Persians at the Battle of Salamis in 480 BC, Grumman added: "If power over the sea will do so much, of how much more importance will be . . . power over the air—which extends over both land and sea and breaks down the barriers between all nations." Not a new thought today, but here was a high school graduate in his teens talking in 1911 when airplanes were still essentially big box kites. Roy Grumman clearly had a visionary spark beneath his reserved exterior.

Did Grumman designers consciously trade off performance for ruggedness? I think so. They realized that the planes they designed were going into battle. One of the most dramatic pictures, everybody's seen it time and time again, was of the F6F landing on the carrier deck off center and hitting the island. The engine section broke off cleanly at the bulkhead aft of the cockpit, leaving the pilot sitting in the cockpit uninjured and the tail section off, lying behind. I've run into many former Grumman aviators who reached flag rank. When they met me they would say, "Thank God for Grumman." Grumman's healthy business with the Navy over the next four decades came from those pilots that got back home in a rugged Grumman airplane.

3

ADJUSTING TO PEACE

GRUMMAN—AND THE AIRCRAFT INDUSTRY IN GENERAL—COULD do no wrong while the fighting lasted. Attitudes were going to change, however, as I found out right after VJ day, when Japan surrendered in August of 1945. I was told to go home, as many of us were. "What's happening here? Do I have to go look for another job?" I asked, and they answered, "Well, probably not." Roy Grumman was very interested in keeping the younger engineers, and I was lucky. They did let me go—with everybody else—but they called me back to do stress analysis, where I sweat bullets trying to perform new tasks.

Roy Grumman, Jake Swirbul, Bill Schwendler, and Clint Towl had far more massive challenges to keep afloat what was now a big company. As a navy contractor, the company had to worry about whether the jet engine, born in Europe during the late hostilities, could coexist with the aircraft carrier. Did carrier aviation and Grumman have a future?

Jet engines in those early days accelerated slowly, so slowly that navy pilots wondered whether they could spool up fast enough for a wave off in the ultimate seconds at the end of a carrier approach, twenty feet or so above the deck, if something wasn't right. Ryan Aeronautical had a compromise, a fighter called the Fireball with a piston engine and propeller at the nose and a jet engine in the tail for a kick in combat. As it turned out, the problem wasn't as bad as feared. Jet power brought changes in operations, though. Catapult takeoffs became mandatory, not the alternative to a flyaway roll down the carrier deck with propellers. Approaches no longer were flown just above stall speed, hanging on the prop. Eventually the angled deck allowed the pilot to come aboard with high power and go around safely after touchdown if he missed an arresting wire—what naval aviators call "bolters."

Another problem arose for Grumman, too. Not only did its traditional competitors like Vought and Douglas begin moving into jet power, but a new rival in St. Louis took on Grumman with its own jet fighters, the McDonnell Phantom and Banshee FH-1 and F2H. Grumman had started working on what became its first jet fighter, XF9F-1, in 1946, what became the F9F-2, -3, -4, and -5 versions of the Panther, all with a straight wing, and the F9F-6, -7, and -8 Cougar with a swept wing. The F9F-2 became the first navy jet fighter to go into combat during the Korean War, in 1950. But the Banshee, which McDonnell had started to develop in 1943, made the first landing by a pure jet aircraft on a carrier in 1946. McDonnell had tough times with a successor, the F3H Demon, when its power plant failed to deliver its required performance. Yet the subsequent F4H Phantom 2, along with the Vought F8U, had displaced Grumman fighters on carrier decks by the start of the 1960s for the first time in thirty years.

As a junior engineer, I wasn't privy to the agonizing in the front offices over building a jet fighter. When I came off of the shop floor after my first eight months doing loop assignments (going to various departments from hydraulic press to final assembly) with the war still on, they put me briefly—for about six months—in liaison engineering, upstairs in Plant Two. It meant signing off on drawings, not very high-level stuff, and learning a little about some of the engineering procedures. Liaison engineering went with big engineering staffs and lots of strict specifications. Interfaces had to be created between the people on the production line who needed changes to make something work and the engineers who had to figure out what the changes had to be. Say somebody cut a part and it didn't fit. Back they'd go to engineering and say, "We've got a problem here," except usually in more colorful language. I was the runner between them. Liaison engineering also covered incorporation of new change orders, ECPs or engineering change proposals as we still call them. It was a minor job, looking over what the changes were and making sure that everything was complete as far as what had to go into the check-off boxes on the drawings themselves. But I learned about the demons in change orders and what they can do to manufacturing and costs.

When I then moved over to Plant Five and went to work in the stress department, Grumman was still a very cozy operation. All the engineers for the most part were in Plant Five on one floor. There were some engineers in Plant Two and some in Plant One as well, but Plant Five was the big engineering stronghold of Grumman. Built late in the war, Plant Five must have been at least one hundred yards long, like an indoor football field with hundreds of people. At lunchtime, engineers could be found flying their model airplanes; Ping-Pong tournaments were going on. Talk about open landscaping. If you stood at one end of the floor, someone way at the other end was easy to see. True there were offices along the side, but it was mostly a big open bullpen. Spotted around the floor were, here, the stress department and there the loads department. Beyond them might be a project engineer, then draftsmen or perhaps hydraulics engineers. Finally there was the engineering counter. Really simplistic it was.

My desk was at one end, with the stress analysis and applied loads people. We worked with slide rules and the drafting people with hand styluses and compasses. Computers that sprouted on engineers' desktops by the 1980s had barely been invented, and if there was one, it filled a room. Offices in the very front of the building housed the engineering vice presidents, like Bill Schwendler or Bob Hall. There were men's rooms here and there all the way down the floor. When I had to go to men's room, I would walk way the hell down to the opposite end. On the way I would schmooze, as they call it now, and on way back I'd do the same. That was a good way for an ambitious young guy to get known, and it turned out to be a good thing.

Stress analysis and a junior engineer's duties need explanation. This was a whole department, some engineers doing wings, some tails, some fuselages or landing gear. Larry Mead was the stress-analysis whiz kid there, though there were others like John Miers and Connie Sweeser. I would struggle, and then go to Larry, because I always felt like I was a dumbbell. Larry wrote NACA Report 4, which was all about how to do stress analysis of a wing and get all the shears figured out. I remember reading that thing ten times, trying to understand it, and using what I learned in working problems I ran into later. Stress analysis wasn't an overall responsibility for me at first. Rather I was asked to work initially with some senior stress analysts on specific parts of the airplane. Eventually they let me do a few things on my own. Much later I was head of product engineering, with about six thousand engineering and other personnel to manage. Yet I never projected myself as a real smart slide-rule engineer. Rather I fit the Grumman mold of getting the job done and the airplane out the door.

Be it civil engineering or aeronautical engineering, stress analysis underlies design, whether of an aircraft, a bridge, or an office building. Stress analysts matched the calculated stress against a known stress limit of the material as determined from testing in the lab. Samples were put under increasing load to find out what material was good for, given a particular heat treat. In stress analysis, we always wanted to have a positive margin at limit load, the applied loads, which designers said the airplane would probably experience. On top, the analyst added a 50 percent factor. Take a 6-g airplane, which meant the limit load factor was 6 and the ultimate load factor, where it was supposed to break, would be 50 percent more or about 9 g, which, sustained, was probably more than the pilot could take without injury. Stress analysis and margins were vital to Grumman's goal of ruggedness.

Still, the slide-rule calculations had to be verified in flight. One of our test pilots on the F4F, Carl Alber, was supposed to pull a limit g on a flight one day. There were no sophisticated g meters then so instead there was a piece of glass freshly smoked before takeoff. A stylus would be used to scratch a line on the smoke that had been calibrated on the ground in order to measure how much g had been pulled. In the air Alber didn't quite get the load he wanted. So he tried again and still couldn't get the g. He tried again. Finally he landed. The accelerometer on the cockpit panel had stuck, so he had just kept trying and trying again. On the ground they found out that he had pulled close to 14 g. The wings were buckled and there was other damage. He was lucky he didn't pull the wings off!

* * *

Grumman had made its reputation with durable piston airplanes, a record that took time to match in the jet era. For example, one of the first airplanes I worked on then was the F8F Bearcat, one of the best performing, possibly even the best propeller-driven piston-engine fighters ever built. Grumman had developed the F8F, a Bill Schwendler concept that was light and fast and maneuverable enough to dogfight with a Zero. Though short legged, it demonstrated an initial rate of climb at forty-eight hundred feet per minute. The first production F8Fs were being delivered to fighter squadron VF-19 at Norfolk in 1945 and the Navy planned to buy nearly four thousand. But the F8F never got a chance to fire a shot before the war ended. Production continued, unlike with the F6F or the TBF torpedo plane, and reservists called up when the Korean War started had a chance to fly one of around twelve hundred various versions of this wonderful fighter.

My job on the F8F was doing stress analysis on its cockpit over-turn structure. Now, it's a little hard to visualize without a drawing, but in the cockpit, there was a piece of armor plate that went up and bent, and there was also the usual rubber cushion on it at the top to protect the pilot's head. Like any tail dragger, maybe easier than most, the F8F could flip onto its back on the ground if the pilot jammed on the brakes or got into soft ground. Pilots in the F4F, for example, were warned to drop their seat to the low position before landing. Otherwise, if the airplane nosed over, the pilot's head was far enough up in the cockpit that he could break his neck. In one F8F noseover at the Memphis Naval Air Station early in the Korean War, the weight of the airplane jammed the pilot's face into soft mud and he was smothered. So the airplane needed something like the roll bar on an open race car.

Eventually the designers came up with the idea of putting an extruded A-frame on the back of the seat, then adding an extruded skid plate like a hat section. From there, they put a drag brace to the fuselage and picked up the bulkhead to take the vertical and drag loads. So I was given the job of doing the stress analysis, and they asked me to accompany the airplane down to Mustin Field in Philadelphia. There they slung an airplane into a barricade to flip it over and measure the loads with gauges all over the structure to see what actual loads we got, as opposed to what had been designed in the truss work. Every time I see an F8F, I look at that and say, "Hey, that's something I can remember working on." And I remember a navy captain who had an F8F squadron who nosed over on an icy runway. He sent me a picture and said, "Thanks for saving my life."

Another one of my early jobs was on a unique airplane for the time, the F7F. Called the Tigercat, the F7F was the closest the Navy and Grumman came to building a twin-engine carrier-based fighter during the war. It was a handsome airplane but had many problems—specifically cantilever loads that were leading to failures in the wing inner panel when the airplane landed, especially as hard as it always did in carrier suitability testing. With my inexperience at the time, that was another real challenge. My job was to do the stress analysis of one particular fuselage bulkhead and test how the loads had to be carried through to an inner torque box at the wing carry-through. Now I didn't do that on my own. I worked with a couple of senior stress analysts at my side, but I did a lot of the grunt calculations. It was paper and pencil for sure, not a nifty computer. Even all of the applied loads were laboriously cranked out. I can still remember they had a bunch of engineering aides, women, who worked on those old hand-cranked adding machines that rattled away in concert on their desktops.

Engines of the F7F were cantilevered off the leading edge of the wing. The main landing gear was mounted on the wing just about midway between the leading and trailing edge. When any airplane touches down on any runway, the wheels go from zero rotational velocity instantaneously to the equivalent of the forward speed of the airplane. So there is a tremendous kick-load that occurs when the wheel hits. That's why you see that puff of smoke. The wheels snap back. Well, when the wheels snap back like that they tend to twist the whole wing nose down. With a big mass hanging out there like an engine, when it hits, boom! Wing root spars were failing. There was a lot of buckling of the skins. When we finally took an instrumented airplane out on the carrier, we found that landing loads, after we had beefed the airplane up, were about 100 percent of what we had designed for. No wonder we had the failures!

Mostly it was torsion, and if things weren't synchronized, the loads could be magnified and a massive delta twist put on the wing. If one wheel hit first, and the engine was rotating when it hit, it could get even worse. That was the inherent problem and fault in the basic design and no one really figured it out, or didn't know how to figure it out until we finally took an F7F in the test hanger. We'd spin up the wheels on instrumented platforms and we could measure not only the vertical load but also the drag load. Furthermore, there were strain gauges all over the wing box. So we fixed that problem. But, of course, the F7F never made it on a carrier given its design problems. The first deployment was to a marine squadron. I think out of eighteen squadron airplanes, nine or ten of them had major or minor failures in the wing. The F7F, with a radar dish that could go in the nose, stayed in production until late 1946, usually in night-fighter versions. Mostly it served with the Marines after the war, but lots of work was done to try to make it the first twin-engine and first tricycle-gear carrier-based fighter. Despite its design limitations, it was a fabulous airplane.

With time, I got into jets, specifically with the F9F, doing stress analysis on the aft bulkhead, which took loads from the tail. Tail loads weren't deep science, but you've got elevator loads that go one way, lift loads on the rest of stabilizer that go another way, rudder side loads go one way, and fin loads going the other way, due to yaw. Then there's a bit of torque here and there. And finally the balancing loads that kept the airplane flying level. These things have to be transmitted and redistributed. This was in all honesty, not a big challenge to a senior analyst. But for me, starting out, it was another matter. I'd get up at five o'clock in the morning and try to think through problems. While Larry Mead was great, I didn't like to go to the boss and ask him, or admit that I didn't understand. Furthermore the fuselage bulkhead at the tail came right where it's notched, where the engine nozzle exits. This contributed to the headaches because of the discontinuity in the fuselage cross section. From a regular fuselage section suddenly came a cut out, and the tail faired into the notch. All of the tail loads, the vertical loads, and the lateral loads on the fin had to be redistributed, in effect jumping to another cross section forward of the tail section itself. What I worked on was to redistribute these stresses.

Later on we had a problem with a bolted-on joint where the engine used to protrude from the tail. Remember, the tail could be removed. When we went to the Patuxent River Naval Air Station for testing, first-time pilots would hit the tail, which had a solid skid, a bumper, on a landing flare. We actually had movies of the whole back end breaking off and just doing a loop onto the runway while the forward fuselage sailed down the runway on the tricycle gear. So we put a hydraulic strut on the bumper with a hinged Stellite alloy plate. Hit that, and it actually worked like a shock absorber and just folded up.

Wes McDonald, who became commander in chief Atlantic (CincLant) in the mid-1980s as a full four-star admiral—the highest in the Navy except for the World War Two five-star admiral of the fleet not used since—flew a lot of navy airplanes, jets, and props. One thing he agrees with me about was the F8F, "a really neat airplane." He also agrees that the first navy jets, the Banshee and the Panther and the Cougar, were good but not great airplanes. The McDonnell airplane he flew on his first fleet tour was kind of fragile, with many electrical complications, unlike the F9F that was typically a Grumman Iron Works–type airplane. Climb—and the F9F ran out of speed very quickly. But point that thing down. . . . Eventually Grumman approached a monopoly in training, with the F9F, and on the carriers McDonald flew the straight-wing F9F-2 and F9F-5 and the swept-wing F9F-6. All three had good reputations for getting a pilot home in the training and fleet commands. "But it wasn't in the class of the air force F-86," McDonald said, "which I flew in an exchange duty tour with the Air Force, because of the carrier suitability that had be built into it left it less maneuverable. The FJ-4B based on the F-86 was really a good airplane. My impression was that the F9F was good airplane, but that Grumman was beginning to slip a little behind the competition."

And the next round turned on the McDonnell F4H and Vought F8U-3.

Grumman came out of the war as cock of the roost, in the opinion of Rear Adm. Leonard A. Snead, one of the first test pilots for the A-6. "George," he told me one time, "you were the best airplane building company of the whole kit and kaboodle of them." As the Navy moved into the jet age, Grumman built the F9F series and the F11F. These were not great airplanes, but neither were McDonnell's Banshee, nor the F3H, nor the Vought F-8 and A-7 Corsair series. But they were all building blocks in what became a great stable of airplanes. Technology was evolving and the jet engine was evolving. Some of those early engines were dogs. Weapons suits weren't particularly good. When the Navy was trying to break the sound barrier, it couldn't do it with the Panther, but the Cougar, going downhill, could—though not for long. This was nibbling on the edges of technology with equipment that really wasn't there yet. Then Grumman developed the A-6, the F-14, the E-2C and the EA-6B, all new concepts pushing the technical envelope. The initial versions of each of these airplanes needed a lot of work, too, especially the A-6, with not the aerodynamics but the avionics and displays. Not until the A-6E did the Navy get the heavy attack airplane it needed.

Grumman's proposal was picked from among eleven submitted by eight contractors for the initial development of this new breed of airplane, what Swoose Snead considers the first really good jet attack airplane with the weapons system to go with it. (Swoose was a long-standing nickname, probably from his long, thin build that resembled the comic character Alexander the Swoose.) I never worked on or had much involvement with the A-6. So Swoose among others can fill in some of that story. His first trip to Grumman came as a young lieutenant commander just out of test pilot school and assigned to the first A-6 navy preliminary evaluation. That's when he got to know the field organization, Nick Scobbo, Ralph Clark, Terry Newitt, and the others at the Oceana Naval Air Station near Norfolk, who were there on the first cruise on the *Independence* with the A-6. Swoose doesn't remember any talk of cancellation of the A-6, though there was some, but he added: "We lost three airplanes early on in the first deployment in 1965. When I came back to Patuxent River, the Navy loaded an A-6 with bombs and cameras. When the airplane was pushed into a dive and the bombs were salvoed, all hell broke loose. The bombs were hitting each other, coming up bumping the wings, hitting the tail. The fix was to use intervals instead of trying to salvo 500-pound bombs, although we could salvo 2,000-pounders."

When VA-75 deployed with the embryonic A-6 to Southeast Asia later, it had what was called the Golden Fleet: numbers 64 through 75 production line aircraft. Every one of the twelve was different because of the black boxes and wiring. Pilots were flying them up to Grumman and picked up the last one the day before going aboard ship. Grumman was trying to fix the airplane and the whole Navy wanted it fixed. No two airplanes were alike in that entire group. Fixes went in this airplane or that one, but the squadron really didn't know what it had.

Pressing that era's technology, the early A-6 computer was a manual-input monster that sat between the bombardier's legs, something that now probably would fit in a package the size of a mini tape recorder. Weapon system integration was unknown then, and Grumman learned on the A-6. *Independence* was an east coast carrier that deployed around Africa and through the Straits of Malacca to enter the Vietnam War. Snead came under significant heat for pressing to send the A-6 into combat then, but there never would have been funding to fix it if it hadn't gone into combat. Everybody loved it, everybody wanted it, but it had to be fixed.

When Snead came back from Vietnam he was called to Washington immediately to brief the Joint Chiefs of Staff and the entire navy hierarchy. Then he went up to Grumman, got the top engineers together in one big room, and the bottom-kicking contest started. Larry Mead, the project engineer, with Grant Hedrick and Dr. Renso Caporali were there and that meeting room was filled. They were quiet as church mice. The bottom line was that the A-6 was the right airplane for the right mission, but Grumman and the Navy had to fix it. No arguments, no dissenting opinion, for Grumman understood. And it was fixed eventually.

"We had a terrible support problem," Snead continued. "Ralph Clark led the service team of twenty-five Grumman tech reps on board *Independence*. When the ship would go into Subic Bay, Ralph Clark would fly over to Manila and pick up boxes of parts air freighted out within twenty-four hours by Grumman and bring them back to the ship. Unfortunately that was putting a Band-Aid on a shotgun wound. Yet Ralph Clark was a magician who could get on the telephone and make it all happen. Subic Bay was rain and rain, and people would leave canopies open. Pretty soon all the black boxes were wet and had to be removed and dried. The Navy had a learning curve also. Inventory wasn't necessarily sitting on the shelf, because we really didn't know exactly what we had. I've said forever and say today, the navy supply support system never gained the proficiency to support a modern-day jet air wing at sea, deployed. We still have support problems."

Vice Adm. Robert F. (Dutch) Schoultz adds that the Navy had a lot of trouble initially with the electronic warfare development, the EA-6B, when he was commander of naval air forces in the Pacific between 1980 and 1983. "The EA-6B was a very expensive airplane for the time," he said, "maybe $70–80 million. And some of the reasons we lost airplanes were dumber than dirt." Because the EA-6s didn't have weapons, the Navy lost two because crews were doing DCM, defensive air combat maneuvering, to learn how they should react if attacked. Another was lost when the cockpit lights came on for the pods the airplane carried on the belly. The crew didn't know what they were, thought they were alarms, and jumped out of the airplane, which flew on forever and finally crashed. Both A-6s and EA-6s were flying out of Whidbey Island, Washington, but something Schoultz didn't know turned up. The EA-6B looks like an A-6 except it's extended. "But the wing loading is a hell of a lot different with all that stuff in the back end and the four crewmen," he said, "yet pilots were flying it like an A-6, which was a very honest and stable airplane."

Another thing that turned up was that the EA-6B had never been tested completely at Patuxent—no spin testing for one. As a result of Dutch Schoultz and his comments, Grumman and Patuxent derived much information for wing loading and changed some of the procedures in NATOPS. Wing loading was higher than the A-6's. In a tightening turn, when the g-load went up, he recalled, "the EA-6B stalled a lot quicker and it departed a lot faster. We also didn't have very good parameters on how to recover from a spin because the testing hadn't been done."

All this happened after the Korean War reversed the downsizing of defense. Post–World War Two business entailed scrounging and looking under rocks. But it was not that tough either. While the factory wasn't busy, it wasn't that empty in the design floor. We had begun to look at the JR2F in 1944, the first of five designations applied to the Albatross amphibian, as a successor to the JRF Goose of the 1930s. Though it was no big production program, more than a hundred were built into the 1950s, not only for the Navy but also for the Coast Guard and the Air Force for air sea rescue, designated HU-16. We also were looking at the AF-2S and the AF-2W, the Guardian. These had started in 1944 as successors to the fabulous TBF that did so much to make so many small navy carriers in World War Two Grumman decks. Both became part of an antisubmarine hunter-killer team: the AF-2W as the hunter with a big belly radome and the AF-2S that mounted bombs, depth charges, or torpedoes in a weapons bay. We built more than three hundred, so that put something on the floor as well into the early 1950s.

Pushing technology I've dwelt on, but there was another big metamorphosis: government relations. In the old days we did some good handholding, but more with the technical Navy and very little then, as far as I know, with senators or congressmen. When the chief of naval operations at that time said something to Rep. Carl Vinson, who was the autocratic chairman of the House Armed Services Committee, such as, "I need another ship or batch of airplanes," he got them! It wasn't, "Wait a minute, we have to talk to the system analyst." If we had talked to Congress directly then, we'd have got the Navy's nose about six miles out of joint.

Even Jake or Roy at one time could go down to Washington or call up and say, "Admiral, we need some more airplanes to keep the plant running." And he could answer, "Okay we'll give you an order for another two hundred." But those days evaporated very quickly. Of course in the 1960s a whole new generation came along, bean counters or whatever you want to call them, system analysts that Robert S. McNamara, as Jack Kennedy's defense secretary, brought in as his crew. The top people in the flag ranks began listening to those underneath them, whereas before there weren't too many who could talk about systems and trade-offs and so forth. "Personas," like Arleigh Burke with strong navy advocates running the committees in Congress—including Carl Vinson, Sen. John Stennis, and Sen. John McClellan—would just say, "Go build them." They had the Congress in their hands so it wasn't hard. I remember later sitting on the porch with Carl Vinson down in Milledgeville, Georgia, his hometown, where we built a military glass fiber parts plant. Sitting there with Vinson was his nephew, Sen. Sam Nunn, who was chairman of the Senate Armed Services Committee. "We're bringing business down here," I told him, "and a lot is for the F-14. We'd appreciate your help." He did help. I still have an autographed picture from Carl Vinson, who was a legend in Congress. That was later, when I wound up in the front office.

My dealings in the early postwar period, like most in Grumman, were with the Navy, not with the flag officers but with the technical interface. What was then the Bureau of Aeronautics handled aircraft requirements, engineering, and procurement. Veterans from the 1930s were still there, like the Navy's Mr. Fighter, George Spangenburg. As a matter of fact, Grant Hedrick used to go down once a week just to keep in touch and to discuss any problems our airplanes might have. There was great mutual respect between Hedrick and some of our hotshots, like Larry Mead, and with Ralph Creel, who was the head structures man, and Ed Ryan, his deputy. The structures guys were very good. But I was a young guy at that time, only thirty years old at the most, so I was just a minor player in that league.

Still I was taken down once in a while and picked up some of the flavor of dealing with the Navy. I got involved with the Patuxent people because right after the war, as I said, in 1946, we had brought down the F7F to do some field carrier landing testing. Patuxent at that time had a wooden turntable with a couple of wires across it. They didn't even have a landing signal officer in residence but had to bring one down from Philadelphia! We went out on the *Franklin D. Roosevelt* and we did some testing on that carrier, which turned out to be okay. On that particular cruise I saw World War Two marine ace, Col. Marion Carl, make one of the first jet takeoffs and landings on a carrier, not long after the initial Phantom did. This was in a P-80, a Shooting Star, a Lockheed airplane. The Navy had bought three P-80As from the Air Force for deck landing tests. While the airplane didn't make it past carrier suitability trials, it did evolve into the T-33 trainer for both the Air Force and the Navy.

Jet carrier operations were pretty sporty in those days, not to mention later on. Carl made a running takeoff. They pushed him aft so the tailpipe was over the ramp, and he ran down the deck, took off, and went around and landed and did it again. Of course the carrier was making thirty knots over the deck. He was light so he got off, and there were no heart-stopping moments.

Carl was a character. At that time he was operating out of Patuxent, and he had the reputation of relishing the challenge of flying an F8F in bad weather. Before he did the carrier jet takeoffs and landings, I remember standing in the back of the ready room, which was packed with people. They were briefing away about what they were going to do and all the things that had to be taken care of first. I looked around for the pilot who's going to do this risky thing. And there to one side, ten feet away from me, leaning casually against a door was Marion Carl, just like he was an outsider poking his head in to see what was going on. That was a big moment for a young engineer. I wouldn't call Carl antisocial, but he was reticent—like Roy Grumman.

While the F9F continued Grumman navy fighter dominance into the jet era, things were changing. The McDonnell fighters came along. Personalities figured here, especially in Roy Grumman's reserve and reluctance to expand, which always struck me as being very symbolic of where Grumman didn't measure up. We went into business in 1930. James S. McDonnell, old man Mac or Mr. Mac, as he called himself around the plant, was cut of the same cloth as Roy Grumman: he was an engineer and a flyer. He went into business in late 1939 or 1940 as a lower-tier subcontractor building parts and pieces for other people in what was then the aircraft industry. Yet he emerged after the war and put the first jet on a carrier. Mr. Mac went after everything. He won the Mercury contract from NASA to build the spacecraft that placed the first American into space. He saw the role of the commercial jet aircraft. His own business jet didn't make it, but he thought big and bought the nearly bankrupt Douglas Aircraft to get into the commercial jet airliner business.

I met him by coincidence on a carrier when they had the F3H performing trials; the fighter struggled with a Westinghouse engine that left it grossly underpowered. Here's this fellow, standing at the railing alongside the stack, watching. I'm there, with my Grumman hat on. But he asked me anyway, "You with Grumman?" "Yes." "What do you do?" "Test engineer. We got an instrumented airplane making arrested landings and catapult launches, working out of Patuxent." I think it was an F9F-5P, a photo version of the F9F-5, which still had a straight wing.

McDonnell had on his company hat. He was wearing glasses, and he had a jacket on as I did. "I see you're with McDonnell," I said. "What do you do?" "My name is McDonnell." "McDonnell?" I said with a start. "Yeah, I'm James McDonnell, Jim McDonnell." Jake Swirbul might have played that same scene, out on a carrier, but probably never Roy Grumman.

Though I didn't know it then, I was about to move into other fields, but before that happened, I relocated into a group in the stress department known as the structural flight test group. Its mission in life was to use the then newfangled strain gauge and measure loads on the airplane in flight and send the data to the ground using a new kind of radio called telemetry to match them against design loads. Subsequently, that was melded that into the Structural Flight Research Group, which I eventually headed. As a lead engineer in all of the structural flight demonstration work we did at Patuxent as well as the carrier suitability work we had to do to specification, I got to be a pretty good expert in buffet boundaries. Everybody learned about buffet after the hit movie *Breaking the Sound Barrier* came out in the early 1950s. Technically what happens is that as an airplane gets near Mach 1 the center of pressure on a wing begins to shift and the nose starts to turn down, tucking under. In those days airplanes didn't have enough elevator power to overcome transonic aerodynamic forces. So designers resorted to putting on dive brakes on the underside of the wing to help the elevator pick up the nose. Buffet boundary was something that could be predicted. I had a famous diagram in Grumman that all the front office engineers used to come around and check for the latest on buffet. It plotted all the different airplanes we could get data on, from the NACA and our own. Transonic drag suddenly spiked at around .84 or .85 Mach number, and that's where all the buffeting and instability and control surface stiffening showed up. Eventually the solution was the hydraulic-powered flying tail, where the whole damn surface moved, not just the aft elevator section.

Just to get a flavor of what those days were like, I looked back at some structural flight test research reports I wrote. I read some of the formulas, and now I don't understand them. I can't believe I wrote them, like equations on buffet boundary and stability and control. So I had background in sophisticated technology, although I was not an aerodynamicist, although I had studied the field in college. But then my career went more into running the operational stuff.

Looking back now, those were rewarding days in the early 1950s—a lot of first flights, of one airplane version or another. Of course the last first flight of a Grumman fighter was the F-14 in December 1970. So the F-14, for that reason and many others, is the crux of the Grumman story.

4

LEW EVANS BUYS
INTO THE F-14

T WO EVENTS COULD BE CONSIDERED WATERSHED MOMENTS FOR
Grumman—and they coincided. One was its winning the contract to develop the Navy's new air superiority fighter to go into the
fleet in the late 1960s. The other was the death, at the worst possible
time, of a relatively young Lew Evans in 1972. Both are intertwined,
because Evans had been the Grumman strategist that sold the F-14 to
the Navy in a bid against McDonnell Douglas. And he also was
responsible for executing, if not technically signing, what was known
as a total package procurement contract for the airplane that almost
bankrupted the company in the 1970s. What the F-14 and its initial
contract did to Grumman's relations with the Navy is a subject for
argument, but it clearly did cause heartburn with Congress.

First, to tell the Lew Evans story, I reiterate that Grumman's hall-
mark is one of "unfulfilled destiny." This has to do with Lew Evans,
who had the ideas and the personality to build the company but
whose life span ran out before he could do so. I feel certain of this
because I had many discussions with Lew, and I had worked for him
on Long Island. After I went down to Cape Canaveral in the mid-
1960s to run the Apollo lunar module operations, I had Lew in my
house more than once. Lew was always after the brass ring. If Lew had
lived, Grumman might have fulfilled its destiny, I thought, for he was

an expansionist, unlike Roy Grumman. He was on the prowl. If Lew had lived, Grumman could have been like Lockheed Martin today.

Even so, he was trapped, because he was working under Clint Towl and Roy Grumman. Besides, he was a lousy administrator. His office had too many people running all over the place. No question about it, Lew had detractors in the company as well as fans. Even when Jake Swirbul was alive, and even though Jake was Lew's mentor as much as anybody, Lew didn't have a free hand. At one time Lew was trying to promote the construction of aluminum railroad cars for the Long Island Railroad. Funny thing, he stuck me, too, with the project of building passenger-loading bridges at the airport. He had me charging here and there, designing those things and talking to the union heads in New York City. Would we have had any trouble building them as a nonunion company and putting it at the unionized airport like Kennedy or LaGuardia? Probably.

On the railroad thing, he had Lennie on it. That was Leonard Sullivan, later an upper-level aide in the Pentagon with the Office of the Secretary of Defense, where, incidentally, he used to give some of the government and the industry people fits. So did his buddy, Russ Murray, in Program Analysis and Review, the offspring of McNamara's whiz kids, who could turn the services livid in the Kennedy days. Both worked at Grumman, Lennie as the A-6 project engineer in the preliminary design group. Lew had Lennie make a wooden mock-up of the train, which I never saw, so it must have been kept behind locked doors. Lew then was a brash young guy, about forty-eight, but he got Mr. Grumman to come down there after lunch one day to take a look at it. Roy walked into one of the back hangars, and Lew introduced Lennie Sullivan to Mr. Grumman. Lennie started talking about building trains of aluminum, aerospace structure, all of that stuff that we heard about later in the post-Vietnam days. Roy just walked around the mock-up and said: "I don't know why we're doing this. I don't know why we're doing this. This is not our cup of tea."

Born to a missionary family in Korea, Lew Evans was a B-29 flight engineer in World War Two and a Harvard Law School graduate who worked for the Navy in contracting. Jake Swirbul brought Lew into the company after Evans impressed him as the navy lawyer on the acquisition of the Calverton plant property on the eastern tip of Long Island. Swirbul in his later days began to talk a lot with Lew, with Jack Rettaliata, who was a public relations guy and political emissary, and with Roger Wolfe Kahn, who was head of the service department. Presumably he was looking for talent, a successor. Roger was wealthy, the son of financier Otto Kahn, a wonderful person, a talented and successful society orchestra leader and composer before he got patriotic in the war and, with other socialite test pilots like Tommy Leboutillier, went to work for Grumman. Roger was famous for writing "Crazy Rhythm," a favorite with jazz musicians, and for his short-lived (1931–33) marriage to musical-comedy actress Hannah Williams, who later married boxing legend Jack Dempsey. Slightly built, dark, very unassuming, considerate of his people almost to a fault, Roger was famous for wearing a trench coat, winter and summer, and a slouch fedora because he was always cold. His second wife, Daisy, was also a New York City socialite. Stories began to circulate nevertheless about how Jake was beginning to home in more on Lew.

Lew had a sponsor in Charley Kingsley, who had come from Remington Rand, and who was the corporate counsel and a very close friend of Roy Grumman. He pushed Lew forward until Jake then took a shine to him. Eventually Jake made Lew and Jack Rettaliata (I think at one time he was Roy Grumman's office boy) vice presidents. But he didn't make Roger Kahn one, and Roger was crushed. That was sad because Roger had built a superb service and support organization at Grumman, something an aerospace company rises or falls on. Roger felt that because he was Jewish there was an element of discrimination there. People say he went into his office and didn't come out for three days, except to go to the men's room.

With Jake's blessing Lew began to develop. Before Lew came along, Grumman didn't even have a marketing department. Now times were changing and we had to go sell ourselves. He decided we should have a business development organization, which had weekly meetings where certain people were invited. I got invited to one or two of the meetings, or somebody took me, but I was in the bleachers so to speak. His troops would preach about what the situation was in Washington. How we have to do this, what the next big program would be, how we have to go after this or that and on and on.

By that time the company began to realize that it needed more ongoing and frequent contact with the Navy—and Washington in general. Initially Oscar Olsen, who was an engineering fellow with a nice personality, would go down to Washington and talk to people mostly in BuAer, the Bureau of Aeronautics, and circulate. There was hardly any political activism that I can recall. When Lew Evans, then a vice president, began to pump up business development, he took the lead with Jake Swirbul's blessing and galvanized all of the Grumman company. Clint Towl was vice president of the corporation, and aerospace had not been split out yet as a subsidiary so it was still Grumman Aircraft. When Jake died, Clint became president.

Lew became the Washington operator, taking the hurdles down there. Having worked as a lawyer in BuAer—dapper, energetic, and gregarious with a gift for gab—he knew the navy people we needed to deal with. He began to cultivate not only local politicians, who quickly embraced him, but he also began to network with the politicians in Washington. This was something different for Grumman's historic hewing to the navy technical types. Using his farm near Warrenton, Virginia, Lew developed a routine, flying down on Thursdays in the Gulfstream to Washington. After scooting around Washington all day, and maybe spending Friday down there, going from office to office and hustling for the programs we were after, he would then come back to New York on Monday on the Gulfstream. During the weekends, he would entertain congressional or military people at his farm. So he was suddenly going to make the presence of Grumman felt in Washington in a new postwar manner.

Tom Kane, who retired after the Northrop acquisition as vice president of marketing, started in flight test and later moved into business development to work for Evans. Lew was very discrete in his entertaining and his friendships, using the privacy of his farm, Kane told me. "He could have walked into the Pentagon with his navy background and knocked on doors," Kane said, "but he didn't. I don't think he ever asked for anything that wasn't achievable and for no more than his share." Lew Evans took Tom Kane, a former A-4 pilot, and Eddie Dalva along with him when he spent two weeks riding on the carriers during the Vietnam War and made a big impression on the Navy. "I didn't realize how frail his health was until that trip," Kane said as a portent of things to come. "He had only one lung, and his father had died at the age of fifty-two."

Before Evans came aboard, Grumman was an internal company, concentrated on engineering and product development. "What Evans did," Kane recalled, "was to make the customer a lot more important in the eyes of the Grummanites. Until then Grumman had concentrated on the technical sections of the Navy, the Coast Guard, and the Air Force, though it didn't make much headway with the latter until later. What Lew did was bring the company out into the open."

Grumman in the early years didn't have a marketing organization or a very high-powered Washington office. Mostly it was a combination of Roy Grumman himself and Jake Swirbul. Later we brought in some former navy people, like Adm. Frederick M. Trapnell. He personally signed off on the F6F after a three-hour test flight to get it into the fleet and combat without waiting for the normal navy six- or eight-month test cycle. Roy said later that he didn't think the formal approval came through until after the war and a bag of 5,155 Japanese airplanes had been shot down. Another in the Washington office was Adm. Joe Bolger. We started to cozy up to the Navy through their own kind. Lew was a born politician who reveled in Potomac fever. Then, when Lew died in 1972, Clint Towl tried to shut down the Washington office.

George Spangenberg, reminiscing before his death in an auto accident, recalled being summoned to a meeting with Lew Evans in Washington on promoting the F-14 in Congress. Sometimes called Mr. Fighter within the Navy, Spangenberg ran the design requirements desk in BuAer as a civil servant. Such talk from Lew Evans about lobbying congressmen left him very uncomfortable and his view of Lew Evans was that of an engineer wondering whether massaging politicians was the way to develop a new fighter. His fears were not idle ones because he had suffered through the battles in the 1960s over the controversial TFX that became the F-111 that then Defense Secretary Robert S. McNamara insisted on building as one airplane for both the Air Force and the Navy. The F-111 was a waypoint on the road to the F-14 and had a lot to do with why the Navy and Air Force took separate paths on a new air superiority fighter that some in the Defense Department thought could be met also with one air-plane. After all, they thought, the Navy had developed the F-4 Phantom 2 and the Air Force had later bought it and liked it.

Spangenberg's F-14 history begins in 1955, the genesis of the navy competition for the Eagle long-range air-to-air missile and its Missileer launch platform, a forerunner of the TFX and of the F-14. Threat projections were warning of difficulties in protecting the fleet against Mach 2 aircraft that were coming off the drawing boards. The Navy needed something better than it had with operational deck launch aircraft. "All the studies showed you just couldn't get there in time to shoot down enough attacking aircraft to protect a battle group," Spangenberg recalled. "Surface-to-air missiles at that time just couldn't handle the threat either. But studies in the mid-fifties also indicated that microwave state of the art was such that we could do a long-range radar—it would take probably a five-foot dish—and get it into an airplane." All this led to perhaps the biggest study effort in the operations analysis field that the Navy had conducted up to that point on how best execute the fleet defense mission. Out of that came a determination that the only real way to do the job was with a com-bat air patrol airplane, a subsonic long-endurance airplane loitering a hundred miles or farther from the fleet, carrying a big load of long-range missiles. It was far superior to trying to accomplish high-speed intercept. With the projected threat of Mach 2 performance com-bined with air-launched nuclear missiles it was imperative the attack-ers be stopped or thinned out as far away as possible.

Larger carriers weren't an option, not to mention an expensive way to do it. So the Navy sold Eagle/Missileer to Congress. Eagle itself was a one-hundred-mile-range missile with mid-course guidance and terminal homing and weighed on the order of thirteen hundred pounds, coupled with a Westinghouse fire control system begun a couple of years before the airplane. The Pratt & Whitney TF-30 engine got started about that time in order to provide the engine as well as the missile system in time to match the airplane. Starting long lead items was a custom then because airframe development time is shorter. By the time of the Eagle competition, Grumman had won a whole batch of programs: the E-2C, the army Mohawk, and the A-6. The Chief of the Bureau of Aeronautics then was Adm. Bob Dixon, and he told

Grumman unofficially that he didn't think that they should win the next competition, that the company would be overloaded.

Unfortunately for that notion, Grumman was really on a roll after a reorganization that placed good engineers in charge of all the forward-looking programs. Grumman foxed the Navy and ended up as a subcontractor to Bendix, which won the Eagle competition with Grumman heavily involved. The Eagle program went along well enough for the Missileer airplane part of it to start on schedule in 1959. It was a controversial airplane because of its low performance: subsonic with two turbofan engines and a two-place, side-by-side cockpit with a five-foot radar dish in the nose. The airframe part of the game was really not too difficult technically. Obviously it was much easier than trying to do a supersonic airplane with that big radar. Pre-merger Douglas won with a very straightforward design with six missiles mounted on the wings, three on each side, externally.

To the detriment of the Missileer Robert S. McNamara arrived in the Pentagon in 1960 as John Kennedy's secretary of defense. The outgoing administration did not want to award a full development contract until the incoming administration approved the program. So the Navy kept Douglas on a low-level engineering effort, probably under $1 million, for some preliminary engineering. McNamara's crew could see the Navy had a new airplane started, and the Air Force had a new fighter started called TFX. They're going to fight the same enemy. Why don't they do it with one airplane? On the working level, the general impression was that the conversation must have been almost that casual, the decision that led to the TFX mess.

McNamara was supposed to be proving to the services that he could wear them down, and the military was supposed to be fighting civilian rule. That wasn't the case at all. The Air Force and Navy really were trying to backstop the technical job that McNamara's crew was screwing up. Up to that time the Office of the Secretary of Defense staff might question something, but would usually accept the reasoning or the technical input from the services. McNamara's crew, which Spangenberg considered incompetent, just didn't believe the services. Consequently the McNamara crowd canceled the airplane, the Missileer, but the Eagle missile continued into early 1960 before it, too, finally was chopped. Thus ended the Eagle/Missileer program, but it set the stage then for the things that came later, the TFX, the A-7, and the F-14.

While the A-7, which Vought won and which became an one-airplane-fits-all program later, had nothing to do with the F-14 directly, it had a great deal to do with it indirectly. The Navy had an A-7 contract through about 200 airplanes and the last lot was for 140 production planes. The airplane was going great. The program manager found some additional money and wanted to buy another half dozen airplanes to add to the original 140. When Vought responded, those extra airplanes were priced at more than those already on contract, despite learning curve theory that they should be cheaper. Trying to sell the idea on Capitol Hill that you want to buy seven more airplanes that cost more than the ones already under contract raises welts. As a result, programs from that point began to incorporate variable lot pricing in the production options—abbreviated as VarLot. The Navy made the contractors give quotes based on what it expected to buy, a normal rate at which they did their basic pricing. But then the contractors also had to quote prices on a curve if the Navy bought as few as 50 percent of normal or 50 percent more.

Later that became real trouble on the F-14 program. "We were ordered to buy only half the original lot size," Spangenberg recalled, "and the variable lot pricing formula was screwed up. The unit price didn't go up enough with the rate cut in half. Having VarLot pricing in the contract allowed the government to cut the rate of production much easier than if, say, we cut the rate and the price went up by 30 percent. Then there would be a better chance of holding the original deal and getting the original figure from Congress. Variable lot pricing made writing the contract very, very difficult and complex."

Raphael Mur, a Grumman lawyer who negotiated many contracts, notes one other thing the F-14 contract had. The Navy usually bought engines and furnished them to the airframe contractor as government furnished equipment (GFE). But with the F-14 the Navy made Grumman responsible for the total package, for total system integration. "I don't think even the C-5 had this," he recalls. Mur insisted, and so did the engineers, that if Grumman was going to do that, it had to have a very detailed specification on the engine and how it was to be tested. For example, there were changes to the inlets because of the engine that Grumman negotiated with the Navy. Until that time, is Mur's point, Grumman never had that kind of an obligation.

Back to Spangenberg's story: The A-7 is really tied in with TFX because at the time TFX was under way the Navy had started the VAX development for an attack aircraft. Navy types all ran around with lapel buttons that said "VAX. I like VAX." The ones that said "We don't like TFX" they didn't dare wear in the Pentagon. A batch of studies (the sea-based strike study must have been done about then) all showed the Navy needed roughly twice the capability of an A-4. The Navy had tried earlier to develop a swept-wing version replacing the A-4's delta, which would have given that capability, or would have if there had been a fan engine to install at the same time. That program, the A4D-3, had to be canceled when the Navy ran out of money.

Vought was playing around with versions of the F-8 without changing the engine. Grumman did all kinds of studies, from brand-new airplanes to versions of the A-6. And North American was doing the same with a follow-on to its FJ-4. In the end the Navy was forced into an off-the-shelf competition because the Office of the Secretary of Defense (OSD) didn't want a high-priced full development. McNamara games again. The requirement said in effect that the airplane had to be a modification of an airplane already developed. It was a good competition, Spangenberg thought, and four designs made the finals. Northrop dropped out, leaving Douglas, Vought, North American, and Grumman. Grumman submitted a kind of a stripped A-6. The other three designs were very close to the same kind of a job.

Vought, with brass, gave up on holding the fuselage and engine of an F-8, and designed a brand-new airplane. The vertical tail was the same, or at least the same shape. Eliminated was the F-8's variable incidence wing, replaced with a thicker cross section. It had a better high lift system, retained experience from the F-8, and saved some of the systems. Probably that was a mistake because putting in ten-year-old hydraulic components in a new airplane doesn't make sense. But Vought was more or less forced into it to make a pretense at off-the-shelf, and it got the contract. From a technical standpoint the competition was extremely tight between North American and Vought. Their two airplanes were almost the same on payload range, the real criteria in the competition. On the other hand, Vought and Douglas were almost identical in cost, but with Vought having a substantial payload radius advantage. "Why Douglas wasn't a heck of a lot more competitive on price was the thing that puzzled me the most at the time," Spangenberg recalled. "It turned out that there was a great difference in those days in the labor rates in Texas versus Long Island and Los Angeles, again, something that came back to haunt the F-14 program. There was no question that General Dynamics and Vought had a 30 percent edge in labor costs. Vought was eager too. They did a good job."

The Navy really needed a six-hundred-mile operational radius from the carrier. "From that day on we tried to get there," he said, "but we haven't yet. In fact we've backed up a bit. With the combination of the F-14, the A-7, and the A-6 we had hoped to get an honest-to-god five-hundred-mile operational radius to do a useful mission. The F-14 ended up shorter than we wanted, but primarily because we didn't get the new engine, got forced into some compromises we didn't have to make and shouldn't have made. But with that combination of airplanes we were getting closer to where we wanted to be. When we get to the F-18 range performance it's obviously a step back to what the A-4 was. That made the fleet very unhappy, and when the operators saw what was coming they came back to Washington and just raised hell. I got called in, after I was retired and a consultant, to talk with a navy captain and he was angry. We chewed for about three hours over how we got to where we were. It was a great help to him because he was scheduled for a three-year tour in Washington and he came in with the idea that the Naval Air Systems Command was nuts." Then Spangenberg switched to another side of acquisition.

"Let's talk about money," he suggested, "and how the Navy developed and bought airplanes then through two distinct accounts: Research, Development, Test and Evaluation (RDT&E) and Procurement, the latter for production where the big dollars were. Between 1955 and 1960, the Navy had three airplanes under development at the same time. All used cost-plus fixed fee contracts, although fixed price was gaining, setting the scenery for the way we procured airplanes in the future. Overruns every year on some of those programs—the North American AJ-1 Savage twin piston attack airplane was one I remember especially—were enough that the Navy kept having to cancel the little R&D programs that are the seed for the future, undermining the whole purpose of R&D.

"In part we thought we had solved the problem with the FIRM plan, which stood for Fleet Introduction of Replacement Models, only supporting airplanes with R&D funds through the mock-up stage. After that it would be production funds. A whole series of airplanes that we did in that 1950 time period were only funded R&D-wise at very small levels, and everything else was done on production funding, where the big money was and where there was more flexibility to operate. The F-4 got started with perhaps no R&D funding. We did it on the tail end of the F3H contract. For the A3J [later the RA-5C] I think something like $4 million was all the R&D money that was involved. Anyway, that windfall allowed the Navy to start too many airplanes. Instead of funding a whole program out of R&D it only had to fund the beginning of it.

"Money was becoming more important at the decision phases. In the 1950s one scarcely mentioned money in a design competition. The concept had all been approved with paper studies within the Navy and reinforced by airplane studies by the contractors that gave a second check on what the designers in the bureau were saying could be done. When we got a line item in the budget we would then do a competition, but we wouldn't fund anything until we had congressional approval to get the program started. McNamara's crew changed all of that, and the change is still causing problems today. Programs are well along before any approval on the Hill.

"A word of caution on this business. Most of the preliminary design people whether in government or in industry tend to be somewhat more optimistic than those who are building and testing, those concerned with the operational side of aircraft development. Part of the reason that the TFX got into trouble was so much of the early work was based on NASA studies done by John Stack and the high-speed aero group of the Langley research organization. Many of the designs when we finally got a look at them in detail, usually years later, were much too optimistic. The cockpits were too small. The radar antennas, when shown at all, were maybe a foot in diameter instead of two or three feet. Preliminary design people tend to get results that are more optimistic than they should be. Many of us believe that the so-called Navy TFX designs were probably incapable of being built, but they were much closer to being realistic than OSD's.

"In the year or two before the end of the F-111, studies were being done both in and out of the Navy, some funded, some unfunded, on how best to solve the needs of the fleet for an F-4 replacement. When it was apparent that the F-111B was not going to make it, the concept turned toward an airplane similar to the VFAX, adding the Phoenix missile system to it. After the Eagle was canceled, the Bendix drawings were turned over to Hughes, and eventually the weapon was reincarnated in 1965 in the AIM-54 with the AWG-9 fire control system. I'm not sure how many other people were inventing that airplane at the same time, but I remember being in Fred Gloeckler's office with a group of Grumman people for a VFAX discussion, and I think Fred first suggested it. The more we looked, the better solution seemed to be a new fighter that would carry the Phoenix and still have enough performance to do the other fighter missions. In short order Grumman came up with studies for that kind of an airplane and all looked attractive. Adm. Elmo Zumwalt in this case was the designated leader of the study group while Capt. Mike Ames, later F-14 program manager, was usually my point of contact.

"It was a big effort. The cost effectiveness studies that used to be done routinely in Gloeckler's shop with his small group escalated to major efforts, extending over a month of work by lots of people. Our old back of the envelope studies were just as reliable. Needless to say that fighter study then justified the need for the new airplane, called VFX. We had the usual trouble with OSD wanting to approve every sentence in the specification and in the Request for Proposals. To comply with the rules coming out of OSD, the RFP grew into a two- or three-inch-thick document rather than the half inch–thick ones that we were used to. But it was better to try to comply than to fight the system.

"Another big difference at the time was in funding design competitions. Heretofore we let the contractors gamble on who was going to get a production contract, which came from winning the experimental contract. This time OSD forced a funded effort for the four companies in this design area, Grumman, North American, McDonnell Douglas, and General Dynamics. Grumman was a hands-down winner. All of the airplanes were variable sweep wing with the exception of North American, a product of design studies up to that point that agreed variable sweep produced a better airplane.

The Navy did not accept the performance claims of North American. However, NASA generally supported our position, forestalling any real controversy."

Mike Pelehach ran preliminary design at Grumman early in his career and led the early study efforts to supersede the F-111B. He was involved in the F-111B meetings at General Dynamics in Fort Worth, where he would sit next to George Spangenberg. "You know, George, this damn thing is not going to go," he whispered to Spangenberg. "It'll fly, but it's not going to be a carrier-suitable airplane." With all the things that had to be there for the Air Force, especially with the escape capsule, it was just going to be too heavy. "Why," Mike thought, "don't we take all the technology that's available—the titanium, the boron, the AWG-9/Phoenix missile systems—and start laying out another airplane?" Pelehach stopped going to the meetings. Although he was convinced the airplane was going to get built, it wasn't going anywhere. "Even before the F-14 competition got under way," Mike recalled, "I had seventeen hundred engineers working trying to put an airplane together, pushing, shoving, and squeezing."

His rule-of-thumb design law for what became the F-14 was his insistence that, instead of fourteen thousand pounds of fuel, it have sixteen thousand pounds. The first thing that happens in laying out an airplane, in Pelehach's experience, is that people try to squeeze on more fuel later and that's the wrong way to do it. If the Navy knows there's sixteen thousand pounds of fuel in this thing, that's part of the gross weight, so, therefore, you've got to make all the structures strong enough for that. Grumman did end up laying the airplane for sixteen thousand pounds. In the middle of this, Lew Evans sent Pelehach off to school at Harvard. While he was gone, Pelehach said, the designers back at the plant "were monkeying around with these rules. You know, save a little bit on weight here or there." Things got out of whack, and Lew Evans summoned Pelehach back from Cambridge. "For the last month of school I would run to Logan Airport and jump on the two o'clock shuttle. A driver met me at LaGuardia in New York, and I would work at the plant until seven or eight o'clock then jump on the last shuttle back to Logan! And I did that for four weeks!" He burst into laughter. Later on, when Pelehach went aboard the carrier and talked with F-14 pilots, they told him, "We love the F-14 because of that extra fuel—for the wife and kids."

When the Navy started the F-14 program, as Spangenberg continued his story, the normal number of production airplanes to be bought was something like 463 at a normal production rate of 8 a month or 96 a year. If the Navy had had its way, the contractor would have bid fixed price on 6 R&D airplanes with production ceiling options for perhaps another 100 airplanes. We tried to get that kind of a contract through OSD, but the whiz kids refused and forced it to include fixed price ceiling options for the entire planned buy, which was quite unreasonable. The financial risks seemed too great for any manufacturer to assume. The program initially adopted the TF30-P12 engines that were already in the F-111B and fully developed, but planned to shift over to a new engine in development under air force management, the Pratt & Whitney F401. It would produce a marked increase in thrust and a better specific fuel consumption. The airplane then would be called the F-14B.

A second step was to install a new avionic suite that would have all-weather attack capability so that it could do the job of the A-6 without a major increase in the system's complexity—the F-14C. It was a good idea, and within the state of the art. The F-14C dropped out of the picture first, and eventually our new engine got canceled as well, so we were stuck for a long time with the engines that had been developed initially for the Missileer and then used with an afterburner for the F-111 program. The basic design mission of the F-14 included four Sparrows, and the six Phoenix fleet air defense mission would be considered an overload. We also had the complete A-7 level of attack capability built into the system from the beginning, although that feature was dropped later. The reason for its elimination was to reduce costs associated with flight test clearance of navy conventional stores at all wing sweeps. At the time, the production program had been cut back to levels that made it appear that all the F-14s would be needed for the pure fighter roles.

"Proposal evaluation went off very well," Spangenberg said, "with Grumman selected as the winner almost hands down. However, to meet the rules that were being laid on by OSD, the Navy had to carry two contractors until it negotiated complete contracts. McDonnell Douglas was selected to provide the competition for Grumman. Outsiders all seem to think that that competitive step is necessary, that it keeps the first contractor honest. My experience is that it just complicates the acquisition and increases total cost. People doing the negotiating know full well whether or not they can reach a contract. If they need competition, then make the decision on a case-by-case basis. Don't make it a requirement and don't get into "best and final" offers to make the contractor reduce his price that is usually too low already. It just breeds more trouble.

"What eventually gave us most of the contract problems in the F-14 was the variable quantity lot requirement, the VarLot that stemmed from the A-7. Grumman in pricing the variable lot quantity made the near-fatal assumption that its business base would stay the same whether the company was building 50 percent of the specified F-14 contract numbers or 150 percent. As a result, the variation of price with production rate was very flat. The F-14 had about one-third the increase in unit price with the production rate reduced by half of what the Lockheed S-3 antisubmarine hunter had and one-quarter in the increase specified for the F-15—facts that were known to us at the time we negotiated the contract. Our contracts people agreed that these price variations were not reasonable. Furthermore they obliquely informed Grumman that we believed there might be a problem with the VarLot pricing. Grumman, after study, didn't agree so the clause remained as bid. It is seldom that a contracting officer will suggest raising a bid price. It just isn't done. In retrospect, we should have been more specific. If I had it to do over, I think I would find an ethical way to let the contractor know."

The effect of that VarLot mistake was huge. The unit price differential between the normal and half production rates was so low that it invited the budgeteers to cut the numbers of airplanes being procured. As they got to the point where they could take advantage of that contract clause they did just that. The discussion went like this: "How much does the price go up if we only buy half as many?" "Well, it only costs another few percentage points." "Oh, well, then let's do it, it won't break the contract." Everybody would have been in far better shape if we had never had the low side of that variable lot pricing clause.

Grumman had another chance to recover. "I remember a trip to Bethpage with Vice Adm. Tom Connolly, then OP 05, Mike Ames, and probably Capt. Scotty Lamoreaux in connection with Grumman's losses," Spangenberg said. "My recommendation was that Grumman could ask for relief under the Armed Services Procurement Regulations by admitting that they had made a mistake and that the Navy was aware that it was a mistake. We could treat it as a mutual mistake and rewrite that clause. For reasons I still don't understand, Grumman elected not to do that. It probably would have created a hassle at the time but it would have saved a lot of effort farther down the road and the Navy might have been allowed to produce more aircraft."

Raphael Mur, who worked his way up in Grumman's legal department, was involved in the F-14 contract negotiations. He echoes George Spangenberg's points about VarLot pricing, but he was aghast at some things that went on within Grumman. "Talk about stupidity," he said. "I don't talk ill of the dead, but Lew Evans comes up with what seemed to be a bright idea, as the archetypal super sales-man. Though he was a lawyer, and a good lawyer, here he was the antithesis of a lawyer. All the things one would have anticipated as a lawyer he just chucked them all aside. His idea was to give the Navy a signed contract. We gave them the proposal as required, but with the proposal went a signed contract. Just sign here, Grumman said in effect, and we have a contract. This is crazy, I argued. First of all, the Navy didn't ask for it. Second, we might give the Navy things the Navy never thought of and doesn't want. Third, it may have things that annoy the Navy because we put them in, and the Navy didn't want them. And most significant of all, they're going to negotiate anyway. They're not going to sign this thing." Not only was it a point for the Navy to negotiate Grumman down from, but Mur thought it was insulting. "But he was chairman of the board and I was the lawyer, so we did."

Technically the F-14 program went very well. To contrast the F-111 and F-14 programs: Spangenberg made three trips to Grumman on the F-14, including the visit to the mock-up. On the F-111 he had been forced to go there thirty-five times for conferences about problems. "The F-14 went like a Navy airplane should go," he contends. "True there were glitches, but they were recognized and solved. Dive brakes had to be redesigned and we had a big hassle on the design of the landing gear. We saved a few hundred pounds with a clever redesign. All kinds of troubles were predicted on that one, but, as so often happens, when you do a good detail design job you can solve the problem before it appears. The airplane flew for the first time on December 21, 1970, a month or two ahead of schedule."

Unfortunately, maybe an omen for the history of the program, the first airplane crashed on its second flight. The problem was in its then relatively new titanium hydraulic lines and a complicated hydraulic pump system with numerous cylinders. What Grumman missed was that there were vibration modes. Everything was working out fine on the second flight when the test pilot elected to check single engine flight characteristics. Instead of shutting down the engine, he pulled it back to idle. That set up a harmonic vibration mode and ruptured a hydraulic line. Although the crew tried to get back to Calverton, the airplane went inverted and the crew punched out. All the fix took was moving a clamp to damp out the harmonic. While the recovery was good, the crash did set the program back a long time.

The program progressed normally in 1971, Spangenberg thought, until negotiations started over the target price of lot 4, undoubtedly due to that VarLot foul-up. Somehow or another the negotiations escalated to the deputy secretary of defense level with David Packard and Grumman CEO Lew Evans. From then on, there was obvious OSD bias against the F-14 program. Packard reached the conclusion that the airplane was too expensive and instituted programs seeking a lower cost alternative. These, of course, revealed the fact that there weren't any. When Packard was being considered for the deputy secretary of defense job, before it was announced, Spangenberg's group was asked to give him a presentation on the F-14. Secrecy enveloped the process, and the navy team wasn't really sure whom the presentation was for. They met with Packard alone in the Naval Air Systems Command's boardroom.

"Capt. Mike Ames, the F-14 program manager, gave a good presentation on the F-14, where we were, why we were doing what we were doing, and so on," Spangenberg related. "When we got through, Packard said, 'Well, you guys seem to know what you're doing. I'll leave you alone. Call me if you need me.' And we thought, this is the first deputy secretary of defense in years that has recognized what he knows and what he doesn't know. But it wasn't long before he stopped leaving us alone to do our jobs. We got into it later with him on the Lockheed S-3 antisubmarine aircraft program. My problem was with the milestone system he introduced as another way OSD was going to fix all our problems. The Navy didn't need milestone contracting, many of us thought, and I was giving him a presentation that we had structured to show why. We already had tight engineering control, tight schedule control, and could change things when we needed to change them. Packard interrupted me at about the third chart and said in very stern tones: 'We're not here to discuss whether we're going to have it. We're here to discuss how we're going to have it.' Needless to say I blew my stack. After this episode and the complete lack of understanding of acquisition, at least in the aircraft industry, as opposed to theory, I lost all respect for Packard and the rest of those OSD people."

The second F-14 low cost alternative phase came during a congressional hearing when Sen. Stuart Symington of Missouri, a former air force secretary, suggested a carrier version of the F-15. Studies that he claimed were ready were not. Spangenberg's efforts to find out their status ran into air force objections to the Navy dealing directly with McDonnell. In the end, the F-15 modification was considerably more expensive than the F-14, so it didn't make any sense. The only real proposal was for a version of the F-15 carrying four Sparrows, putting it into the effectiveness ballpark of the F-4 or a little below because it was a single- instead of a two-seat airplane. The Navy tried to get from McDonnell Douglas a proposal incorporating Phoenix for a more direct comparison of capability, but the Air Force said that McDonnell Douglas could not do that job within the time, money, and resources available. The Navy, it seemed, did a thousand cost studies and every time found it was cheaper just to buy more F-14s than to buy half as many and supplement them with something else.

After OSD found out that there was no single low cost alternative to the F-14, the high-low mix idea surfaced in OSD. Rather than one for one replacement of F-4s by F-14s, some lesser capability (and much cheaper) aircraft would substitute for F-14s. A study of replacements reached the stupendous conclusion that total expenditures down the pike surpassed current defense budgets. Of course, this has always been true. Long-range plans always exceed any current budget. Fiscal sanity finally comes in the upcoming year's budget. The study solution: buy some high-capability aircraft to meet high threats and a flock of low-capability aircraft to meet the low-technology threats. To the Navy, the idea was naive, particularly for carrier aviation. High threats were going to take everything the Navy had and then some.

Prototyping, another Dave Packard gospel and a sore memory with Spangenberg, was pushed hard, too, although it was given up before World War Two because it cost too much, took too long, and really wasn't necessary with the state of the art at that time. Those who had no institutional memory maintained that prototyping would solve all known technical and fiscal problems. Ridiculous, but it cost an enormous amount of time. The high-low concept led to OSD arguing that Phoenix wasn't necessary. The Marines complicated the problem by jumping in and out of the F-14—one year in, next year out. Replacement of marine F-4s added to the Navy's required 729 or so airplanes, which could have salved the airplane's economic abrasions. In early 1973 William H. Clements Jr., a Texas oil man and former governor who had become deputy secretary of defense when Packard became secretary, appointed an ad hoc committee to look into naval aircraft modernization. Dr. Alexander Flax, its head and well-known and respected in the aero field, had run Cornell Aeronautical Laboratory. The Flax committee report, like all other studies, concluded that the Navy needed something better than the F-4 but less expensive than an F-14. Happy as the Navy would have been to get F-14 capability cheaper, it didn't know how.

Clements finally sent a memo to Secretary of the Navy John Warner concerning the fighter modernization program directing us to study versions of both the F-14 and the F-15 and some kind of a modified aircraft and reply in one week, which Spangenberg protested in a memo to the secretary that disappeared in the bureaucracy. Then came a Clements request for funding estimates for his prototype scheme including development, testing, and production. NavAir prepared the data and forwarded it either to or via the CNO. Again the whole idea made no sense to Spangenberg, unless costs were aggregated of the prototype plans plus the production of the selected prototype plus the production of reduced numbers of F-14s, and compared to the normal F-14 costs.

All this headed for a climax in a hearing before the tactical air subcommittee of the Senate Armed Services Committee. Clements testified there from notes that, after studying the fighter modernization program, he concluded the Navy didn't need Phoenix in all of its fighters but that the Navy had found no lower cost alternatives to a Phoenix-carrying airplane. So he was embarking on a prototype program to determine what was the best non–Phoenix carrying airplane to supplement the F-14. He still wanted the Navy to prototype a stripped F-14 and to get an F-15 carrier-suitable airplane from McDonnell to test. He defended his program in the usual manner of "preliminary data, more later, etc." Secretary Warner and Adm. Mickey Weisner, then acting CNO, were less adversarial to the prototype program than Spangenberg hoped, and they concentrated on supporting the budget request for fifty F-14s. As usual Clements had undercut them by saying that everybody was in agreement and that the Navy was supporting his program, but Spangenberg knew everybody was not. In the end, Congress refused to fund the Clements prototype program.

Using less than a one-to-one replacement of navy F-4s was still an idea in being. The total number of F-14s talked about then was in the low 300s. Grumman had produced or had agreed to produce through lot 5 something on the order of 122 airplanes, which were being built at the minimum contractual rate. Grumman had refused to build lots 6 and 7 under the terms of the contract because the company would have gone bankrupt. At that time the Marines were back in the program, after dropping out earlier. If the Navy was to complete the VF modernization, that is replace all the F-4s without any production gaps, 174 more F-14s were needed in fiscal years through 1977, a total of about 400 F-14s. Unfortunately, the new engine slated to go in airplane No. 68 was in the process of cancellation, and the GE 101 engine hadn't come along far enough to be considered.

From an acquisition policy standpoint, forcing Grumman to fixed price ceilings in the original contract, for 463 airplanes—the normal quantity—was obviously a mistake. It had been forced upon us by OSD, however. We should have held the fixed price ceiling requirement to only about 100 aircraft. That would have been more or less equivalent to the 200 that we had on the A-7 program. Try to go too far and the system falls apart. The contractor should not have to risk his entire company. Anyone with even a moderate background of airplane design would have recognized that the program pushed by OSD had absolutely no hope of success.

* * *

Vice Adm. William D. Houser came back from the Mediterranean in 1972 to relieve Adm. Mickey Weisner as OP 05 (naval shorthand for deputy chief of naval operations for air) and landed in the middle of the F-14's troubles. "It was a very tough time," he recalled. "As I said then, 'I'm going to put on my tombstone, the F-14 did it.' Clint Towl hadn't helped any when he testified before the Senate Armed Services Committee. He and the committee got into a heated argument about losing money under this contract. 'I'll close my doors,' he told the committee. The hair came up on the backs of the necks of these senators, as if they were thinking, 'Go ahead and close the doors you SOB.' I had to live with that for the next three years." Grumman people, though, claim that Towl was misunderstood, that he was simply stating an unwelcome reality.

Houser got the residue. His testimony up there embittered the Senate against the airplane, which the crash on the second flight didn't help. In some cases opponents within the Navy were trying to cancel the F-14. Adm. Kent Lee became the commander of Naval Air Systems Command, an officer Houser considers a great nuts-and-bolts and logistics guy but who didn't understand, who didn't want to talk about what the F-14 could do and what the mission was. He wanted to talk about availability, about how much trouble it is to change out the engine. He didn't really trust Grumman as far as I could see. He was totally antagonistic toward Tom Connolly—Mickey Weisner succeeded him as OP 05—who he thought brought the F-14 in and who then went to work in Grumman's Washington office.

"It was a bad situation," Houser lamented. "I had to fight within the Navy and deal with the Air Force as well, although they were pretty good about it. The Air Force, of course, would have liked to see F-15s in the Navy. Senator Symington from McDonnell Douglas's home city of St. Louis was pushing this. So were some others in Congress, who didn't like the F-14. Despite the problems of adapting land-based airplanes to sea duty, the F-15 could have operated on carrier. By the time it was modified with folding wings and generally marinized, though, it would have been as costly as an F-14. Remember, the F-14 took the mission of the Eagle/Missileer, yet it was also was a very good combat fighter."

Agitation for the lightweight fighter had started when Houser left the Navy, which was being told to have two fighters. "That's nonsense," Houser objected. "We can't support two fighters when we can't even support one fighter now. Why do we need another fighter?" The Navy, in his view, had a perfectly good airplane (the F-14). If there was going to be another fighter, a supplemental fighter, it should be able to do something more, such as take the strike fighter role from the A-7. Besides in the F-14 he liked getting back to Grumman products and their reputation in the fleet for ruggedness.

"I had commanded the *Constellation*, which was one of the large decks at the time, and which Lew Evans visited when he came out to Vietnam. I had the F-4s, two versions of A-4, the A-4C, and the A-4E—all from McDonnell Douglas. We had the A-6s from Grumman. We had the RA-5C, that great big Vigilante, and we had our COD and the E-2Cs. The E-2C was a wonderful airplane and a great credit to Grumman. Nevertheless I contended that this was a great burden we're putting on ourselves unnecessarily, all these different types of airplanes from different manufacturers. The F-14 is a great fighter with long-range missile capability. It would also be a very fine two-place attack airplane with a radome big enough for a thirty-six-inch diameter flat pulse Doppler attack radar antenna."

What killed the attack F-14, Grumman marketing vice president Tom Kane says, were the divergent ideas of these two communities in naval aviation: fighter and attack. "The F-14 community was basically ruled by the pilots," he said, "and the A-6 by the BNs, the bombardier navigators, the electronics types. So it was the perceptions of the pilots against the attack guys. The latter liked what they had in the A-6 and didn't want to lose their uniqueness. We actually had an A-6 system in the F-14 that we were flying, but the A-6 community, where I had a lot of friends, told me: no soap."

Bill Houser reiterates the value of a common airplane on carriers, which, with the F-18, to Grumman's ill fortune, is what the Navy is coming to. There could have been an AF-14, Houser believes, which the Navy could have modified into an RF-14 to replace the Vigilantes. Someday, he thought, the F-14 could have become an EF-14, like the EF-111. "This is a great opportunity, I said at the time, to take a wonderful tested airframe, the same wing, same landing gear, plus all the rest and save on training. The F-14 could have carried other stores where Phoenix was hung. And it had the structural strength to take carrier operations with six Phoenix missiles in an overload condition.

"We would have had money enough to have developed the big engine to replace the TF-30," Houser said. "Finally the TF-30 got to working pretty well. But in the early days it was really bad. Squadrons were having to pull engines after five flights or something. And it was a big job. The TF-30 was not a green engine. Trouble came with the installation, how it fit in the F-14, for one. Second was what we were doing with it in the Navy that the Air Force wasn't doing. I flew the F-111 one time, at Nellis Air Force Base, honking the airplane into buffet and such. My very nice co-pilot in the right seat said, 'Admiral, we don't do that.' 'Why not?' I asked, and he answered, 'We don't know what's going to happen.' Meanwhile, back in the navy court, we were throwing this airplane up to high angles of attack, trying to do all sorts of things that fighters would do, whereas the F-111 was almost a straight-and-level bomber. Originally the F-14 was to have a development engine, the F401. Because of the amount of time and money we had to spend defending the F-14, Lt. Gen. Ben Bellis, who ran the program for the Air Force as program manager for the F-15 and its F100 engine, siphoned away our money. In any case, I think a deck load of F-14s, with the A-6s and the AF-14 as well as the EF-14 and the RF-14, would have made for a really very powerful boat with savings in training and support. Any commanding officer of a carrier who has all these different types of airplanes that need different engines and different systems would agree it just doesn't make any sense. The Navy couldn't simplify with all A-6s, for example, or with all RA-5Cs, or with A-7s, or A-1s. But it could go a long way toward simplifying by using something like this kind of F-14 family."

Another thing that happened then: a lot of criticism about the airplane and crashes started circulating. The airplane was getting compressor stall and pilots were being killed. So there wasn't much sympathy for the airplane on Capitol Hill. Congress didn't want to build very many of them and kept cutting down and cutting down, which meant the unit price of the airplane was going up and up. (Something that also happened with the F-15.)

Grumman dealt with the Hill as best it could, wherever it had friends. Within the Navy Department, Kent Lee did not support the F-14. That was the only time Houser recalls where there was a schism between the Office of the Chief of Naval Operations (OpNav) staff, where he represented aviation, and the Naval Air Systems Command. "Kent Lee," Houser said, "was very logistics oriented. He understood logistics, but I don't think he understood tactics. And I don't think he understood applications very much at all. If the airplane engines were working and the availability was up, he seemed not to care much what the airplane could do as long as the systems were working."

Clint Towl's testimony still resonated because the Hill felt he was threatening Congress, or at least the Senate Armed Services Committee did. Grumman's relations with the Navy started to un-ravel with the F-14, Houser believes, and the Naval Air Systems Command lost faith in the F-14. And they were looking at how many other airplanes that Grumman was also supplying, E-2Cs, EA-6Bs, A-6Es, as well as the F-14. In that sense, the F-14 was a spoiler. "I don't blame that on the Grummies as much as on the Naval Air Systems Command," Houser said. "But the bad decision was that Congress was dictating types of airplanes the services were going to buy, and Grumman was the victim. When Congress dictates that a follow-on airplane had to be an F-18 or F-17 or F-16 derivative, that's wrong. With almost no aeronautical knowledge Congress invariably makes mistakes. Sure there was a budget squeeze at the time. But we always have serious budget problems. All my life they have been terribly serious. So what did OSD do but put several billions of dollars into developing the F-18."

5
THE LIGHTWEIGHT FIGHTER DILEMMA

*L*IGHTWEIGHT FIGHTER, THE F/A-18, COULD BE ETCHED ON GRUMMAN'S tombstone. Clearly, though, the F/A-18 didn't destroy the F-14 program directly. While it siphoned money from the F-14 as a fighter, the F/A-18 was not a competitor for the original F-14 standoff fleet defense mission. How much it drained from the F-14 attack version was debatable, for it also impinged on other airplanes—such as the Grumman A-6 and the Vought A-7. Again, I was doing other things when this fundamental program came along, as I was with the start of the F-14. For the story that follows, I'll have to draw once more on those who were there.

To many in the Navy, the distaste of George Spangenberg or Bill Houser for a lightweight fighter rang a bell. There were others who had a much different view. One was Adm. Wesley McDonnell, who followed Houser later as OP 05 and became CincLant before he retired. Another was Vice Adm. Robert F. (Dutch) Schoultz, also a later OP 05.

Sortie generation was the rationale for the F/A-18, as Admiral Schoultz points out. Yet at the time of its gestation, its opponents also included Ronald Reagan's secretary of the navy, John Lehman, who had more influence on defense policy than either of the other service secretaries at the time. The Office of the Secretary of Defense had made it clear, Admiral Schoultz says, that the Navy was going to have the F/A-18, but John Lehman was a big Grumman supporter. "He loved the A-6," Schoultz recalled, "because he flew it [as a naval flight officer] all the time. He wanted to get rid of light attack airplanes. Yet he made a statement at an Intruder Ball, which was a function for the A-6 community down at Oceana, that I as OP 05—and it got back to me in a minute—had killed light attack." Light attack encompassed the A-7 and the old A-4 as well as, prospectively, the F/A-18. "That was my community. But I wasn't interested in the community. What we needed, something that the A-6 could not provide, was sortie generation rate. The A-6 was a long-range, heavy airplane with a great role and a good mission but you couldn't turn around if you got in close. If you needed a lot of sorties it wasn't the best airplane. A light attack, a light quick airplane, is cheaper and faster."

Bickering over the short legs of the first F/A-18 versions, in Admiral Schoultz's view, wasn't relevant because the mission for it didn't need long legs. A-6s were for long-range operations. For close in would come something that would generate sorties very rapidly, an element in the carrier air wing. "Lehman's thinking," Admiral Schoultz said, "was to buy an F/A-18, just a small number of them, and take that community out as a major player."

Despite contrary and firmly held opinions from others, including George Spangenberg and Bill Houser, an attack version of the F-14 was no longer a consideration by the mid-1980s. Grumman had insisted that it was a great air-to-ground weapon, Schoultz said, yet the whole fighter community just absolutely threw its hands up. "Fighters look at the ground as dangerous," he observed. "They're fighters, they do the ying yang and pulling back and stuff and they didn't want to do that other stuff." So the navy fighter community fought the attack F-14 version, which could have saved Grumman's bacon. But it is a big airplane, and in today's world with the precision weapon zealots it's a whole new game. If they'd have pushed the F-14 more for air to ground, Schoultz believes, Grumman might have antagonized the whole damn fighter community.

Actually the F-18 came into being while Houser was there, Schoultz recalls, and his successor as OP 05, Wes McDonald, pushed it. "The secretary wanted to make all-Grumman air wings with A-6s and F-14s and that's all," Schoultz says, "but I told him we needed something else for sortie generation. I finally convinced him to do one of each, two light attack squadrons on one carrier, one on the other. Unfortunately, he crowded me into putting the ones with the light attacks on the smaller carriers, which wasn't quite an even balance."

Yet, Schoultz never was a really hard-core supporter of the F/A-18, which did have some real problems, like the landing gear with double drag links and the fuel tank. At one meeting he got up said, "I don't know how the hell we ever approved that airplane." It had something like thirty-four penetrations of the fuel tank with stuff going through pipes, through wires, around corners. They almost had to take the airplane apart to get the fuel tank out of it. "Anyway," he said, "I got in trouble with the secretary, who said I was not a team player. I was a team player. I was playing for the naval aviation team, not necessarily on all of his ideas."

Grumman had a concept that could have filled the light attack role. Tom Kane worked on it as vice president of marketing with Jack Welch of Vought, who later headed acquisition for the Air Force. This was a twin, re-engined version of the Vought A-7. New engines would have given the A-7 all it didn't have, Kane told me later. "NavAir thought it was great," Kane said, "but it ran into the juggernaut of the F-18 and couldn't get funded." Chuck Meyers in the Office of the Secretary of Defense told the Navy that it could have the F-18 or nothing.

What irritated Grumman is that it felt it was frozen out of the lightweight fighter competition by Bill Clements, as deputy secretary of defense. Exactly what his hostility to Grumman stemmed from is unclear, although he reportedly did not like that the F-14s were being delivered to Iran in the quantities that they were. Clements, Kane says, was quoted by someone in the Pentagon as saying, "I got the lightweight fighter and it's coming to Texas." Which it did in the form of the Air Force's F-16, built by General Dynamics, now part of Lockheed Martin, in Fort Worth. Grumman wanted to team with McDonnell Douglas in the lightweight fighter competition, but, as Kane recalled, the word came back that Clements said, "No!" Then the Navy decided it wanted its own lightweight fighter, not the single-engine F-16, and Grumman sent feelers to Northrop. Tom Jones, the legendary chairman of Northrop, called back in a few days to say, sorry, but it was too late. Northrop had designed the YF-17 that became the F-18, but joined with McDonnell Douglas to build the fuselage sections, but as a follower—what amounted to a joint but junior contractor.

George Spangenberg had a historical outlook on the F/A-18 and the lightweight fighter program, which started with the Air Force and with some of the same kind of community battles as the Navy had experienced. In the Air Force, proponents of the F-15 air superiority all-weather, day-night fighter looked skeptically at the day-fighter limitations of the original F-16. All this, in Spangenberg's view, eventually and significantly affected the way the F-14 program proceeded from 1973 onward. Prototyping was the buzzword in the 1970s when the F-18 was conceived. Dr. John Foster in the office of the director of defense research and engineering (DDR&E) supported it, and Dave Packard as deputy secretary of defense did as well, and he directed the services to submit possible projects, amid wishful thinking that the dollars for it were going to be extra dollars.

The Air Force submitted its list of perhaps ten programs, and about halfway down was a lightweight fighter, promulgated by what Spangenberg called the "gum on the windshield" fighter types in and out of the Pentagon. In retrospect, the prototype program may have been designed to get a lightweight fighter started. Whatever the case, the lightweight fighter for the Air Force was the program that actually got funded. Maximum dogfight capability and minimum control by the Air Force as well as reduced life cycle cost were the guidelines. Rules of the competition strongly emphasized use of an engine already in service, which meant a proposal had better have the F100 engine that was already in the F-15.

"The Air Force was in a bind because it had looked at lightweight fighters in setting the requirements for the F-15 and had rejected them," Spangenberg recalled. "Those requirements aimed at the most capable fighter possible that would not conflict with the F-14. Those of us in the Navy thought that the airplane in reality probably didn't offer much over the F-4 program. Obviously the Air Force could not get a new program of its own if it was going to be analogous to the F-14." When the lightweight fighter came along, the Air Force didn't want it to be an F-15 competitor and specified that the light fighter program was solely a technology program. Proposals came to the Air Force from General Dynamics, Vought (then part of LTV), Boeing,

Northrop, and Lockheed, all with the F100 engine. Northrop also submitted a twin-engine design using GE 101 engines. "After the proposals were in," Spangenberg said, "the Air Force invited the Navy to take a look, so four or five of us did, me among them. Kelly Johnson, then running the Skunk Works at Lockheed, had just ignored all the rules and tried to build the best airplane he could that would be a replacement for the F-104. It did have a reasonable capability with enough fuel to have a decent radius, but it obviously wasn't going to win that competition under the ground rules."

General Dynamics, Boeing, LTV, and the Northrop's single engine were all very similar. At first, Northrop's twin-engine design did not seem to be considered very seriously by the Air Force, undoubtedly because of the ground rules on life cycle cost that almost doubled if there were two engines. When the Air Force finally made a decision it selected two proposals: the General Dynamics design that became the YF-16 and the Northrop twin that became the YF-17 —the latter picked in Washington. Boeing was upset about the twin award in the face of the ground rules, as were others. That decision loomed large later for the Navy.

Although Congress had refused to fund what Spangenberg regarded as Clements's ill-considered prototype program in 1973, the issue did not go away. Clements and OSD still insisted upon the Navy getting a low-cost alternative. By that fall the Navy had conceived of something called the F-14X as a solution, scrubbing everything possible from the airplane. Out went the Phoenix, but with provisions it could go back in again.

In 1974 congressional hearings Clements told the tactical air subcommittee that the Navy had been directed to buy a lower-cost alternative fighter to the F-14. Apparently, by that time the F-14X ploy had failed, and OSD settled down to get a lightweight fighter. Fighter Study 4 was organized. Through most of 1974 the Navy vigorously fought low-cost alternatives and lightweight fighter low-capability approaches. In the budgets prepared within the Navy, F-14s were included. By the time budgets passed through the system, however, the F-14s had been trimmed and the VFAX or F-14X or Naval Air Combat Fighters (NACFs) were back in the picture. Fighter Study 4 people argued the Navy would get either low somethings, or nothing. From the fighter study emerged a reinvented VFAX and permission to go out to the industry with something called a presolicitation package for a Naval Air Combat Fighter.

Congress got into the act at the end of 1974 and specified that the Naval Air Combat Fighter had to be a carrier version of the airplane that the Air Force selected as its air combat fighter. So, in essence, the Navy was told to develop a version of either the F-16 or the F-17, whichever airplane the Air Force selected. A competition followed near the end of the year, and both General Dynamics and Northrop were asked to submit proposals to requirements. Each was to maximize commonality with the air force lightweight air combat fighters, and they were to do the best they could meeting the VFAX requirements. The Navy was then going to pick the best airplane out of the batch.

By the following spring the decision within the Navy had been made to select the twin-engine version of the Northrop YF-17. So many changes were necessary that it was redesignated the XF-18. The Navy had eliminated consideration of the General Dynamics F-16 navy version, primarily on grounds of carrier suitability. Vought formally protested the award, the first official protest in many years of navy aircraft competition. McDonnell Douglas was named prime contractor based on its carrier aircraft experience, with Northrop, which had none, as a principal subcontractor for the fuselage. The F-18 engine bypass ratio had to be increased to get more thrust and better cruise specific fuel consumption. Overall weight increase was something over eight thousand pounds, from twenty-five thousand pounds to thirty-three thousand pounds. There was really very little commonality left with the F-17, but it didn't matter anyway since the Air Force had bought the other airplane, the F-16.

Attack requirements were something else. Spangenberg remembers some exercises in the fleet where an F-4 was able to penetrate two targets yet more heavily loaded and slower A-7s could not. That brought more support from the Fighter Study 4 group for the F-18 concept. "The whole effort still didn't make any sense to me," Spangenberg said, "that we would stop buying our most capable airplanes in favor of something that was intended to be cheaper and which, in my opinion, had less capability than the airplanes we already had in the fleet. Whether the F-18 really was cheaper depended on how the analysis ground rules were defined. Whatever, the whole exercise didn't seem to reflect much credit on OSD."

What Bill Houser had to say publicly on the lightweight fighter and what he said inside the Navy were a bit different. Congress had soured on the F-14, so the Navy offered to do something else to the airplane. But Congress insisted on a version of the lightweight fighter. Specifically the lightweight fighter was forced on the Navy by a staffer over in the House Appropriations Committee, who had it written in the bill that the Navy would have to choose the YF-16 or the YF-17. As OP-05, Houser recalled with a grimace, he testified before various committees at least a dozen times in one year: "I was up to my eyeballs in the F-18," he added.

Houser concurs that the Navy tried to fend off the lightweight fighter with the Naval Air Combat Fighter, which would have been a George Spangenberg–type airplane: enough fuel, strength, and hard points. "Trying to make the YF-17 into this was a terrible job, one we're still trying to do," Houser said. "About 80 to 90 percent of it was new. The point is that it wasn't designed as a navy airplane. Good airplane, true, but it really had to have a lot of compromises to become a navy airplane." Did the F-14 have enough stores capacity to function in strike role? Bill Houser thought so. Hard points for the four-thousand-pound Phoenix were adaptable to other ordnance, and fuel capacity was ample, as Afghanistan demonstrated. And in the F-14 the Navy was getting back to Grumman products and the comfort zone of Grumman's reputation for survivability and product support.

"There was a group, including Kent Lee," Houser said, "that wanted a lightweight fighter, though not necessarily the F-18. The F-14 was too big and too expensive, they thought. Chuck Meyers personified the lightweight fighter, too, and I knew he was pushing it in DoD. But they believed the lightweight fighter was our destiny. Our destiny should have been that the Navy doesn't prepare for just one thing. Short-range, high-performance fighters, like the Douglas F4D Skyray was supposed to be, don't solve the problem. We had Soviet Backfire maritime bombers to worry about. We needed long range, to intercept as far out from the battle group as possible. A big airplane, right. But that big airplane is apt to save your neck, so believe in it and those missiles."

Talking about the F-4, Spangenberg remembered an odd thing that happened later on when the F-18 came along to challenge the F-14 for funding. Admiral Lee, then head of the successor to BuAer, the Naval Air Systems Command, in the mid-1970s, asked him to come in for a cup of coffee. Admiral Lee started off by saying that he had read a statement that Spangenberg had given to the House Armed Services Committee. He agreed with all of it except the last paragraph. These were Spangenberg's conclusions that the Naval Air Combat Fighter concept, what was subsumed into the F-18, was unsound and shouldn't be supported and that the F-14 and A-7 should continue. His attitude astounded Spangenberg: he couldn't believe that Admiral Lee could agree with a couple of pages of the statement and then not agree with the conclusions. After a good deal more discussion on the subject of complexity in fighters, Lee made another stunning statement: "We should never have started the F-4." Taken aback, Spangenberg asked, "You mean the F-14, don't you?" "No, I mean the F-4." Well, at that time the F-4 had been in the fleet for more than ten years, a capability that we were trying to improve on rather than to degrade from. "So I was absolutely dumbfounded," Spangenberg recalled. Nevertheless Admiral Lee's dislike of complexity on board ship had deep roots in the Navy, which had once resisted hydraulic-actuated landing gear on carrier aircraft in favor of the hand-cranked system on the Grumman World War Two F4F. Lee's dislike of complexity came at a bad time for the F-14.

Many, including myself, considered Kent Lee an F-18 lover. Swoose Snead, who was the navy F-14 program manager in some of its critical days, believes Kent Lee was the father of the F-18, as far as the Navy was concerned. Lee was an A-4 driver, and the lightweight fighter to him was the reincarnation of the A-4: light, simple, easy to maintain—the low end of the high-low mix, a cheap combination of fighter and attack airplane. "He drove the Navy, drove Houser, forced the lightweight fighter on the Navy," Snead contends. "I won't say Chuck Meyers didn't have anything to do with it, but Kent Lee was the mover."

The thing the F-14 had that the lightweight fighter didn't was the range, the long-reach missile, and it could dogfight, too. And it could have been heavy attack, reconnaissance, and the rest. The lightweight fighters, on the other hand, could do one thing very well—dogfight, air-to-air. No way could they provide safety or security for the fleet as the F-14 could.

Irrespective of the F/A-18 competition, the biggest threat to the F-14 was a combination of politics and its power plant. If Adm. Elmo Zumwalt had not placed the personal prestige of his four stars as chief of naval operations on his testimony that he needed the airplane to protect his fleet, Swoose Snead says, the Navy probably wouldn't have saved it. As the navy F-14 program manager, Swoose followed Capt. Mike Ames in the grim days of 1972 and 1973, when Grumman was losing money on every airplane and deliveries were falling behind; he replaced Mike Ames, because Ames and Lew Evans had stopped speaking. That became, to put it mildly, a definite handicap in running a program. Ames had believed what Lew was telling him, that everything was going to be all right. All of a sudden it ain't all right. Because of that, Mike Ames decided Grumman was being somewhat less than honest. The facts were there, but Lew didn't want to address them. Lew just didn't believe there was a financial problem. Again, this was before I moved up to run Calverton, but Towl, I found later, was getting suspicious. After Lew died, Towl said to me, "George, I had to go to Washington and clean up Lew's mess." That's just the way he said it, but he didn't explain exactly what the mess was.

"How did you patch things up with Lew Evans?" I asked Swoose, that is, after he took over the program. "I just walked into his office," Swoose answered, "and said, 'Hi, Lew. Mr. Chairman, we're going to get on with it.'" "Great," Lew replied. "We're here to help and serve. But our engineers are getting tired of going down to NavAir and being told by Kent Lee and company they are a bunch of dummies." As program manager, Swoose Snead worked for Kent Lee, and he remembers the first meeting when Lee assumed command of NavAir. "He called all his program managers together," Snead said. "He looked around the room and the first thing he said was, 'I lead by fear. I'm going to fire somebody in this room to get everybody else's attention.' Then he went into a tirade about how the Navy shouldn't have the F-14, that it was too big, too expensive, too heavy, too this, too that. I was smart enough then not to say anything until after the meeting, when I asked to chat with him. 'Admiral, I'm between a rock and a hard place here,' I said, choosing my words very carefully. 'I thought I was doing what the CNO wanted me to do. I've been traveling the length and the breadth of the Navy trying to convince the Navy and naval aviation that the F-14 is the right airplane. The CNO has testified as such.' After that, he couldn't wait to get rid of me, and it was old Swoose that was the somebody in this room he would fire." The Marine Corps's interest in the F-14, such as it was, surfaced and waned very quickly with Lee in charge. Ultimately, the Marines, for whatever reason, made their own decision, but Swoose blames the choice on Kent Lee and his emphasis on the F-14's maintenance complexity. "Kent Lee was an A-4 guy," Snead said, "which was all he knew and all he flew."

Wes McDonald, who was in the F/A-18 camp as OP 05—though he does not consider himself anti-F-14 either—adds to the marine story. "I relieved Fox Turner," he said, "who was having big fights with the Marine Corps on the programs we were trying to budget. Of course the F/A-18 was the Navy's big plan at that time, but the competition in the Marines was what became of the AV-8B version of the British Harrier." Marines to this day have not changed. If there is a program they consider vital for Marine Corps aviation, they really fight for that program, and, as the V-22 Osprey shows, usually win against the odds. "Sometimes," McDonald said, "the Marines will not even support the Navy. Or they'll work Congress." George Spangenberg smarted over the Marines not supporting the F-14, and Wes McDonald added: "They did the same thing to the new F-18E/F recently. They saw the AV8B as what they needed to push, plus the Joint Strike Fighter, the JSF, again because it has a V/STOL capability built specifically for the Marine Corps."

As a squadron and air group commander, Wes McDonald dealt both with McDonnell Douglas and Grumman field service representatives but did not meet me until his days in Washington. "George Skurla always came across as very honest, straightforward, protecting his programs, but with a sense of balance," a comment from him I was happy to hear, but not necessarily what followed. "Even at that time, in the early 1980s, there were some of the people working out of the Washington office, names I've lost, and just as well, who were really doing counterproductive things as far as the Navy was concerned. I had explained to some of them personally, 'I can't push any farther this year. We don't have enough money. And I've got to pay for this and that and the next thing.' And they'd still go work the Hill."

Sometimes it was a positive sell of Grumman programs, but there was a bit of mixing, of knifing other programs. Competition turned rougher after McDonald went to Norfolk and then retired in 1985. "Quite a few very bitter confrontations with DoD on F-14 funding followed," McDonald recalled. There were battles over improving the F-14, although the Navy maintained the modifications couldn't be funded. Or there were whispers that the F/A-18 was in deep trouble or that efforts should be made to tank the airplane. Grumman was not alone, for as McDonald agreed: "Absolutely, there was an F-14 mafia in the Navy that still lives." Nevertheless, McDonald thinks there was some pushing on Grumman's part after he left that diminished Grumman's gold-and-silver reputation in its dealings with the Navy.

Wes McDonald didn't see arrogance on Grumman's part during his tenure, but he says others might hang the "Big A" on the company. It's a chronic complaint by the military that contractors try to tell them what they should do rather than support what they are doing. "Things started coming apart a little bit later," he said, "say the mid-1980s, when Grumman began to press very hard, when the F/A-18 was gaining numbers as a portent of where it might be going. Grumman started playing hardball, and a couple of Washington reps were abrasive at times. Not Ralph Clark, who had been around a long time and who would back off if he realized he wasn't accomplishing anything for Grumman or the Navy. But then I was consulting with McDonnell Douglas, so I was looking at it in a parochial manner, as a Hornet guy myself. Herb Hope was another good guy in Grumman's Washington office, who had been an A-6 pilot. Though he could push pretty hard, even though we had disagreements, I don't think he was arrogant. Someplace along the line, though, the corporation was perceived as not listening but telling. As a producer, that got a little beyond Grumman's purview."

Congress was part of the political problem, crystallized by Clint Towl's testimony that Grumman would have to close its doors if it could not modify the F-14 contract. But the F-14's political struggle, Swoose Snead said, started with the Office of the Secretary of Defense. "When I made my manners call on Dr. John Foster, who was heading the then-powerful office of the director of defense research and engineering, he was blunt. 'You, the Navy, jammed this airplane down our throat. So you can't expect any help from us.' I learned early on to eat before going to the breakfast meetings at OSD because I was the weenie at the weenie roast. There was some truth in what Foster said, because, when we parted ways with the F-111, which was an OSD airplane, the whole team of people there supported the boss. They threw us to the dogs. The Navy was out on that limb by itself and they were back there sawing."

Realities—a contract with a huge overrun and severe cost escalation and then the Towl testimony—signaled that things had hit bottom. The Navy, directed by the secretariat, had picked a navy engineering team to take over Grumman and continue production, something I hadn't heard until Swoose told me. NavAir had picked the people from engines, avionics, weapon systems—the whole gamut. As for his own role, Snead considers one of the biggest mistakes he ever made was not forcing the development of the 28,000-pound-thrust Pratt & Whitney 401 engine. The F-14 started life with the 20,000-pound-thrust TF30 engine because it was in production for the F-111 and it was the first turbofan afterburning engine with resultant good fuel specifics and range. Pratt could not bring the 401 engine to fruition in time to catch the first F-14, so airplane No. 64 was designated for the phase-in on the line. Retrofit was always the plan, but not past 64.

"Unfortunately," Swoose said, "and this is where I made a big mistake though I didn't know all of it then, Pratt was developing the F100 for the Air Force F-15 and the 401 for the Navy. But when Pratt looked at the relative size of the two contracts, it put its engineering effort and talent into the development of the bigger-money F100. When I fussed at Ben Bellis, the Air Force's F-15 system program director, he had an answer: 'I've got an airplane and I don't have any engine. You've got an airplane and you've got an engine of some sort.' So I forced a meeting between his boss, who was Gen. Bill Evans at Systems Command, Bill Houser, and myself in Houser's office. 'My bottom line,' I argued, 'is that the Navy is paying half the bill and we're not getting half of the engineering talent and half of the development money or half of anything from Pratt & Whitney. Our engine is suffering.' Pratt did not have the capability to develop both engines at one time, and, at 24,000 pounds of thrust, the F100 was not a big enough jump to be a practical alternative. Because of the TF30's shortcomings, we lost credibility with the operating Navy. The Air

Force accepted the F100 before it was finished development. 'How are you going to finish development of that engine?' I asked Ben. 'I'll pay for it with component improvement money,' he answered. 'That's illegal as hell,' I argued. 'I know that,' he shot back, 'but what the hell do you think I'm going to do?' This was where Ben Bellis was smarter than I was, for he backed off on his engine requirements to the point that whatever he had would fit. What did we do in the Navy? We got that 401 engine to 144 hours in a 150-hour test before it came apart at forty thousand feet at Mach 1.5. We didn't need 150 hours. We didn't need a Mach 2 engine. By the time the airplane gets to Mach 2 it's out of fuel. Dumb, dumb, dumb!"

One of the might-have-beens for Swoose Snead was the visit he had one day about this time from Gerhard Neumann. Born in Germany and a shop-trained engineer, Neumann wound up keeping P-40s operating for the Flying Tigers in China in World War Two, where he got his nickname and autobiography title, Herman the German. When he came to see Snead, he was running General Electric's jet engine division. "Neumann gave me a blackboard drill, and at the end of the hour, this very sage old gent said, 'Admiral, give me $10 million and I'll build you an X engine in thirty months. You may not buy my engine, but you'll get Pratt & Whitney's attention. And you better believe me, you don't have it now.' That was the wisest advice anybody ever gave me, and I was too damn dumb to take it. Only $10 million, but $10 million to a country boy like me was a lot of money under the circumstances, these being we had just pulled $40 million out of the spares and support line to cover part of the overrun."

Why did the Navy not back off its requirements as the Air Force did? Here the engine problem and the political problem played off each other. Any sign of backing off the contract would bring from the critics, "There they go again," and the Navy didn't want to face that image. "When I talked to Houser," Snead recalled, "he said we'll fall in behind the F100 engine down the road. That didn't happen. We had twelve or sixteen engines in the program and we put two in one of the early production airplanes, and it flew like a dream. Development money kept shrinking and it became six engines, then four engines, then two. So I fostered a meeting between Admiral Houser as OP 05, Adm. Kent Lee from NavAir, and Tom Hayward from the money area, and a senior aviator, too. They met at Houser's quarters for lunch to figure out how to come up with the money to force Pratt to continue development of the 401 engine. I sat there by my phone, and when Houser called, it was: 'Swoose, I lost. The vote was three to one against me. Nobody had the money and nobody was willing to try to find the money.'"

Pratt & Whitney paid a price eventually, because General Electric developed the 404 engine with 28,000 pounds of thrust for the F/A-18, and now carrier decks are going with General Electric engines. Eventually the F-14D wound up with another GE engine, a developed version of the F101 that powers the B-1B bomber and designated the F110. Ironically it was in the same 24,000-pound-thrust class as the F100. Swoose and I agree that the F-14 was most victimized by the engine. "If the F-14 had had the 28,000-pound-thrust engine," Swoose says, "I think there would have been no F/A-18. The Navy lost a lot of F-14s, over a hundred out of seven hundred built. But when pilots started flying the engine instead of the airplane, the accident rates dropped."

6

LANDING ON THE MOON

MORE IS TO COME IN THE STORY OF THE F-14'S TRAVAIL, BUT during its initial travails I was off in a different realm—space. How Grumman got into space is a story in itself, for Grumman's founding fathers, and Roy Grumman himself, were not especially interested in the space business, or in missiles for that matter. I doubt that Roy changed his mind, even after the success of Sputnik, whose launch into orbit by the Soviet Union in 1957 electrified the world. Nevertheless it got Grumman's attention, but down on the engineering floor. Within a year or two of Sputnik, Grumman decided to form a space systems department in preliminary design.

Walter Scott wrote the early proposals for the Grumman space program. I worked for him directly in structural flight testing and research at that time. Al Munier ran the space group, and he in turn brought a fellow named Tom Kelly back from Lockheed Sunnyvale. Kelly had worked in Grumman's propulsion section, been called up by the Air Force, and then joined Lockheed to work on space propulsion systems. He has written a fine book called *Moon Lander*, published in the Smithsonian History of Aviation and Space Flight Series, that is an excellent source for Grumman's Apollo program work.

Kelly's book says that Grumman had actually won the NASA competition for the Mercury spacecraft that was to put the first

American into space. But the Navy objected because of all the navy work Grumman had at the time—the A-6 for one—and it didn't want any diversion of effort. Saul Ferdman, a space veteran who had also worked for me in structural flight testing on the F9F, tells it a little differently. Grumman went into the Mercury competition and ended up tying with McDonnell. At that point the Navy wrote a letter to NASA, stating that Grumman was very healthy (we had just won three major navy contracts), but that it would be appreciated it if we weren't picked as the Mercury winner. "When the lunar module came along," Ferdman says, "I saw to it that we wrote a letter first, and no more of that went on."

Saul had also worked for NASA at Langley. His first space program was the passive balloon called Echo, or sometimes O'Sullivan's Ball for its originator at Langley. Ferdman considers it a remarkable achievement: a thin Mylar folded into a launch container that explosively inflated into a huge balloon in orbit, a balloon large enough to see at night without glasses by people on the ground. The idea was to use it as a reflector for a radio signal, and William J. O'Sullivan, the designer, thought it was going to be the greatest deal: "Of course, nobody else did, but what can you do?"

Grumman's reaction to space in the early days—and Ferdman's recollections match Tom Kelly's—was that the Navy knew Grumman's aircraft products and they couldn't be beat. So space was a little of a pain in the rear because Grumman's leaders never saw how they were going to make money on it. Ferdman agrees with me about Al Munier, who did much to inveigle Grumman into the space field. "He was a little bit of a curmudgeon," Ferdman told me later, "but actually, he's never gotten the credit he deserves for hanging in there when nobody was interested. Tom Kelly also worked for him, as you remember, and was a real go-go, eager guy who also wanted to be in space."

The first big space program Grumman won—in the mid-1960s—was the Orbiting Astronomical Observatory, a telescope to be placed in orbit above the distorting atmosphere of the earth and based on an idea conceived in the 1920s in Germany. The OAO ran into lots of problems and suffered several management changes, but the spacecraft evolved into the successful OAO-3, christened Copernicus after the sixteenth-century Polish astronomer who grasped that the earth rotates around the sun, not vice versa. Few realized the extent of Grumman's space facilities then. Furthermore, engineers learned new lessons by hard experience, such as how to handle electronic shielding in the radiation field of space.

Grumman's initial response to space was not so different from that of Pres. Dwight Eisenhower and his staff, who had tended to pooh-pooh the significance of Sputnik as a toy in orbit. But then John F. Kennedy succeeded Ike, and the Soviets did something even more astounding: they put the first man into orbit around the earth. Mercury put an American into space, but in second place, and Jack Kennedy decided to outpoint the Russians decisively. He committed the nation to put a man on the moon by the end of the 1960s in what became NASA's Apollo program. Later, Grumman did go after the Apollo command module and joined with Hilliard Paige at General Electric's re-entry group in Philadelphia before GE established a space center at Valley Forge, Pennsylvania.

Spurred by Kelly's ideas for projects—his group conceived some of the preliminary concepts for the Apollo moon mission— Grumman began to secure million-dollar space contracts here and there. NASA liked what Grumman did, and Grumman emerged as a real contender on the lunar module. While all this was going on I was working in structural flight research, eventually heading the group. Then came the truck bodies and the overrun and working with Lew Evans in the business development world. One of the ideas we had was to do something with all of the big leased IBM computers that we only used internally. Why couldn't we exploit this base like McDonnell Douglas did in building MacAuto? Later that turned into Grumman Data Systems.

Around 1960 there was a change in command. Fred Rowley, who was head of the flight test department, had an assistant, Dr. Ralph H. Tripp, who was big in instrumentation and math. Doc Tripp was asked to take over the OAO, which needed better management. Fred was looking for somebody to replace him. Theodore Moorman suggested me as a replacement, so Fred came to me and asked if I would take the job as his assistant. "Oh, gee, yes," I answered, "it's a promotion." I went with Fred but was unaware for the most part of what Kelly and the rest were doing in space. Although we lost the Apollo command module, Joe Gavin, a senior engineer, had been named to head a team to enter the competition for the lunar module. This was the segment designed to separate from the Apollo command and service modules circling the moon, descend to the surface, take off, and then rendezvous for return to Earth. Grumman won what was to be a critical part of the lunar mission.

At that point I was still assistant director of flight test—and lucky to have that job after an overrun on a navy portable ready room program that I had headed. Fred and I had to alternate between Bethpage and Calverton. One day Fred and I were sitting and talking, and he mentioned the lunar module program. Joe Gavin wanted someone from flight test to be base manager for the lunar module (abbreviated "LM" but pronounced as "LEM") at the Kennedy Space Center in Florida, then under construction for the Apollo launch. "You've got to find somebody," Fred told me. That started me thinking about NASA, the future opportunities there, and what would be a dazzling parade and a new horizon for Grumman. "Fred," I said, "why don't you take the job, and I'll go there with you." "No, no, no," said Fred, who wasn't having any of it. "Those testers down there will all be working for us." We were not only the testers but also final assembly checker outers, and we handled flight activation. His conviction that New York was going to run the lunar module launch operations led to trouble later.

After sifting through the names of candidates, I decided I ought to volunteer. But I still wanted Fred to go, with me as his assistant. We had a good relationship and he had confidence in me, and encouraged me—the best boss I ever had. "George, you don't want to do that," Fred kept arguing. But I wanted to find out. So I called Bob Mullaney, who was Joe Gavin's program manager, and told him, "You guys are pressing us for somebody. Would you consider me?" Mullaney talked to Joe, who now was vice president for the program, called back and said, "Yeah. Joe said he would."

Only once before had I been to Florida, to Palm Beach at a truck body convention. I didn't know whether Cape Canaveral was north or south of Vero Beach, and I just barely knew about Orlando, which was pre-Disney. I also had four little kids and didn't know anything about schools or where to live. So I went back to Gavin and Mullaney and said, "I'd like to go down and look at it." Orlando was the closest "big" airport, and today it is one of the finest airline terminals in the world. Then it was an old air force base, the terminal little more than a shack. Nothing was there. It was awful. I had to wait half an hour or more to get a cab to go to Cocoa Beach, jouncing on old junky country roads. I looked around, and thought, "I don't know about this." But I was interested enough in the challenge to tell Gavin that my family's future is involved. "Take Marie down," Joe said. My wife, Marie, was an Italian girl from Long Island, and we lived amid a slew of relatives next to a golf course. When we flew down there I thought, "She's not going to go for this place." For two days we toured around Cape Canaveral. Finally, on the cab ride back to the airport I got up enough nerve to ask her, "What do you think? You wouldn't want to live down here, would you? There's no four seasons. Look at those scrubby trees and all this gunk." "Why not? Let's go for it," she answered. She surprised the hell out of me. I couldn't believe it. "You're going to come down here, with four little kids to handle?" I asked her. "What will we do with the house? I don't know anything about space or rockets and I don't know what to do," I was filled with questions and doubts. "We can always come back," she answered. "Yeah, sure, I'll probably get canned." With what happened later, that could have been prophetic. On the flight home she talked to me about the prospects, and finally I took the job.

When I moved down in 1965 it was two years before the first lunar module would be delivered to the Kennedy Space Center, where the humongous Vertical Assembly Building, the VAB, was still under construction. In those beginning days it was the blind leading the blind, that is, people with absolutely no field test experience testing. First, I had to sign on an assistant base manager, Chuck Kroupa, who took my place when I went back to New York. All the department heads were offering me people as we started to staff up. Everybody sought a piece of the action and wanted their agent looking over my shoulder. I wasn't going to let this happen and it was time to settle the issue. I took the company Gulfstream 1 back to Bethpage. Upstairs in Joe Gavin's Plant Four office, I walked into a roomful of ground support guys, Edward Dalva and company. Ed Dalva was a longtime Grumman engineer and project engineer and was running the company's Integrated Logistic Support for all its aircraft and spacecraft. "I understand you're coming up here to sell your organization," he said. I was kind of surprised he knew that. "We'd like to see it," he said. Okay. Sure. Unless they supported me, I wouldn't get very far, and I couldn't afford a gunfight with them early on.

As soon as I laid it out, the counterarguments began. Fred Rowley's idea that the launch site would be run from Bethpage had come back to hang around my neck. "We don't think you ought to put this guy in that job. We think our guy over here ought to take that job," and it continued. Finally I said, "Wait a minute. I'm going to be down there running this thing. I've talked to NASA. I've talked to the other people down there. This is the way I'd like to organize it. These are the people I'd like to have in all these jobs, the key people." "We think you're making a mistake," they argued. "I might be," I answered, "but if I'm responsible for this operation, I'm going to say who's doing what." With that I rolled up my big organization chart sheet, with a parting remark: "I have to leave now. I've got a meeting with George Titterton." George was senior vice president at that time, an old engineering hand who had much influence on the lunar module.

Titterton listened to my case for running things at the Cape in my style; I also pointed out that I had campaigned around and checked with people about the best candidates. "These are my choices," I said, "top-notch guys in the senior jobs." He bought it. Then I told him about Ed Dalva and those who wanted in. "We can't have Bethpage crawling all over the Cape. There has to be some autonomy there." This he agreed with, too.

Titterton came down to the Cape and saw Rocco Petrone, a tough West Pointer who was director of launch operations for Apollo. Petrone was a thunderbolt. He deserved a lot of credit for Apollo's success, and I always wondered why he never went as far as he could have. Petrone at first was suspicious of Grumman. We were the new guys, and if we fell out of the tree so did the whole Apollo program. Even Sam Phillips, an air force general and acquisition expert who was brought in to shake up NASA after the command module fire that killed three astronauts, was wondering: "Can these guys hack it down here?" Petrone snapped at Titterton, "Who runs this place? Who does this guy report to? Three or four vice presidents back in New York?" Titterton said, no. He reports to you here and to Joe Gavin. That satisfied Petrone for the moment and we got going. NASA at my suggestion helped me organize our Cape operations, and

NASA fell in with what I was doing. In fact, NASA used it as example for one or two of the other contractors.

As director of operations for Grumman's LM, the reporting line went from me to Gavin. Initially it was going to Ted Moorman, an experienced test engineer who had set up, with North American—as it was known then—the test plan for the LM. Ted antedated me with the program, and it was he who recommended me for the assistant director of flight test position. Ted was in charge of all the testing on the lunar module, including testing at the Cape, so it was natural that I reported directly to him. Once I got down to Florida, I saw this was not going to work. First and foremost, NASA felt all contractors at the Cape responded directly to it, not through a corporate hierarchy. Rocco Petrone was typical of those who didn't want the guy running it at the Cape hobbled by a corporate wiring diagram. They wanted the boss on the scene, me in this case, to go right to the top spot—if not to the president then at least to the vice president for the lunar module, Joe Gavin.

Not only did I win the direct line management case, but I also wanted to move the whole support function from Bethpage down to the Cape. My seventeen years of teamwork with Bob Watkins began then, because Bob had been tapped in 1965 to run field service for the lunar module by Bob Mullaney, who was program manager on the lunar module. Field service was something Grumman had made into a credo with Roger Wolfe Kahn and it became a part of the company's staunch reputation with the Navy. Mullaney felt he needed someone on the LM with field service specifically engraved on his brain. Ted Moorman, to whom Watkins was assigned, was a super guy, but he was out of flight test and didn't have the same service department attitude drilled into him. When I talked to Joe Gavin in 1966 about concentrating the LM program at Cape Kennedy, not at White Sands or Houston, I proposed moving the whole support function to the Cape because of its critical foundation to success. "Then," Watkins recalled, "George came to see me and announced, 'I just moved your job, want to go?' That was an inducement. Actually I jumped at chance."

When Watkins first put together a support budget for the lunar module, he went to see a friend at McDonnell who had worked on the Mercury and Gemini programs. Of the total contract price on the Mercury program, Watkins asked over a couple of beers, how much went toward spares? Mercury, his friend told him, had something like 9 percent and didn't do well in maintenance support. Gemini, at 12 percent for spares, did better. Back home Watkins then sat down with Tom Harding and worked for a week on a set of numbers that came to 17 percent. With Joe Gavin, he flew to Houston for a presentation to Joe Shea, the hard-nosed Apollo program director. Shea sat with feet up on the desk with the red socks he always wore. Tapping on his desk, he said, "You guys always pull that stuff. I know that you're telling me you want 17 percent. You're going to get 14 percent, and that's it." "I only hoped for 12 percent," Watkins chortled. Back outside, Joe Gavin shook hands and said, "I didn't think you'd pull that one off." As it turned out, a lot of money was left over.

Between redundancy and the necessity for absolutely perfect spacecraft components, spare parts usage was low on the lunar module itself. Most spares wound up in the 132 pieces of ground support equipment. Furthermore, spares had to be in the right configuration for this customized and modified hardware. Spacecraft components had been fairly well tested and analyzed by the time the spacecraft was built, and once readied for launch at the Cape it was not the time to find out whether or not a part had a potential to fail. Traditional field service philosophy moved down there, too, with Watkins. He beat on me as well as NASA to get permission to put two trailers right at the foot of the launch pad. NASA had never done that in either the Mercury or Gemini programs. Watkins's concept came from his Gulfstream and navy support days. Put the parts right up against the user, not twenty miles away. On a high-tech program like the lunar module, Watkins predicted that engineers would argue for hours about what spares were needed ultimately, and then not have the part at hand when the crisis came. Trailers at the base of the pad paid off on one or two occasions. No more than that, but it was worth it.

Once at the Cape, at the first meeting Watkins attended, I sat him down next to me at the head of the table after I got through talking to the staff. Watkins remembers it well. "George put a hand on my shoulder and made things clear: 'Bob is the support manager for the base. He has all of the authority of this office. I want every one of you guys to react to that.' Then he squeezed my shoulder and told me, 'I just took away all of your excuses. Don't ever come back and tell me that you can't get so-and-so to cooperate with you.' I got that blanket authority, because George knew he was going to be busy on the technical side, the checkout side, and the launch side, and he was counting on me to do the support side."

At the Cape, Grumman took over the old McDonnnell warehouse that was full of black iron, a bunch of unusable parts. Watkins cleaned it all out. For the next two years Grumman's Cape operation was going to be in an acquisition mode, and he wanted room. Nobody had ever built a lunar module, plus Grumman had those 132 pieces of specialized ground support equipment—brand new, not what Grumman was used to with the Navy. "I didn't know exactly what we needed," Watkins said. "We were running maintenance analysis night and day, as fast as we could, analyzing the tech manual, and our technical writers were writing this stuff up. For two years we acquired things. Then, I said, okay, starting Monday morning I want to get rid of things. I don't care if it's toilet paper or pencils or anything else. Now we clear the decks to get down to what we had determined was a hard-core piece of hardware."

Relations could get sticky with NASA, as they did when I brought in some people from NASA, such as Wylie Williams, who had talent and experience that I lacked. This didn't go over too well. I had to go to New York and talk to Gavin, Titterton, and Lew Evans collectively in one meeting. "If this backfires," Lew warned me, "you're going to be in trouble." "I'll be in trouble if I don't get this fellow," I said, "so it's an easy call." Wylie Williams worked on Gemini, which proved out rendezvous in orbit for the later Apollo program. He was supposed to be the lunar module project man for NASA when I stole him away, which I accomplished through such ploys as talking to him about stock options at night, away from the office. Finally he took the bait, and he did a really good job for us. He was a known quantity. Wylie ran all the checkout, the project engineering world, and safety and quality reported directly to me. This proved successful. Ultimately we wound up with about eighteen hundred people at the space center.

I was smart enough to try to hire in all the hands that were going to become available after the Gemini program phased out, to get their experience on the scene. I went to the base manager for McDonnell operations, Ray Hill, and told him that some of his people were asking to get on board. "I don't want to take them unless you say I can have them," I offered. "We should have some kind of a deal that if somebody applies at Grumman we can find out his availability as far as you're concerned as you are phasing out on Gemini." That worked out very well. Chrysler, the contractor for Saturn 1, which was superseded by Saturn 5, was also quite cooperative. So, in this way, many good folks from other contractors were mixed in with the Grummanites. The whole composite of people turned out to be a winning team. Similarly, the NASA group working for Rocco Petrone had been trained on Mercury and Gemini.

Even so, the delivery of the first lunar module, LM-1, to the space center in 1967, two years after I arrived there, was a disaster. Petrone called me into his office for a classic chewing out. Kelly's book describes Petrone's reaction this way: "George, what kind of a two-bit garage are you running up in Bethpage? The LM you sent us yesterday is supposed to fly in space but I wouldn't even allow it on the launch pad. Its propulsion tanks and plumbing leaked like a sieve. It's a piece of junk, garbage! You should be ashamed. And it's four months late besides." Nothing with the name Grumman on it is junk, I argued, but Petrone went on: "When they turned on the sniffers there were sirens wailing everywhere. What kind of tests did they do in New York before sending this wreck to us? You guys were supposed to be a cut above North American, but now it seems you're even worse. I want you to tell Evans and Gavin that NASA won't stand for this. They had better get this fixed and fast!"

The North American crack stung. After the Apollo pad fire that killed three astronauts North American had gone through several base managers, the last guy a loudmouth and a big troublemaker in a sense. He used to say to me, "Skurla, the way you ought to run your operation to build up morale is to fire a guy every day." No way did that fit the Grumman culture. We generally ran a low-key operation and we wanted to get our credit for doing a damn good job. Several other controversies didn't fit that picture, such as complaints that Grumman workers were writing their names in the LM or sailing paper gliders off the VAB building.

Our good reputation seemed a long way off when I called Gavin and told him about the roasting from Petrone. Tom Kelly's book recalls the explosion. Kelly remembers that I called him up, reamed him out, told him to get it fixed, and that it better never, never happen again. When the roof fell in at Bethpage, Kelly was removed as the LM engineering manager and put in charge of manufacturing and test operations in Plant Five. George Titterton took over the program at the request of Clint Towl and Lew Evans. His blistering speech to the LM team included a comment from Joe Shea, who thought Grumman was complacent and technically arrogant, though that tends to be a typical government manager's view of a contractor midway through the course. Bob Mullaney was taken off the program and went to work for Titterton as a staff man, but not directly on the lunar module program. Joe Shea may have had him in mind, because Mullaney would argue with him. Several people got knocked out of the box, though I didn't know the precise details. I had to have the guts to stand up and say this was the wrong way and now here is the way we're going to do it. My organization did change from the initial site activation and vehicle delivery phase to the lunar module checkout phase. From start to finish, no contractor could claim that they could have accomplished the Apollo mission by themselves. It was NASA input, NASA direction, NASA oversight and demands, and its autocratic ways that kept everything really going. Slowly, Grumman performance at the Cape was accepted.

Ed Markow told me about some of the lunar module nitty-gritty engineering headaches. Trying to reproduce the lunar environment for testing was one. Ed recalls an expert in soil mechanics named John Velaga. Grumman simulated lunar soil using slag from a steel mill, put it in a bell jar, pumped it down to 10^{-6} vacuum, and took it up in the Gulfstream in which it flew one-sixth g parabolic trajectories. John had a penetrometer checking characteristics. These were the days when Tommy Gold at Cornell was saying that lunar soil was cigarette ash and with Grumman building the LM with feet on the bottom it was going to sink right down to the engine bell. "Poor John," Ed recalls, "he was in a flight suit as the Gulfstream oscillated up and down, up and down, taking data. And he comes over to me, and he's smelly. Grabs me around the arm and says, 'Ed, in the name of science-uuurrrpppp.'"

Grumman's conservative philosophy was to have a lot of redundancy. In the lunar module Ed remembers, the only thing that was not redundant was the ascent engine. It had to work. "Just think of the nightmare for the designer to realize that guillotines had to cut all the lines," those connecting the descent engine and landing gear section from the ascent engine and cockpit. "All the fluid lines, all the electrical lines, had to be cut simultaneously as the ascent stage lifted off. If just one hung up a little bit, that was bad trouble." Testing went step by step, from component to subassembly to assembly. The thing that was so exciting to me was to come into Plant Five and watch the LM come alive. There was a big electronic display panel showing the status of the systems. Looking at the status board one could see this thing growing in the shop with more and more lights glowing on the panel as each system came online.

I left Florida around the time of Apollo 13. That story, of how the lunar module served as a lifeboat and got the crew home, has been told and retold so I won't do that again. Grumman was the hero of the mission, and the crew later flew up to Bethpage to give the Grummanites a vote of thanks in person. Yet Bill Zarkowsky remembers a sour note in the aftermath—and represents the plank-holder Grumman manager's view of the space business. The contract kicked off different profit incentives in sequence as the mission proceeded. "After the explosion on the way to the moon," he recalled, "our incentive went out the door. We got nothing. A couple of guys went down to NASA to negotiate after we had done the lifeboat mission and saved their bacon, and they argued that we expected to get all the incentive points. First NASA said, 'You don't get any.' Then they backed down a little and said, 'You do get two or three.' The minute Apollo 13 astronaut Freddie Haise [who later went to work for Grumman] turned on some LM equipment, Grumman did pick up a few incentive points. Moments later came the oxygen tank explosion and that, technically, cut off any more Grumman incentive fees." NASA wasn't being just hard-nosed or legalistic. Unlike the flush days before Apollo 11, when NASA had all the money it wanted, the spigot was turning off as public interest faded. As Ed Markow put it, "What were we going to do on the later missions, just pick up more rocks up there?" NASA was being criticized, Zarkowsky added, for overrunning every program budget, and "therefore, the money people were just trying to do their job."

For the step after Apollo, Grumman as much as anybody conceived of having a shuttle sitting on a centerline propellant tank with a couple of solid boosters strapped to its side. That was the eventual layout NASA selected but Grumman lost out to Rockwell in the competition for the program. Bill Zarkowsky told me why. Grumman was in financial trouble with the F-14 program at the time of the shuttle competition. NASA used to depend on its contractors to swallow part of the costs during a program's build-up stages. Grumman was going to have to borrow money for the program, if it could, and NASA didn't think Grumman could get it. In fact, after Clint Towl said Grumman might have to shut its doors there was no way we would win the shuttle. That was true even though Grumman had completed a study contract and fiddled around with a small orbiter sitting on a big expendable tank with two solid boosters—the eventual layout.

Grumman did get a piece of shuttle support business from Lockheed. I called Roy Anderson, Lockheed's chairman, and asked to join his team. We had helped Lockheed in Washington with a C-5 problem in Congress, and I told Roy it was payback time. Furthermore, I pointed out, Grumman had an astronaut, Fred Haise from Apollo 13, running our space business and Rockwell had Jim McDivitt. Lockheed had nobody, no manned spacecraft experience. "We made that decision eight or ten days ago," Roy demurred, but I assured him. "We're not looking for 50 percent of the action, more like 20–25 percent." When Roy said he'd call back I thought it was the kiss-off. But it wasn't. He had me and Fred Haise run down to Washington to talk with Larry Kitchen and some of the other key people, and Lockheed finally did give us a piece of its support work at the Kennedy Space Center.

Zarkowsky, Markow, and I were talking what-might-have-beens at one of our Grumman reunions. Ed raised a question that is fundamental to my feeling about unfulfilled destiny. Intrigued by Ed's question, I asked Zarkowsky, "Bill, do you think we would have survived had we won the shuttle and lost the F-14?" Zarkowsky thought about that for a minute or two and answered: "After I canceled the original F-14 contract we made money. We never made any money on the LM. That was a WPA project."

"I think," Ed Markow chimed in, "that George Titterton shook hands with NASA on a number we never should have shaken hands on. It was NASA's number. Don't bill us any more than this." Nobody knew what the extent of the program was in the beginning.

Zarkowsky agreed: "Nobody. What followed were lots of risks and plenty of expenses that cost us money. If we weren't making money on the other projects, you guys would have been out of business. We would have shut you down."

Raphael Mur, who handled contracts as a lawyer, tells me the lunar module cost grew from $400 million to $2.1 or $3 billion. One could argue it never should have grown, or by that much. But NASA was much more openhanded with the contractor, trying to get the job done, than the Navy, which was more confrontational on the F-14. NASA could do no wrong, and all the money it needed was shoveled its way—up to a point. After the Kennedy speech, if the contract was within the scope specified, then you could overrun 10,000 percent. But only in the beginning.

Grumman did get some subcontract work on the shuttle orbiter wing. Grummanites see the orbiter tail as a Grumman signature tail. NASA's original concept was for a fully reusable system. But it gave Grumman a Phase B contract to look at the alternatives. Within the first six weeks of the study, Hal Moss recalls, we said the layout should be an orbiter with an expendable external tank and solid rocket boosters. That's exactly what NASA ended up with a year and a half later. Moss, who was director of operational analysis, said the Grumman design rationale was cost. Grumman, Moss said, sent three hundred engineers out to Rockwell on the West Coast to work on the shuttle for the first two years of the program and one of those engineers eventually was in charge of a section of fifty or sixty Rockwell people.

Grumman tried to get into the space station. Ed Markow worked on a robotic device for an early space station concept, but that never went anywhere because of lack of funding. Space as a source of business and a path for Grumman's future gradually dwindled away. But one of the spin-offs from the roving vehicle program was a Grumman concept of a run-flat tire, simply replacing the steel belt in a radial tire with a thin advanced composite band. If it did lose air, it would behave like a bicycle spoke wheel. Markow, who has several patents on the concept, said Firestone has tested it in Mexico.

✳ ✳ ✳

Still the question nags: Was space part of Grumman's unfulfilled destiny? Or was it a money-losing detour? Could Grumman have stayed in the space business? An answer, probably not, came after I had moved out of the Cape and back to New York, not with much enthusiasm.

The company went after the space shuttle as a successor to Apollo. Lew Evans had a grandiose plan to have a shuttle organizational tree of senior guys, including me. It would have meant one awesome responsibility that included final assembly and checkout in Bethpage for the orbiter and launch at Kennedy Space Center. There would be work at the NASA Mississippi engine test center and at Dryden, co-located at Edwards Air Force Base, California. Mind-boggling! Lew took vice presidents from all over and put them on the Christmas tree when the proposal went in—a familiar tactic in aerospace contract selling strategy. I never saw the proposal in writing, but this is what Lew told me: "We'll put in there that your home base is going be Kennedy Space Center, because that's where it's finally going to go from. Now are you happy?" I was happy for the moment. But it never happened. Lew died before the shuttle was awarded. Losing the space shuttle, which had the configuration Grumman created, thus had the same finality as a last chance at bat in the ball game.

Goya Foods built a new facility that stands in the middle of what used to be the runway from which a whole series of Grumman aircraft were test flown or delivered from the company's Bethpage complex.

Courtesy of William Gregory

The Calverton flight line early in December 1973, with tail numbers 46, 48, 49, and 53 visible, a sign of how fast the schedule was being picked up.

One of the first decisions George Skurla made when he took over the flagging F-14 production line at Calverton was to get rid of the trestle that was universally despised by the assembly forces. Both the F-14 and A-6 were assembled on this system. F-14 assembly is on the left, A-6 on the right.

Mixing with the guy on the production line was a tenet in Skurla's management strategy—and his personal inclination as well. Here he is (*center*) talking with one of his troops at the kind of plant open house he liked.

Courtesy of George Skurla

Fuselage sections of the F6F line the plant floor at Bethpage during World War Two, a glimpse of the kind of military aircraft production rates—at its peak more than 600 per month—that have seldom, if ever, been seen since.

One of the favorite moments for Skurla was his chance to fly as a backseater in the F-14. Here he is climbing into the cockpit of an F-14D Super Tomcat at the Calverton assembly facility on Long Island.

Jack Bierwirth (*center, in light suit*) was brought in from National Distillers to become vice chairman of finance of the Grumman Corporation. Here he tours Plant Two with Skurla to see the F-14 wing box in fabrication.

Navy Secretary John Lehman (*right*) was a fan of Grumman aircraft after flying the A-6 as a naval flight officer. That didn't stop Lehman from jousting with Skurla (*left*) over Grumman's pricing or from sending the A-12 stealth attack aircraft contract to other companies.

As director of lunar module launch operations for NASA's Apollo lunar landing program, Skurla (*right*) shows the vehicle in flight preparation at the Kennedy Space Center to Grumman chairman Clint Towl (*far left*) and engineering chief George Titterton.

Grumman's last big aircraft contract before the merger was for the air force–army Joint Surveillance Target Attack Radar System (JointSTARS). Using a synthetic aperture radar concept developed in the company, Grumman beat out some of the more electronically experienced contractors. Retired airline Boeing 707-300B transports were gutted, stuffed with consoles and operators, and fitted with a side-looking radar antenna (ahead of the wing leading edge) to track hostile ground vehicles and forces in Desert Storm, Bosnia, and the war with Iraq.

Re-engined, the F-14D version became much closer in performance and reliability to the original concept for the air superiority fighter.

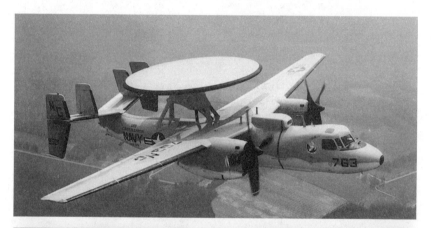

Two of the four aces, the production aircraft that carried Grumman into solid profitability during the late 1970s and early 1980s. The E-2C (*top*) stayed in production after the merger and was sold overseas successfully. The EA-6B (*bottom*) was the Navy's carrier-based electronic warfare stalwart, derived from the A-6 attack aircraft that was the third of the four aces.

Grumman showed that it could carry out a research aircraft flight program with the X-29, financed partly by DARPA, the Defense Department's research agency, and the Air Force. Although it was technically a success, Skurla came to lament the financial losses Grumman took on the program.

One of Grumman's rare military aircraft programs for a service other than the Navy was the Army's OV-1 reconnaissance aircraft.

A gallery of historic aircraft Skurla worked on in his days as a young engineer after World War Two. The F8F came along too late for wartime combat, but its nimble performance made it a favorite of fighter pilots who flew it afterwards (*top*). The F7F pioneered the idea of twin engines for carrier duty, but was turned over to the Marine Corps when it fell short in carrier suitability trials (*middle*). The F9F was Grumman's first jet fighter, and the F9F-6 here was its first swept-wing fighter (*bottom*).

Happier days for John O'Brien (*far left*) receiving a navy award with Skurla (*second from left*). O'Brien became Grumman Corporation chairman after Skurla retired and was subsequently indicted for his political fund-raising missteps.

Grumman introduced the retractable landing gear for carrier aircraft with its FF-1 biplane fighter. The belly-stored, hand-cranked system carried on through Grumman's last navy biplane fighter, the F3F, and its first production low-wing fighter, the F4F.

Grumman's F4F-3 Wildcat World War Two fighter had a wing-folding system that, legend has it, was invented by Roy Grumman toying with a paper clip. Unlocked by a ground crewman, each outer wing panel, on a massive steel cylinder functioning as a pivot, swung down and back. Then it was locked in place parallel to the fuselage to minimize storage space on a carrier's deck. The hand-cranked, belly-stored main landing gear was also Grumman's innovation.

Plant 1 (*upper right*) was the first aircraft-manufacturing plant built at Bethpage. Plant 4 (*upper left*) is where final assembly of many Grumman aircraft took place from the 1940s through the 1980s. Plant 2 (*center*), Grumman's largest aircraft-manufacturing facility, was officially opened on 7 December 1941. These three aircraft-manufacturing plants were at the heart of what became known as the Grumman "Ironworks."

7

FIXING THE F-14

ONCE THE LUNAR MODULE HAD MADE IT TO THE MOON AND landed I was ready to try to enjoy life, at least as much as might be possible in a high-pressure, highly visible program like Apollo. Then, right after Apollo 12, the second landing, Clint Towl and Lew Evans came down to Florida. We were rolling pretty good at the Cape, I felt. It was all very festive with Apollo 13 coming up in April. Instead Towl and Evans dropped a bomb on me. They wanted me to come back to Bethpage.

As the F-14 program sank further into the swamp, the program that Lew had politicked so hard to win was about to drag Grumman into humiliation or even bankruptcy. Exactly how I fit there wasn't clear, but Lew insisted I come back. "I don't want to do that now," I demurred. "I've got a sound operation here, all greased, going along, and we've just landed on the moon a second time." But Lew cajoled me about the problems on the F-14 and argued that the engineering people there were not operationally oriented. "They don't really have a good sense of producibility," he said. "They design things, but then the manufacturing group has a hard time building them." Grumman was not the only aerospace company to have this disease, and the situation got so bad that missionaries from the Naval Air Systems Command had begun going around the country lecturing on how defense companies ought to do better manufacturing with better quality.

Towl was twisting my arm, too, but I had hoped to be the last guy out of the Cape, turn the key on the door, and get assigned to run Grumman's Stuart plant just to the south in Florida, because I was one of four or five who opened that place in 1950 as a winter flight test site. On a visit to Bethpage early in 1970 I was still dissembling. Butch Voris, the first leader of Blue Angels, had become head of public affairs for space. He was very close to Lew, whom I had come up there to see. Lew hadn't gone into all the F-14 problems when he broached the idea of moving, and I found out about them only later the hard way. Butch called me and said, "George, I went to the tennis match at Madison Square Garden last night with Lew [who was a dedicated tennis player]. We went out for a Coke, and Lew was bemoaning the fact that you were giving him a hard time by not accepting reassignment to Bethpage. The boss is not happy about your taking so long to make up your mind, showing every sign of not wanting to come back. He wouldn't be asking for you if he didn't think he wanted somebody like you. George, you better think this over."

Next came a call to have breakfast with Lew at his home in Brookville on Long Island. Lew lived in an older house, with big rooms, including one that could hold a grand piano, and there was a telephone wire that must have run twenty-five feet or more so he could walk all over the place while he talked. He was always on the phone, like Generation X folks today with their cell phones in their SUVs. Lew started working me over once more as we ate: "George, we're going to need you up here, need you up here, need you up here." No question, whatever his reasoning, he wanted me up in Bethpage. "Lew," I argued, "I spent five years running that thing at the Cape. I've got my family there. Now I'm in for another wild swing. I'd just like to ride this out where I am." Lew's pulse-beat response went on. "We need help, we need help, we need help." Finally he drove me back to the plant and parked his car right in front of Plant Five, where I subsequently parked my car when I became president. I left him saying I would think it over. Back in the hotel room, I was tormented. Finally I remembered something a friend told me who owned a big supermarket chain and lived in the same Long Island neighborhood where our kids used play together. "As you go through your business life," he said, "remember that if the company wants you to do something and you turn it down, you're probably not going to get another chance." That had drifted back into my mind when I had to decide whether to go to the Cape. I did, and it was good that I did. Furthermore, there were all kinds of hints being dropped about the advantages of coming back to Bethpage. "You come up here and we're going to make you a vice president," was one, which was a big carrot. Grumman didn't have many vice presidents at the time. Personally, I thought I should have become a vice president at the Cape. Clint Towl took the blame, saying the board was chary of program vice presidencies. Programs had a way of going away, leaving vice presidents without a home.

So finally I went to Lew's office, adjacent to my eventual office years later in the corner of Plant Five on the third floor. I knocked on the door, and he got off the phone and stared at me. "Well Lew, you've got yourself a boy," I announced. So he jumped up and said, "Oh gee, that's great. We really need you up here." And on and on and on. Complications were there though, I told Lew. "I got a family and I'd rather have them stay in Florida. Where am I going to live up here?" "Don't worry about it," he said. "I'll take care of everything. We'll get you an apartment, we'll get you furniture, get you a car. We'll take care of you. If want to go home to see the family, go. But I need you up here." In February or March Grumman had a board meeting and elected me as vice president for product engineering, and I got the word direct from Clint Towl.

My product engineering operation reported to Grant Hedrick, who also had the research department as well as preliminary design and advanced development. All the engineers on the airplane programs, the space program, and the marine program were technically generated from my department. As I saw it, I was the protector of Grumman's legacy in design excellence and integrity. The responsible department, within the engineering world, would assign these people to various programs. My doctrine was that product engineering would oversee, but the main responsibility for running those people was the program director, not me.

Mike Pelehach, whose preliminary design talents I've mentioned, came to see me right away. "George it's great that you're here," he assured me. "We need somebody like you." Nice to hear. But then I discovered some of the labored routines they had. Processing ECPs, engineering change proposals, would take us two weeks, for example. I had heard that old man Mac, when he was running McDonnell during development of the F4H, had a desk where he would approve every ECP just by throwing it into one of the drawers. He thought they were worthless.

Quickly enough my new responsibility, product engineering, got me enmeshed in the F-14 program. It was a jumble. We had some weekly meetings with Lew and representatives from all of the departments in the boardroom. Lew was very, very optimistic, positive that we were going to be able to pull it off—his "don't worry no matter how bad it is" leadership mode. But I was quite friendly with the comptroller of the company, Pat Cherry. Even as Lew made optimistic noises, Pat was saying that Grumman was going to lose a bundle on the program. Then came the demands and complaints: cut this and cut that, trim it down, the Navy's unhappy, the F-14's overrunning, we're in a box here—with a fixed price contract projecting only 3 percent escalation and inflation hitting double digits.

So we had to reorganize, and, because of the F-14 overrun, we had to cut back. Timing was bad, for the lunar module was topping out as the F-14 was starting to settle in the groove. Product engineering was the home department for all the people who worked on the F-14, and they had nothing to do with preliminary design or research. My job was not to manufacture and roll stuff out the door. Managing the engineering world was my job, and producibility became a dogma. The Navy was saying we had too many people on the F-14 program, and too much overhead in Grumman in general. The Navy began to make noises about Grumman restructuring, downsizing.

Shrinking my "empire," cutting one layer after another out of an engineering hierarchy, had become a prime task. When I came back to New York we must have had perhaps fifty-eight hundred people in product engineering, including some of the secretaries. Roughly half that force was gone in eighteen months. Painful! As home department vice president, and as a company rule, I had to talk to anybody that had more than fifteen or twenty years with the company, and it could be agonizing. Some who had been given notice would come to see me, often angry and very aggressive. The best thing to do, I told them, is call on your contacts, network inside the company, help yourself, talk to anybody you know about another slot. Others would come in like sheep. Looking out my window in the afternoon at quitting time, these fellows would be carrying brown boxes, with all their stuff, slide rules, desk things. It wasn't hard to imagine what kind of night they would have once they got home and had to tell their families.

Terrible as the layoffs were, there were compelling reasons for them, a subject Swoose Snead and I jousted over when he and I told sea stories one day after the both of us had retired to Florida for good. Swoose, Rear Adm. Leonard A. Snead, was the navy program manager for the F-14 during the delivery crisis, as I've said before, and later worked for Grumman and then Pratt & Whitney. "One of the things I used to harp on when I joined Grumman," he recalled, "was having somebody in charge. Grumman being Grumman, nobody ever was in charge. True, that's an overstatement, but Grumman did allow a lot of flexibility at various levels of management. Unfortunately it had too damn many levels of management. John Lehman was exactly right when, as secretary of the navy, he told Grumman it had too many people building too few airplanes. Grumman didn't skinny itself down in a very timely manner."

Sadly, that's exactly the dilemma I ran into when Lew Evans pulled me out of Florida to run product engineering; too many people on the job. This was especially true of the F-14 program. Building up for the F-14 put layer on top of layer, workers five deep when they should have been one deep. My disagreement with Swoose is that we did respond, but in the traditional Grumman way toward its employees. Swoose didn't have any problem with building up for the F-14 since it was Grumman's primary program and deserved foremost consideration. "After you got over the hump," Swoose argued, "Grumman got down to producing one or two airplanes per month yet holding on to that basic organization, past the program peak." "Now wait a minute," I interjected, "we were building about sixty F-14s a year." "But, George," he insisted, "Grumman got down to the point where it was not building very many airplanes, just onesies and twosies." Swoose and I didn't exactly agree, although we were talking about different times. But he wouldn't back off his contention that once Grumman got over the F-14 production line peak it still had those layers of people.

Remember, though, Grumman had buildups from two big programs winding down in sequence, the residue of the big Apollo program and then the F-14. Grumman's head count drifted down. It was not hammered down. Once the F-14 RDT&E was more or less behind us, we had people still hanging on as we cut down slowly, not sharply. But we did finally respond. My former assistant, Bob Watkins, points out something else: the program management role had evolved. From a functional organization with centralized services like product engineering, the new government-encouraged organization of program managers meant each one was a vice president and each had his own team. So we had team after team after team with stand-alone organizations—and many people. "Whatever, George," Swoose said, "the best present you ever gave me was December of 1973, when I sent my boss a memo saying Grumman's F-14 production line is now on schedule." And in a sense that made me a hero for a second time after the Cape.

Lew thought the restructuring I did was so good he took the new organization chart down to Washington to show the Navy and bragged that he had Skurla up in New York cutting costs and raising hell about gold plating and too many vice presidents. That didn't make me feel any better inside, though. Engineering on F-14 development work was cresting, for this was 1970 and we flew the airplane in December of that year. As I noted, the lunar module was starting to come down, too, because the last Apollo, Apollo 17, flew in December of 1972, and the pressure was dwindling. People down at the Cape wanted to come back, and they were good. So they were bumping one another out of positions. Anybody who is vulnerable, I thought, ought to be informed as soon as possible, even a month ahead of time. "Oh, no, you can't do that," I was told. "We'll have all kinds of trouble, sabotage, disruptions." Instead I argued: "I don't want some guy we're going to let go a month from now—and we know it, or probably know it—buying a new house or a new car, or thinking he's still going to have a job. We owe it to these people." I was overly sensitive to this in the minds of some of my colleagues. But I felt rotten about it.

Of course, I was not the one who had to deliver the bad news initially. I can imagine how those conversations went: "We can't use you in the department. We can only have ten slots and there are fifteen engineers here. So five of you have to go." In other words, they were expendable. But, as I said, I had to talk to them if they had fifteen or more years in the company, which was a long time by corporate standards. So I wanted these people forewarned as soon as possible, given at least two weeks notice. Some people disagreed and thought it was disruptive. It wasn't.

Working for Grant Hedrick, who was very technically minded, was doable because I did have a technical background. Since I hewed more to the operational management side, though, I still worried about what future I had there. But then Northrop came along and flew me out to California, where I met Tom Jones, the legendary head of Northrop, and had lunch with him and Welko Gasich, who was the executive vice president and another fabled name in aerospace. They were talking about hiring me as the vice president in charge of all technical operations and flight test. I started looking around for a home in the plush section of Palos Verdes.

At the same time I was making noises at Grumman because I wanted to enroll in one of Harvard Business School's advanced management programs, which ran for sixteen to eighteen weeks. Other senior managers, including John O'Brien and Ed Dalva, had gone, and I wanted to as well. "You don't want to go to that," Hedrick scoffed. "You want to go to some technical course." Bill Schwendler heard about it and called me in. "You don't want to go up there, do you?" he said in his most avuncular, listen-to-my-advice style. "All these other guys are getting educated," I countered. "What about me? I busted my can down there in Kennedy, and now I am up here in engineering. I would like to go to something like that, but Hedrick doesn't want me to." "You really want to go?" Schwendler repeated. "I really do want to go." "All right," he said, "I'll talk to Hedrick."

Concurrently, Northrop made me a great job offer. On top of that I was impressed with Tom Jones and Welko Gasich. Still I called back and said, "I'm giving up twenty-five years of Grumman, walking away from whatever I have in the way of perks. If I'm going out there, I'd like a three-year contract to cover me. Your people will be sniffing around at me coming over the horizon, asking, 'Who's he?' First thing you know there will be politics all over the place. That could knock me out of the box at Northrop and I'd be out of Grumman." Tom Jones disagreed: "George, we don't give contracts to anybody. I don't have a contract. You have nothing to worry about. We checked you out." "That's great," I answered, "but you may run off with a blonde next month and I'll never see you again. I'm going to Harvard." Fine, they answered, go to Harvard and think about it. I thought about it: no contract, no job. Northrop's headhunter called one more time while I was at Harvard and asked whether I was going to make up my mind. "I don't think I'll come," I finally said.

In the meantime, Pat Cherry had been sitting in on all the meetings on the F-14. He told me subsequently that he had gone to Joe Gavin, now president of Grumman Aerospace, and told him who could probably straighten out the F-14 production mess—me. George Skurla, he argued, has been down at the Kennedy Space Center working for a hard-nosed customer, and he was responsible for final acceptance, assembly and checkout, and selling off the lunar module. Besides he's worked in flight test, structural flight test. Then came a surprise phone call to me from Frank Edwards, who was the head of the pilots out at the Calverton F-14 final assembly facility at the eastern end of Long Island. "Is there anything you want us to do for you?" Frank asked. "We understand you're going to come out here to run this place." News to me.

Pat Cherry, as this incident shows, was a great supporter of mine. A story in himself, Pat was one of the old-timers, and at one point Roy Grumman's caddy. Had he played his cards right, grown as a person and networked, he could have made it to chairman of the corporation —and probably been a good one, for he was an expansionist. Unfortunately, he was a financial type who liked to roam around the shop where his friends were, a guy who would put on a good suit and then wear white socks. This was fatal after Jack Bierwirth came in to run finance. Though an impressive-looking man, Pat would walk around chewing cigars, and there were piles of stuff on his desk. "This old pro is not going to take any of this stuff from Bierwirth," he told me, and I warned him he'd better be careful or he'd be tossed out. Sure enough, I was at the meeting at Stuart when Bierwirth proposed letting him go. There wasn't much discussion, a shock to me, except Clint Towl said to make sure that he was well taken care of. But he wasn't. Instead he was eased out at sixty with peanuts after all that time with the company. He lost a lot of benefits and sued.

Grumman sent me up to Cambridge in January 1973. Before I left for Harvard, Gavin had in fact called me in and told me that he'd like me to go to Calverton, responding to Pat Cherry's recommendation. "Corky Meyer's running that world," I told Joe. "Other people are involved, especially Mike Pelehach who is emotionally wound up with F-14. I'd only go out there on one condition, that you split the company in half, Grumman east and Grumman west. I'll run Grumman east, and Grumman west will support it. But I don't think you have the guts to do that." He sat back and half laughed, with one of those "we'll see" looks. Swallowing, he finally said, "Why don't you write your thoughts down." This was a Thursday or Friday, and I was leaving Sunday. I followed his recommendation, in words like this: "Joe, you want me go out to Calverton, but that would be like going out there with a BB gun to shoot an elephant. I'm not about to run something with a lot of vice presidents back in Bethpage shooting torpedoes at me. I know what the problem is, or at least have a sense of what it is. I think I know what has to be done, and I know the people I could get it done with. I have to be el supremo there."

I put the thing on his desk late on a Friday and went off to Harvard. Until around Easter I heard nothing from him. Then he called, casually asked how I was doing and when school would be over. "What's up?" I asked. "Oh nothing," he answered. "Just checking up on you, and thought I'd give you a call." Was I coming to New York for the holiday and was there any chance for me to stop and to see him? I did, and he had Corky Meyer and Ed Dalva and some others there. Gavin repeated the final assembly problems at Calverton and said he was going to put me out there to run the thing. "I want you guys to support him," he said. "Things are critical and we could lose the whole F-14 program. Proxmire's after us, we're going bankrupt, and we've lost all our commercial bank credit." He was referring to Sen. William Proxmire of Wisconsin, a dedicated defense industry critic and sometime bane of the Pentagon.

When I came back from Harvard, I walked into the Calverton plant with my wife at an open house. "My god," Marie exclaimed, "you're going to build airplanes in here?" Is the chaos out here that obvious, I wondered? Just in subcontracting alone, vendors were delivering hardware that passed source inspection and then couldn't pass delivery inspection, screwing up everything. When I finally did go out there in May 1973, it was as vice president and general manager of the whole Calverton operation, which included flight test, F-14 final assembly, and also A-6 and EA-6B assembly. Gavin reduced my marching orders to one: Get fifty-four airplanes off the F-14 line and delivered to the Navy by year's end and have No. 58 flying, meeting the company's existing commitment. Skeptics in the Navy and Congress doubted whether Grumman could get within ten of that number.

Man-hours for final assembly were running around thirty-five thousand and had to come down. Out-of-station work on the F-14—that is costly cases where the airplane had to be pulled off the assembly line and specially worked before it could go back in sequence—had hit 65 percent, and design modification introductions were falling behind. Paperwork was late, and airplanes arriving for preflight checkout were essentially unfinished. Not only was there an inordinate amount of difficulty in building the airplane, but also in selling the airplane to the Navy Plant representative for acceptance. When I got out there Grumman hadn't sold an airplane to the Navy in two or three months. Modification of A-6s to the A-6E version and EA-6B production work were also late. So there was a daunting commitment to get A-6E tail No. 36 and EA-6B tail No. 40 delivered by the end of the year as well. These became the letters etched in fire: 58-36-40.

An article in *Aviation Week & Space Technology* (July 1, 1974) laid out the problem:

> Plant 6, as the final assembly area is designated, has a T-shaped assembly area, with the flow starting at the base of the T. At that point it was criss-crossed with air hoses and electrical wires for the tools and equipment used by assemblers because of remotely located connection points. Half the line was occupied by a structure called the trestle. This was an elevated platform for A-6 assembly that was conceived as an automated conveyor to move aircraft along the line and at the same time make sections accessible for the assemblers without their reaching or stooping. Its bulk created the impression of a traffic jam on the F-14 side of the line. Compounding the space squeeze were a large roll-over fixture on the F-14 line—for rotating complete assemblies to drop out loose bolts, metal, tools or whatever foreign objects might have been left in the

assembly process—and a DIT-MCO automatic checkout fixed position station. Not so obvious but much more fundamental to the delivery problem for the F-14 was the concept for final assembly. Work was organized along functional lines—electronics, hydraulics, structure. Assemblers and technicians in these functional groups pursued the aircraft to wherever it might be. Workstations were floating stations, not fixed points. Assembly crews went to the storeroom to draw parts for jobs. If a part was not available, the assembler would try to track it down—or left the job undone until the part materialized.

Most hated by the plant force was the trestle. Fire codes forced it to be built higher than specified, so work could not be done at shoulder level. Besides, the idea of moving six airplanes at once to the next station never worked, for all six were seldom ready at the same time. While the trestle was not a total impediment to putting the plant back on schedule, out it went as a morale builder. I cut the last remaining I-beam with a torch while a volunteer bugler played taps. So also went the roll-over fixture for the F-14. Eight fixed stations replaced the F-14 floating workstations. Paperwork was brought up to date simply by working long tedious hours. Some shifts went to twelve hours. Calverton won the race. The Navy signed off on the fifty-fourth delivery just before the plant shut down for Christmas, and No. 58 got a break in the usual eastern Long Island fog and rain to fly at the same time. Stars fell on me after that.

Five years at the Cape running the lunar module launch operation was like running the New York marathon. Though I'd never want to do it again, Apollo was a wonderful experience. Calverton was like running the 440, foam coming out of your mouth all the way. Pilots were flying test hops at night, and they thought I was crazy. "What do you mean we're going to fly on Saturday?" "Not only Saturday," I told them, "but you'll fly on Sunday." Wives called me on Thanksgiving Day asking who the hell I thought I was, working their husbands then. Neighbors complained about our suicide pilots, running engines up at nine or ten o'clock at night. I was hyperactive: Get rid of that, cut that down, you can't cut that down, get that damn trestle down by end of the week. All of it was just rolling the dice that I could get away with anything I wanted. John O'Brien was administrative vice president then and he told some of the maintenance people he had at Calverton not to put down the rug I wanted in my office. "Get that damn rug in there," I shouted, and the rug went down. Then the joke was when I finally became president—remember, this is a joke—John O'Brien calls up and asks me, "What color rug do you want on the runways?"

The F-14 was really screwed up, and the A-6 suffered from it. With sudden expansion and increased production rates, Grumman began to hire everyone from delicatessen baloney slicers to former nurserymen or truck drivers and just threw them on the line—unskilled and uncertified. It was then I met an uncompromising Irishman, a who-the-hell-are-you–type foreman, as I walked the line at Plant Six, because I knew we had to get the airplanes over to Plant Seven before they could fly. Eventually Eddie O'Donnell and I wound up with a very tight, good relationship. (His daughter is Rosie O'Donnell, the television star. She writes about how her father neglected the family, working for Grumman at Calverton, coming home at all hours. I felt like writing her a letter, telling her that her father did great job, a great thing for the country, and put bread and butter on the table for his family. But how would that sound when I was the bad guy, keeping everybody working seven days a week.)

Over it all came the umbrella of producibility. Some engineers, as times changed, never flew an airplane, and worked only on the computer. There was no feeling for how something was created in the shop because engineers were transfixed by computer-aided design. Often enough, employees didn't care about airplanes; they just worked there. They didn't make model airplanes as I did, or get a pilot's license. Once at Calverton I told the personnel people to get retired navy chiefs or air force techs, trained by the military to work on airplanes, who knew what safety and discipline were all about. "Get as many as you can in here," I ordered, "because I don't want tomato farmers from Riverhead who just work to get a paycheck." That was one good reason the F-14 learning curve came down like a ski slope and deliveries picked up.

* * *

Fixing the F-14 had two halves, and I've dwelt on the production side. The other half was the financial half. So to back up a bit, it's time to take a look at what was going on in the administrative world. While the manufacturing battle was under way, Grumman's new vice president of finance, John C. Bierwirth, was making the rounds of financial institutions to get the company back on the credit rails. Bierwirth, who moved over from National Distillers in 1972, had planned to take a vacation before he started his new job, but then Lew Evans died. Bierwirth went to his funeral and on the way he said to Clint Towl, "Look, if you really need me earlier, I'll come. I can't do very much, but I can at least get started earlier." Towl's response was, "Maybe you and George Titterton can take a look at the financial situation of the F-14." Bierwirth was hired on so to speak as a consultant for the month of July. By about the middle of July, he went to Clint Towl and said, "Give or take two weeks, by the middle of next April you're going into bankruptcy." Startled, all Clint could say was, "Really?" "I didn't surprise him too much," Bierwirth said with a rueful laugh. "Clint added that things hadn't looked too good, but Grumman had declared a profit on the F-14 the year before. 'Look at the 1971 financial statements and you'll see that the F-14 was profitable.' Of course it wasn't at all."

Jack and I shared this memory when we met in May 2000, and we chimed in together: "We were losing about $2 million a copy." Jack elaborated: "They hadn't recognized that they had used up all the development money and still hadn't finished the development. By using up all the development funds that they had planned to spend, they could turn a slight profit. But what they were going to be paid for those airplanes wasn't going to cover their costs. The guys that are selling canoes can sell canoes like they were going out of style and it might make three days' difference to which day we went bankrupt. The Navy didn't want to recognize that we were telling the truth because the Navy had a fixed price, which they liked, and the Navy didn't want to forget about it. So the trick was to go down there to explain to the Navy how things were going to go. Every time you'd explain that to an admiral, you were talking to someone who had no financial expertise telling him something he didn't want to hear."

I wasn't involved in the contract or the settlement, but I knew about the original eight-lot procurement fixed price on the F-14, the total package. Of course, what the Navy liked was the long-term price guarantee, without considering whether any private company could deliver on that commitment. After Jack convinced Clint that it looked like the company would go bankrupt, Clint made his celebrated appearance before Congress, where he predicted Grumman would have to close its doors. Finally Jack and John Warner, who was secretary of the navy then, came to a decision: Grumman would swallow the losses up through lot 5. After that Grumman would go on a year-by-year contract.

Although Jack Bierwirth thought he was breaking bad news for the first time, Carl Palladino was the first one that had to ring the tocsin. Much earlier, in December 1971, he had told Lew Evans and the board of directors that Grumman had a loss on its hands with the F-14 contract and that its financials looked sick. Palladino became senior vice president and treasurer for Grumman Aerospace when I became president. It was Carl who coined the nickname for those next ten years—1974 to 1984—as the "Golden Decade of Grumman Aerospace." Production lines were humming with the four aces—the F-14, A-6, E-2C, and EA-6B—and profits were climbing every year. In the flush early years for defense of Ronald Reagan's presidency, business couldn't seem to get better. That was not the outlook at all when Carl, then Grumman comptroller, began to worry about the F-14 womb-to-tomb, ten-year fixed-price total package contract. Palladino started in 1963 as what was then called the chief accountant. Grumman was doing around $300 million a year then, which literally exploded to a billion in three years.

Carl and I were having coffee many years later after I had just talked with Jack, and he remembered the warning and the reply from Lew Evans: "Carl, it's the only ball game in town so we signed up for it." In other words, it was take it or leave it. "Lew was in denial, not trying to mislead anyone," Carl told me, and I buy it because I heard Lew argue that Grumman had to win this or be out of the fighter game forever—he was absolutely convinced Grumman was going to make money on the project. Lew almost hired a new comptroller when Palladino first gave him the news, but contented himself with throwing Palladino out of his office. When it was all over years down the road, Grumman did make money on the F-14, with profit margins of 11 percent. The last loss-leader airplane was No. 134, delivered about the time I became president.

Inflation, pegged at 3 percent in the initial contract, ballooned into double digits as the F-14 went into production. Still Grumman was sure it was going to fill the skies with A-6Es for a much bigger business base. Post-Vietnam budget shrinkage forced the Navy to back off those plans, so Grumman's overhead fell more heavily on the F-14. Palladino's first loss estimate was $60–80 million, and Clint Towl had Palladino make a presentation to a special board meeting in January 1972. Grumman had to close its books on 1971, and Palladino recommended declaring the loss on the first four lots and filing the company's tax return the next month, in order to secure an accelerated refund from the Internal Revenue Service. That $20 million helped to tide Grumman over from April until August, along with creditor games. "I called in the major ones," Palladino said, "and told them, 'I'm not going to be able to pay you like I used to, promptly, take discounts, and the like. But when I tell you that you are going to get a check for so many dollars, you can count on that. I'm not going to string you along and say the check is in the mail or all those other excuses people use to delay payment.' One asked what if they didn't go along. 'Well,' I said, 'don't put your bill in the bank.' They laughed and that broke the tension."

Bankers Trust pulled the plug in the midst of Palladino's scraping and skimping. "I used to call and get $20 million over the phone," he recalled, "and pay it down as the money came in from the government." Then came the shambles at the Senate Armed Services Committee when Clint Towl seemed to be threatening to shut down the company. "I glanced around and our friendly bankers were there looking very concerned," he recalls. "After this disaster I knew we were going to need some money, and I called the bank. 'Carl, we've got some bad news for you,' came the answer. 'Your credit line has been cut off.' 'How can you do that?' I demanded. 'We've been doing business since 1927.'" Grumman had been pushing for a revolving credit line against which it could draw as needed. Instead it was restricted to what are called "overnights," short-term money on an as-needed basis. In effect, it was no credit at all.

Again, pre-Bierwirth, Grumman went to the Navy to negotiate an advance payment agreement, as opposed to progress payments, permissible under certain terms and conditions. Palladino's Washington treadmill started, with him and one other Grummanite locked into a small room with maybe twenty negotiators from the Navy. "They insisted," he recalled, "on a formal advanced payments contract with all kinds of covenants, including limitations of raises to officers, where the company could invest, and so on. The prime bank rate at the time was 4 percent, but they insisted on sticking us with 6.5 percent, which I said was unreasonable. They insisted, but I did ask for the ability to invest excess cash in Treasury notes that were paying 2 or 3 percent. Peanuts! We signed this in August of 1972, and it was working out fairly well when Bierwirth and Warner signed the final F-14 settlement in March of the following year." The advance payments contract stayed in place into the Reagan years, by which time interest rates had soared. "When Reagan became president," Palladino said, "the prime rate went to double digits. Now I was able to invest excess cash at 7 or 8 or 9 percent and pay 6.5 percent for the money. It was their doing."

After much shuttling back and forth, and with Bierwirth on board, he, Joe Gavin, and Palladino went down to Washington the week before Washington's birthday and made some progress with Secretary Warner by the Friday before the long weekend. Warner asked whether they could be back at his office at nine AM Tuesday, the day after the holiday, with an analysis of the potential solutions they had reached. Palladino called his office before he left Washington and brought in twenty or thirty of his key financial people who worked every day over the holiday until two o'clock in the morning. They finished the reports in time for the Tuesday meeting. These were the basis for the Bierwirth-Warner agreement the following month.

Grumman ate the losses on the first five lots, about $250 million all told, broke the old contract, and started anew. With that agreement, Grumman then went back to Bankers Trust to renegotiate its credit line, tided over by a loan later from Iran that financed Iran's eighty F-14s. Palladino told me about one last miserable negotiation with Bankers Trust that started about nine AM and went on until midnight. "The air conditioner was off," he said, "it was boiling hot and we were almost down to our undershorts." But Grumman did get its credit back, as Jack Bierwirth will explain.

Why did Grumman bid and stick to a price that even the Navy, sailing close to the procurement law wind, hinted was too low? Mostly because the idea snaked through Grumman that the bid of its prime competitor, McDonnell Douglas, was lower. But McDonnell couldn't match Grumman on performance, and Grumman had the swing wing and Phoenix missile. Lew Evans set the doctrine, though: Either Grumman was going to win this damn fighter or it was going to be out of the fighter business forever. Concurrently Grumman was going after the S-3, the new antisubmarine aircraft to carry on the role of the S2F. If we're going to win only one, was Lew's rationale, we want to win the fighter because the Navy's going to fill the sky with them. Lew Evans primarily, but probably with Clint Towl's approval, turned down a navy offer to renegotiate the F-14 price in the early days. His reasoning died with him, but Lew, the unwavering optimist, was convinced to the end that the F-14 would be profitable.

By the time I got to Calverton in 1973, the financial situation had been resolved, and by the following year the Navy had recognized that Towl's financial warning was accurate. Then followed the F-14 shuttle diplomacy, in the fashion Henry Kissinger made famous in flitting back and forth between the Egyptians and the Israelis to bring peace in the Nixon Administration. What it finally got down to was that Bierwirth called up the secretary and warned him, "We're going to have a board meeting on Thursday. We are going to make one of two decisions. Either we are going to go bankrupt and sink quietly beneath the waves. Or we are going to go into bankruptcy and sue you for breach of contract and all the costs we've incurred. I've got three law firms that tell me we've got a reasonable shot on winning that case." Warner asked whether he could come up that Thursday, which was fine with Bierwirth.

"To my amazement," Bierwirth said, "he sat in my office and we talked. Then I would go in the boardroom and explain to the board what he had said. Then I'd come back to him and explain what the board had said. I didn't want to bring him into the boardroom. It was a much better position for me to be in, and he didn't ask to go in. So I got to interpret what he said to the board, and I got to interpret to him what the board said. On top of that I got time in between to think about it. At the end, we had an agreement. Typically, though, it took another two or three months and several trips before we finally got it settled." Bierwirth thought Warner did well in the negotiations, dealing with a situation for which he had no responsibility, but for which he had to work out a solution.

Suing would have been convoluted, using the theory that the Navy, by insisting on changes, had also changed the contract. Much as contractors don't like to sue the government customer, a contractor being forced into bankruptcy might as well do so. Bierwirth thought chances of winning were no better than about 30 percent. But it was worth a shot. "What the hell?" Bierwirth said. "You owed that to your stockholders." And it got the government's attention, finally. My question to Bierwirth was "Couldn't the suit have contended that after the contract was signed Grumman's business base had shrunk unexpectedly? We thought we were going to have X much business base as we went forward, but the government cut that back and ran the overhead up." Bierwirth was dubious. "I don't think the Navy had an obligation to maintain the business base. But they did want that airplane and they wanted all the others, too."

"Didn't you bargain for another thing, Jack," I asked him, "for the government to bank us for a while somehow?" "That came from Warner," he answered. "There was a law that said the government could make a finding that a company needed financing. Then the government could go ahead and do so for a defense contractor if it decided it had to have the product. The interest rate was set by law, on a formula. At the time, the prime rate was around 4 percent but the rate in our loan was to be 6 percent. We were, in effect, being penalized. But what happened was that in the summer of 1973 we had one of those financial crises that comes every once in a while. The prime rate went all the way to 12 percent, when the administration was trying to put the brakes on inflation. We were still paying 6 percent. McDonnell Douglas was fit to be tied that we were paying 6 percent and it ended up paying 12 percent."

When Grumman lost its traditional line of credit from Bankers Trust Bierwirth invented something that worked. He had represented banks as a lawyer and then had been a banker. By coincidence most of the bank presidents in New York were his friends, or at least the senior people in the banks were. "We have to have $12 million working capital," he would say to one or another. "If Grumman had a million dollars in your bank, and if we decided that we were creditworthy at some point in the future, I would like to be able to come to you and ask you for a $10 million line of credit. A $1 million deposit would normally support a $10 million line of credit." "Who is going to decide whether you're creditworthy?" they asked. "I'm not going to come to you until I think we're creditworthy. But then if you tell me you don't think we are, I'll just take the million dollars out and just walk away. You have no obligation to decide that we're creditworthy. But if you decide that we are, I'd just like your oral promise that we would be able to get a $10 million line of credit from you." They were a bit incredulous: "Gee, you're not asking very much." Even though there was a credit crunch in the United States then, Bierwirth was faced with going around and saying, "Now we're ready." But not one of the ten banks let us down and it meant about a hundred million bucks.

What the Navy did in the end was to take the total net worth out of Grumman in two bites. The second time around they took everything Grumman ever made except for the dividends that were paid. "They took us right down to zero," Bierwirth said. "The settlement was that we make one more lot for the Navy at the old price and accept a $200 million loss. Because of the subsequent Iranian contract and because of the way we were managing our affairs, we had rebuilt that net worth within three years. We never looked like zero, because by the time they took the second bite we had already made back some. Extra volume on the F-14 made the F-14 profitable." In the process Grumman cut its overhead rates. Some layoffs were the price, but, as Bierwirth noted, people come and go in a big company. Attrition is the jargon. More business came along, too. "When I arrived at Grumman," he said, "the sales level was about $670 million a year. When I left, it was over $4 billion and the line was steady."

The trouble was, to use Bill Houser's phrase, those four aces, the stalwart Navy airplanes, were going to pay off one day.

8

IRAN: A LIFELINE FOR THE F-14

WHEN THE F-14 WAS MIRED IN THE WORST OF ITS FUNDING AND manufacturing stresses, the Shah of Iran reached out from Tehran with a lifeline. He decided to buy eighty F-14s in a procurement spectacle that had everything: international politics, suspense, danger, intrigue, mysterious agents, industrial competition, rivalry between the U.S. Air Force and the Navy, and, not the least, one of the relatively rare high-performance air show fly-offs that directly affected a huge order.

Henry Kissinger and President Nixon had stopped in Tehran on one of their world trips and were involved in getting the competitive demonstration started. They had bypassed the national security apparatus and had gone directly to the services. Gen. Hassan Toufanian, the Iranian vice minister of war, came to see Grumman in the fall of 1972 with Adm. Swoose Snead, then the Navy's F-14 program manager. The Iranians were interested in buying the latest U.S. air superiority fighter, either the F-14 or the Air Force's F-15 or a mixed bag. If the Iranians did buy the F-14, they told Swoose, the Navy was going to have to sit on top of Grumman to ensure that it performed. This was before the crucial flight demonstration.

Dennis Romano, a Grumman engineering flight tester who later became a marketing vice president, was the F-14 backseater at the

114

demonstration, and it was he who later filled me in on the details. This came after the Paris Air Show in the spring of 1973, Romano recalls, at Andrews Air Force Base, in the suburbs east of Washington, D.C. Grumman took the demonstration's potential seriously enough that Don Evans, the pilot Romano was flying structural test programs with, and Romano performed in a series of practice air shows at Calverton before they actually took the airplane down to Andrews. Both wanted to make the show look as crisp as possible.

Their airplane, an early production model, left for the show at Andrews at about three o'clock in the afternoon. Grumman's veteran test pilot, Chuck Sewell, brought down F-14 No. 2, which was the spin airplane. Capt. Jimmie Taylor and his backseater, Cdr. Kurt Strauss, who had wowed a Paris Air Show audience in the F-14's first appearance there, brought an airplane in from the naval flight test center at Patuxent River, Maryland.

"Between Calverton and Andrews," Romano told me, "we wanted to take the fuel load down to about eight thousand pounds to make the airplane light and a lot more maneuverable for the show the next day. So, on the outskirts of Andrews, we opened a dump valve to get down to our final target fuel load, which almost gave our strategy away when it stuck open. Since we were performing the show at an air force base, the Air Force was especially sensitive to the kind of flying that we were going to do. Their troops really wanted to sell the F-15 to the Shah as much as Grumman did the F-14. So they kept telling us repeatedly that the two shows were to be the same. There would be no difference in maneuvers, and the Shah could make his decision on the same baseline. Andrews had an FAA control tower, not military like most air force bases, because Air Force 1 and Air Force 2 operated from there to civilian fields. Don and I took the time to go over to the tower and thoroughly brief the controllers on what we were going to do for the Shah the next day. They simply cautioned us to be sure we didn't get too far to the west, because they didn't want to encroach on the airspace of neighboring Washington National Airport."

Evans and Romano wound up at the Officers' Club that night after dinner. A bunch of young air force officers were there, claiming that the newer and hence better F-15 would clearly outpoint the F-14. At the end of the evening, after listening to all this for half an hour, Evans simply turned to the group and suggested they just come out the following day and see.

"Next morning," Romano went on, "the weather was not great for demonstration flying, a typical warm-front day in August, with lowering clouds and four or five miles visibility. But in a weather briefing from the tower, we noticed there was low altitude wind shear. At the surface the wind was blowing from the south. At one thousand feet it was 180 degrees the other way around. That made a big difference later in the show."

What the crowd at the Officers' Club may or may not have known was that the F-15, flown by McDonnell test pilot Irv Burrows, was fairly new in its flight test regime, and its envelope had not been opened as far as the F-14's. Thus it was operating with restrictions the F-14 did not have. McDonnell was going for light, too, offloading the Sparrow missiles that were on the airplane to save weight. The F-15 was going to fly first, while the F-14 sat at the end of the runway with the engines up at a fairly high power to burn fuel down, maybe to seventy-five hundred pounds. After a maximum performance takeoff, the F-15 disappeared into the overcast sky. For much of the show, the F-15 was out of sight. It would do a steep vertical climb and disappear. Then it would come back, execute a high-speed pass and disappear. While the vertical performance of the airplane was truly impressive, because of its very high thrust-to-weight ratio, the fact that it took so much airspace was a detriment.

"When our turn came," Romano related, "we pointed the airplane to the north, and staged the afterburners up. The F-14A in those days had five zones of afterburning. Takeoff technique was to stand on the brakes until the tires begin to slide, then release. We took the airplane up into the vertical, cleaned up the gear and flaps, pulled it upside down, and rolled out at about eight hundred to a thousand feet headed south. Then came a 90-degree turn to the right, followed by a 270-degree turn to the left to come back to runway heading. Next came a knife-edge pass, the airplane rolled 90 degrees, to the vertical, to give reviewing stands a plan view of the variable sweep wing. This meant sweeping the wings manually from 68 degrees full aft to full forward, 22 degrees—a very uncomfortable maneuver. We had about five hundred feet and were pulling 1 g, but laterally. Nevertheless it came off quite well and looked good."

There was more, with changes in wing sweep and acceleration into an 8.5-g 360-degree turn around the runway that stayed inside the field boundary. Then followed a turn downwind for a low-speed pass, indicating ninety-five knots with the gear, flaps, and hook down. With a twenty-knot headwind, the airplane seemed to take forever to pass the reviewing stand.

"After a pull-up and cleanup," Romano said, "we did a touch-and-go landing and lit the burners. By now the airplane probably had about twenty-five hundred pounds of fuel left, not a whole lot. We pulled up into a vertical climb with the gear and flaps down, and, right over the Shah's parked airplane, went inverted, dirty with gear and flaps down. Then we did a quarter roll right over the top of where the Shah was standing. Then we landed with a maximum-performance braking maneuver, stopping the airplane probably in about twelve hundred feet. The F-14 was never outside the field boundaries for the entire air show, it was always visible."

Not only was the Shah very impressed, but also, in another way, so were all the air force guys at Andrews. They were furious. They wasted no time going over to the control tower in an attempt to file a flight violation against us for performing low-level acrobatics over a crowd. Because of the briefing that Evans and Romano had given the tower, however, the FAA knew what was coming, and the Air Force never did file a flight violation.

That show probably was the seminal event that convinced the Shah that the F-14 was the airplane he wanted. He was obviously impressed, and he commented about the high-quality flight crew which flew an absolutely first-class, high-quality airplane. That show clearly demonstrated the maneuverability of the F-14, its low- and high-speed flying qualities, to the point that he ultimately bought eighty from Grumman. Peter B. Oram, who had been Grumman's F-14 program manager and head of the company's international operations during the Iranian sale, reiterates that important test phase point. Because the F-14 was at least a year further along in its test program than the F-15, and had cleared much more of its performance envelope, it did have a big advantage in what it could do at Andrews.

Dennis Romano's story of the Iranian F-14 is from the performance side. By that time I had finished fixing the F-14's production near-disaster at Calverton and Grumman had become a ward of the Navy. After we won the Iranian $2 billion contract for eighty airplanes—I had become president of Grumman Aerospace by then—the Navy was able to back away from sending us money every month to keep us floating. Still there was bitterness. The Navy complained about this and that and everything else, and former navy flag officers tend to agree that the F-14 was the point at which a long love affair with Grumman ran not onto the rocks, but into cooler water.

Lifeline that it was, the F-14 sale to Iran placed what had been a rather conservative, straitlaced company into the fringes of the overseas payment scandals that had so besmirched other aerospace companies in the 1970s. Grumman's predicament came with a family firm headed by Houshang Lavi, whose exact role still mystifies me now. For all their reputed siphoning of cash, they lived in very modest homes on Long Island. Where did all that money go?

Grumman's retired general counsel, John Carr, who later headed its Washington office, has his own suspicions. But he says the $25 million commission, originally $28 million, for the agents who dealt with Iran is something of an oversimplification. Butch Satterfield and Tom Kane, both senior marketing people, had gone to Iran early on to case the area and talk to other contractors. Aerospace companies were inexperienced at doing business in the Middle East or the Third World then, and the common wisdom was that, without an agent, a company couldn't get anywhere in countries like Iran. Somewhere on their rounds, Satterfield and Kane met the agents, the Lavi group, and became convinced that they were the people Grumman should have. Everybody else was using them, and Grumman fell in line. Then there was General Toufanian, the 5-percent general. "I don't know how much went into his pocket," Carr says, "but some did at any rate. Later we found out the Lavi family was in ill repute in Iran. We were told to change agents, and we tried to do that, managing to secure a written agreement from the Lavis to surrender their rights to another group. But then it all blew up. George and I had to go to the Waldorf in Manhattan to meet with General Toufanian and explain our position to him. He came in ranting and raving, cursing us up and down. Then his son came in with his little grandson. In the space of ten seconds, Toufanian turned into the nicest, kindest man imaginable as he greeted this little boy. As soon as they had gone, back he went to yelling at us. Finally we negotiated a deal where there was $18 million owed, and we were going to pay it in spare parts. In the meantime, one of the Lavi brothers, Houshang, sued us. A family member had signed the agreement, but claimed he was forced to through threats—not from Grumman, but from the other agents. It looked as though we were going to get stuck twice, that we were going to lose the lawsuit. But then the Iranian revolution came, and we never did deliver the spares."

Because of Grumman's credit starvation, financing the Iranian program was not so easy, no matter that it was to be a foreign military sales program. Once, after I became president of aerospace, I asked Jack Bierwirth about his dealings with the Iranian Bank Melli, which had coughed up the loans to get the program moving after the U.S. government backed away. Grumman's financial condition caused the U.S. government to worry that the company couldn't carry the Iranian sale, what with contract disputes and overruns. Jack laughed and pointed out that having been a banker, he knew Bank Melli but not the people there. For a defense contractor to borrow internationally, it needed permission from Washington. Grumman was having trouble because it had refused to support Nixon but several competitors had—some legally, some illegally. When Bierwirth went to Washington to tell Deputy Defense Secretary Bill Clements that he wanted to go to Bank Melli for financing, it came as a bit of a surprise. Clements shied away, then finally told him to go ahead. Bierwirth went to Tehran after the contract was signed in 1974 and told the Iranians, "You've got to come up with seventy-five million bucks if you want to have your F-14 purchase financed." There was consternation. "We already have an agreement with the United States and we've already delivered $250 million to your Treasury," they responded. "Yes," Bierwirth answered, "but they haven't given any of it to us." "We have a contract for the F-14," they protested. "Not with us you don't," Bierwirth pointed out. "We're not going to build the F-14 for you because we don't have any contract directly with you to build them. So we have no obligation to you unless we have your $75 million." Then came the really hard part for them. "Because this is a foreign loan," he explained, "you have to be subordinated to all the American banks." This was the Fourth of July weekend, and hotter than hell. It was July 3 when he told them his story, and there was a Fourth of July party at the U.S. Embassy to attend. "I'm leaving on July fifth," Bierwirth warned them. "If you can't work it out, that's your decision, of course. But if you don't I will set the wheels in motion to make sure we do not produce the F-14 for Iran. Just let me know what you want me to do." The Iranians decided to go ahead.

Selling the F-14 to Iran was a marketing and finance coup. To those who had to get the airplanes up and flying in Iran it was anything but romance in exotic realms. Dick Barton, who was a right-hand man at Cape Canaveral for the lunar module support, came back with me to Calverton. There he was handed one of his toughest assignments: to run the F-14 support operations in the Shah's homeland. Of course there was a memorandum of understanding, a government-to-government agreement. Nevertheless, as Dick Barton said, "They just never considered support services. In other words they didn't take into account that there was no housing in many of these areas, particularly in Isfahan, one of the bases for the F-14, where there were only forty houses in the whole damn place."

Military hardware is sold overseas in two different ways. One is a straight commercial sale, where the U.S. seller goes through the U.S. government for the necessary clearances and export licenses. The other is through the Pentagon's foreign military sales office, where the foreign government is required to put money in a U.S.–owned bank and maintain a running balance, a revolving fund, which is usually replenished on a quarterly basis. Then the U.S. government pays the contractor from that account. Minimum levels are established for the fund, and regulations prohibit any U.S. agency from expending funds on a foreign military sales case that is not covered in that account. So it's against the law, actually, for any government procurement officer to allocate or obligate funds not covered by deposits from the foreign government. This became a wrestling match for Dick Barton by the time Adm. John Alvis had replaced Swoose Snead as navy program manager for the F-14.

Alvis wanted Barton to review the briefing for the F-14 foreign military sales case. Booz Allen Hamilton, the consulting firm that prepared the case, had people who had made several trips through the Middle East, and a retired navy admiral with Booz Allen was in charge of their input. "That was about the worst foreign military sales briefing I'd ever heard," Barton recalled, "though not from the stand-point of the briefer, but because the case itself was really vague. I could see $250 million worth of costs accruing that were not even funded in the case, which really put Alvis in one hell of a spot." When Barton gave Alvis the bad news, Alvis reddened and demanded an explanation. Here was a sophisticated airplane going to a country that didn't have the skills and the infrastructure we did, and there was no line item for support. That left Alvis with the daunting prospect of recalling the case during processing, amending it, and going back to renegotiate it with the Shah and his people—all out of the question because there already was a tacit agreement. The only other thing to do was to get a memorandum of understanding, a government-to-government agreement, and offset all these additional costs. How long would that take Barton, Alvis asked, and he knew Barton had been in the Air Force Strategic Air Command and had negotiated agreements for many of our overseas SAC bases. Three days was his guess, and he got the go-ahead.

"Back in Bethpage," Barton said, "I wrote the draft in about four hours, which would have to be signed by officials of both the U.S. and Iranian governments. After a forty-minute briefing I gave the next day in Washington, and a lot of questions, everyone was happy. 'All you have to do Admiral,' I explained, 'is send a TWX through contracts to Grumman saying you want Dick Barton to negotiate a government-to-government agreement with Iran dealing with all the support services that have been left out of the foreign military service case.' He did just that. 'I'm just a contractor,' I told him, 'and over there they will all ask who the hell am I. That is, unless you've got some holy water sprinkled on me from this government.' Just after the first of the year, 1975, I arrived in Iran with the agreement and a presentation."

In any foreign country, Barton knew, the first thing in starting a new project is find out what the national budget is and its priorities. For $25 he got a copy of Iran's five-year budget plan and stayed up all night memorizing it. The total budget was around $41 billion, and about $29 billion came from oil revenue. The Shah had massive programs for forestry, housing, and highways, and Barton had to know the setting to understand the logistics challenge and where to get the kind of support he needed. Grumman would have to build livable houses from scratch, as well as roads, sewage, and everything its employees needed to work. Then he was ready to take on the U.S. Embassy, the first place for a contractor to negotiate, not the military assistance group. There he briefed the embassy finance officer for an hour, without generating many questions. "These Iranians never will sign an agreement," the officer told Barton. "It's against their philosophy." "Just don't get in my way and I'll get this agreement signed," Barton answered. As he walked out the officer called after me, "Rots o' ruck."

Since it was an Iranian Air Force program, the air force section of the Military Assistance Advisory Group (MAAG) would be responsible to support the Iranian government. So next came a meeting with a brigadier general at the air force section, who was cool to Barton's briefing because he, too, doubted whether we would ever get such an agreement by the Iranian officials. "Just stay out of my way," Barton repeated, "and I'll come back with the signatures." Still more briefings followed, to the army section. The Army had sold, in an earlier foreign military sales case, legions of Bell helicopters to the Shah, the biggest foreign military sales order Bell had ever had.

Then Barton had to tackle the Iranians. Negotiating overseas base rights in his USAF days left Barton not as daunted as he should have been, and he chose to begin with Gen. Abdolhosain Minousepehr as a direct link to the F-14. At that time a brigadier, Minousepehr headed the F-14 program at all the planned bases. After briefing Minousepehr, Barton had him arrange a meeting with Gen. Ali Mohammad Khatami, who was commander of the Iranian Air Force. The briefing for Khatami at headquarters in Tehran took maybe thirty minutes.

"After Minousepehr introduced me, he and Khatami talked in Farsi for fifteen minutes," Barton said. "I didn't have a clue to what they were saying, just hints from body language. Yet I wanted to touch base with the Iranian Air Force before I met with Gen. Hassan Toufanian, the vice minister of war for Iran and a four-star general. The situation, as Minousepehr described it to me, was literally Byzantine. General Khatami had been air force commander since 1958 and had married a sister of the Shah, making him part of the dynasty. He was junior to Toufanian, but Toufanian was not part of the dynasty."

General Khatami was all smiles after the conversation in Farsi and told Barton he would support the program. When Barton said he needed to see General Toufanian, Khatami picked up his phone and arranged a meeting for two or three days later. Khatami did not attend, Barton assumed, out of discretion. Instead, he sent Minousepehr along. Four general officers besides Toufanian, three senior civil servants, and the air force military assistance section chief met at a big conference table in Toufanian's huge office.

"The crux of my one hour briefing to Toufanian," Barton said, "was that he could save at least 30 percent of $250–300 million if he agreed to the memo of understanding. If the Iranian government goes to the U.S. government to contract for support, I pointed out, the government adds a 12 percent fee to the total. On top of that comes at least 30 percent more in fees from contractors providing the service. So, it was more than 30 percent, but I tried to be conservative. In addition are travel costs and pay differentials overseas. Toufanian stopped me periodically, and he and General Minousepehr went over to the other side of his big office and looked out the windows, talking in Farsi. Then he would come back and say 'Okay, Mr. Barton, go ahead.' With that I skipped through the rest of my long financial briefing. Later, to my surprise, it turned out one of the senior civilians there was a top Iranian finance expert, who liked the proposal."

"This is the first time that any contractor has come to Iran and briefed me on how to save money," Toufanian told Barton in his adequate, but not polished English. "All of them before thought the streets in Iran were paved with gold." Clearly Barton was going to get his signature, and the MAAG chief had already signed it. Barton later insisted that Minousepehr become the single point of contact with the Iranian Air Force. Toufanian wanted to talk to the Shah first, whom Khatami had already briefed. So when Toufanian called the Shah—and this was big money for Iran—the Shah gave the approval to go ahead. That one document was the crux of Grumman's success in Iran. Without it, the situation would have been the same as with every other contractor over there, no housing and no furniture—no way to work effectively. Other contractors were building tables out of shipping crates and sitting on boxes.

Only runways and taxiways were in place, and Grumman had just six months to get the first site activated, checked out, and ready for delivery of the first airplanes in order to start training 110 Iranian Air Force two-man front/back–seat crews, as well as the Iranian technical enlisted maintenance people. The latter could speak broken English, but all the pilots were English-language trained, fairly fluent, and young. During the negotiations on the agreement, Barton had warned both General Minousepehr and through him Khatami that the F-14 was the most sophisticated aircraft in the world at the time. Transfer as many pilots as they could out of F-4 or F-5 active units, he suggested, who had preferably one thousand to two thousand hours of fighter time, as a cadre for the F-14 program. They understood, and the first classes were just that.

Grumman's Flight Test Development Section at Calverton selected retired navy F-14 flight crews to work with Iranian flight crews. They would fly check flights and verify when an Iranian was ready. The initial two or three classes comprised experienced people and they did great. Still there was the language barrier, and while the crews spoke good English they didn't understand everything they heard. Delivery rates at two or three a month were slow. Still, when eleven airplanes had been delivered, there were eleven qualified F-14 crews completely checked out through transition but not in combat maneuvers.

One squadron deployed on schedule to Shiraz and one later to Meribad in Tehran, leaving the third at Isfahan. Grumman sent a handful of tech reps—about forty people for logistics activation. Eight of those were to deal with the horrible Iranian supply system. Hardly anyone in Iran or the Navy believed Grumman could bring in the spares and other supplies on schedule, but it did. OTUs, operational training units, were set up to which, after transition, Iranian flight and ground crews were assigned to train as a squadron and then sent to operate on their own for a month or six weeks.

"As we were getting ready to move the next squadron to Tehran," Barton recalled with dismay, "the political bombs began to fall. Khomeini hadn't yet entered the country, but his supporters were attacking government buildings with firebombs. In Isfahan alone there were 275 Iranians, family groups, in a theater one night at a movie. After it started a mob arrived, rolled fifty-five-gallon drums of gasoline into the lobby, poured it down the aisles, locked the doors, and lit it off. All 275 burned to death. Ambassador Sullivan, a good, seasoned diplomat, tried but failed to get the secretary of state, Cyrus Vance, and President Carter to lay out a government evacuation plan for all of the American contractors. Vance and Carter were going in another direction, and Sullivan also felt that the Shah, militarily, would be able to quell any uprising. Given the fire bombings of government facilities, I argued, that was all protection after the fact. An army battalion had a command post set up around the periphery at Isfahan by this time. True, there were armored vehicles and tanks, but if an uprising exploded in the middle of town it would take them fifteen minutes to get there, and the damage would be done. As a result, I had no alternative but to arrange for our own evacuation plans."

The result was an on-call commercial airline contract. In November 1978 Grumman started pulling out women and children. Then in December the rest of the dependents plus all the non-essential employees came out. By that time there was no question that Grumman was going to have to fold its tent. In early January 1979, it pulled everybody except fifty-eight people back, then cut that number to thirteen.

Khatami was dead by this time, in a purported hang-glider accident. In order to get himself and his dynasty out of the country as the bombings escalated, the Shah abdicated without telling the military. The generals were really teed off. In what had been an authoritarian government, where little power was delegated, the military chiefs were left without a rudder when the captain abandoned ship. Ruhollah Khomeini closed the borders and the airports. His followers had a hit list. Khatami's successor was hauled before a kangaroo court and shot two days later. They shot some of the F-14 pilots later, Barton was told. Toufanian got out of the country, for a price, and died later in the United States.

Grumman had 895 people at Isfahan, 38 at Shiraz, and 28 near Tehran executing two contracts for the F-14 and for the support services. Besides Grumman employees and dependents there were also associate contract employees and dependents from other companies including Hughes and Pratt & Whitney. All told, the total contractor contingent was close to two thousand. All but one of the eighty airplanes in the contract were delivered before the revolution. The reason the eightieth wasn't delivered was because the Iranian Air Force, or the Shah, wanted the last one modified for air refueling with the type of tankers they had. Calverton was working on the modification when Khomeini moved in, and the airplane later went to storage in Tucson.

Dick Barton's story of Iran ends there, but there was more to the Grumman tale. Barton did a magnificent job in my opinion. If it weren't for him, I don't think the Iranians could ever have handled the F-14, so I was one of his fans. Not only did he have responsibility for the Grumman contingent, but also for Hughes, Pratt & Whitney, and other subcontractors. Superb a job as he did, though, Barton ran into trouble, which carried a hard lesson about selling overseas. Barton was a chain smoker, and the Iranians objected to this enough to invite him out. Barton and I sat in front of General Toufanian, who told me he wasn't too happy with what was going on. After that Grumman made the decision to bring Barton back home and sent Swoose Snead over to replace him. Snead had retired from the Navy and had joined Grumman International in Europe. "Then," Swoose recalled, "George called me and said he needed somebody to go to Iran. What George wanted, George got as far as I was concerned. George told me I didn't have to go, but I said, 'You're not listening to me. What George wants, George gets.' Off I went."

Despite the benefit of foreign sales to overheads, Swoose says the Navy had blinders on sometimes. This coincides with my recollection of how passive the Navy was toward export orders, and Swoose agrees. There was no F-14 system program office like the Air Force had, and the various program and separate functional groups, such as contracts or support, saw the Iranian sale as just another program dumped on them without any more support personnel to make it happen. "So," Snead said, "they could give a lesser damn about the overall impact of the eighty airplanes on the production line. Some of us recognized what it would do to the cost of our own airplanes, spares, and support, but there was not what could be called an outpouring of backing from the navy management hierarchy for the Iranians buying the F-14. The Air Force is more oriented to sell to foreign countries. They're good salesmen for their products and they've got good military assistance groups, too."

Swoose had cause to wonder about the Shah's political wisdom when he landed in country. From the good homes that Barton had built for the Grumman employees at Isfahan and Shiraz, the employees had to drive over roads with potholes so deep it was better to plow through open fields, this to reach a brand-new base to fly twenty-million-dollar airplanes. "Such was enough to make us wonder about their sense of values," Swoose said. "Nevertheless, that was the way it was."

Before Swoose was there very long, the revolution really started to boil faster. "One day the general commanding the base telephoned an order for us not to come out to the base again," he said. "Their equivalents to our chief warrant officers and chief petty officers who ran things had beaten the hell out of him in his own office. They had exploded over a big levy laid on them for a going-away party for a general they identified with the F-14."

Although most of the Grummanites had gone home, the company still had some retired military personnel, the kind who would stay. Snead was called to Tehran for a tongue-lashing by the Iranian Air Force chief of staff, Gen. Amir Hossain Rabii. "You Americans and your President Carter and your human rights," he snapped at Snead. "This country isn't ready for human rights. Besides, you don't have sixteen hundred miles of common border with the USSR." Then the Iranian Air Force two star there, Rabii pointed out that the Shah had not gone yet. The United States didn't want to put another nail in the Shah's coffin, so Rabii asked Snead to stay, with as many people for as long as possible. "I've got a group who will stay until hell freezes over," Snead told him. By then Grumman was hanging by its thumbs, and I called Snead with an order as aerospace president: "Admiral, get the containers packed and get them all out."

An Iranian Air Force enlisted troop was on Snead's roof twenty-four hours a day as a guard. One night he just disappeared. A couple of days later the compound was overrun. Snead's car was surrounded by a mob when he drove in. "I'm the leader here," he shouted. "Who's your leader?" They chattered among themselves for a while and finally one stepped forward. They were looking for General Koshradad. One of the Iranian generals had quarters there in our compound at Isfahan, but it was not Koshradad, who had suggested to the Shah that he could level Tehran. "I do not think General Koshradad is here," Snead told them, "but please search the compound. Just let me get the keys to open the doors. Don't kick the windows in and kick the doors down to search." "No, general (he called me general), if you say he's not here, he's not here," the leader replied.

"A couple of nights later," Snead continued, "came a hurry-up call from our central command post that had all our communications flashing computer alarm gee-whiz lights. Milling around in it was a gang, something between Arafat and Zapata, wearing bandoliers and waving guns around." When Snead asked one of his Iranian staff what they were saying, he translated, "Let's shoot a couple of these Americans and let the whole world know the CIA is here." With massive understatement Snead suggested that the odds didn't look very good. To this day he's not sure how he talked his way out of that one. "By this time," Snead said, "we had skinnied down to the dirty dozen. We had some Air America C-130s, and a bunch of Bell guys also stood by. They were the toughest crowd I've ever seen, right out of Vietnam with their Vietnamese women. They would ride through the local hotel on their motorcycles, with their hair down to here. But they were great. They knew I was a retired admiral and worked like Trojans loading those airplanes and getting our stuff out."

A retired navy senior chief had set up a ham radio station upstairs in one of the back bedrooms in his quarters. When the army compound in Tehran was overrun, Grumman had the only contact with the outside world. It stayed in constant touch with the commander in chief, Europe (CincEur), but the Iranians found out and talked about taking them before the revolutionary committee. "Get a bus," Snead told an aide, Marty Clark, "but leave everything here. We're getting out after sunset." Clark found the bus and the group made a midnight run up through Qom to Tehran to find the last evacuation plane loading.

"We didn't bring a thing with us," Snead said, "but just got on the bus and left. Going up the road in the dark, the driver kept falling asleep, and I spent the trip up front poking him. We rolled up over a knoll and there was another bus ahead of us with an old pickup truck next to it. Revolutionaries with guns were holding up the bus. Our driver started to stop, but I yelled 'Go! Go! Go!' Around we went, and they never chased us. At seven AM one of the revolutionary guards boarded our bus, stayed with us through road blocks, got us to the airport, and we got the hell out of there. A great story, but never again."

All sorts of rumors have circulated as to what happened to the Iranian F-14 aircraft and the Phoenix missiles. Iran bought a hell of a lot of spares and support, Snead says, and they could do things with their hands. "But they were not aggressive pilots. A thirty-degree bank was an unusual attitude for them. Mostly those airplanes were a big showpiece for the Shah when he would come down to Isfahan. When he did, there would be water and new plants and he only saw things that he wanted to see. He didn't see the potholes. After we left only the F-14 radar operated, for all the Phoenix missiles had been disabled." By this time, Snead suspects there are just sixty or seventy hunks of junk left. For a time, though, they could have been cannibalized for maintenance, and Grumman had trained many people to do that work.

Without Grumman integrated support, the presumption is that the seventy-nine delivered F-14s would not have remained flyable very long. For a while after the Shah fell, there were calls to Grumman, presumably from Iranians, trying to buy verboten spares. Dennis Romano thinks a couple of them found their way into Russia. The Iranians may have flown them in the war with Iraq, using the AWG-9 radar just to look at the battle line. At least eight of them were lost in crashes.

Grumman had a good team of people across the spectrum of maintenance and instruction, and Barton had established a well-oiled organization that didn't need changing. Swoose gives him the highest grades. "This is where Dick Barton showed his organizational skills," Swoose said, and I agreed. But he wouldn't stop smoking. Barton moved up to Calverton with me from Cape Canaveral to set up the F-14 maintenance center, always smoking and puffing on his pipe. Ask him what time it was, and half an hour later he would still be telling you how the watch was invented. Jack Bierwirth didn't appreciate him. Barton wrote a memo that he wanted me to bless and send on to Jack about what Grumman should do in the wake of Iran. Jack fancied himself as an internationalist, which he was, and he brought into Grumman a sense of international culture that we previously lacked. I tried to discourage Dick, but he insisted. My policy as president, if someone had strong feelings, was to go ahead, for maybe some good would come out of it. Jack called me later and said, in effect, that he was less than enthused. Finally Barton wound up as a vice president at Grumman Technical Services in shuttle support, a fabulous guy on organization and maintenance and on proposals. "That's good air force training," Swoose added. "Navy, we're a lot more relaxed and loose." And so was Grumman, which came back to bite it.

9

SELLING THE GULFSTREAM

O F ALL THE TWISTS AND TURNS IN PLAYING OUT GRUMMAN'S unfulfilled destiny, one of the hardest to understand was the sale of the Gulfstream. What started out as a medium-size twin-turboprop powered by the Rolls Royce Dart turned into a family of increasingly larger and longer-range jets that are, by coincidence, the Rolls Royce of business aircraft today—and to someone else's profit. To me, the decision was incomprehensible. As I said before, once into Gulf-stream 1, the twin turboprop, we didn't have enough drive or imagination to go for a DC-9 type airliner, which the later Gulfstreams almost became. But John Carr, who was general counsel at Grumman at the time, and Jack Bierwirth, who made the decision as chairman of the corporation, contend that there were compelling reasons for the sale.

The story of the Gulfstream begins with Mike Pelehach. He was in preliminary design in the 1960s and trying to turn the piston-engine-powered S2F antisubmarine aircraft into a carrier-on-board-delivery (COD) transport airplane. The S2F was too small, though, and needed aviation gasoline that would eventually disappear from carriers. A colleague happened to show Mike's rough sketches to Roy Grumman, who thought they were lousy. Nevertheless, Mike wound up talking with Roy, who, out of the blue, enunciated a policy: "It's time for us to build a good reliable business airplane." Mike demurred, because he was strictly a military designer, but Roy dismissed those objections and told Mike and production test pilot Henry Schiebel: "Take your golf clubs, get on the company airplane, and for two or three weeks go out and visit people from U.S. Steel and Ford and the like." They did. Among other things, they landed in Detroit to see Willow Run airport, where the airplane they designed would have to take off in four thousand feet. "Make sure that it is a reliable airplane," Roy told Pelehach, "because it's going to end up as the airplane that the Board of Directors and families are going to fly. It absolutely must be reliable." So Mike started to lay out alternatives: high-wing airplanes, low-wing airplanes, as well as their specifications. What resulted was a low-wing, twin-turboprop—the Gulfstream 1. Then Roy asked him, "Mike, what engine are you going to use?" Mike's thought was a General Electric turboprop engine that had great thrust-to-weight ratio for the time. "Mike," Roy asked, "what is the most reliable engine there is?" "It's the British Dart," Pelehach answered. "That's the engine we are going to use," Grumman ordered. "Everything's going be too heavy," Pelehach protested. "It's the most reliable engine," Roy reiterated, "so you put the Dart engine in there, with five thousand hours between overhauls." Accordingly, Pelehach laid out the airplane with the Dart. "GE was going bananas," Pelehach recalled. "They couldn't understand what the hell was the matter with me. All I could say was, that's what Mr. Grumman wants."

Grumman was building the first Gulfstream 1 when I had my one-to-one meeting with Roy. "The Gulfstream is different," he emphasized. "We got into that to preserve jobs at Grumman. We weren't sure it was going to make money." He didn't say it this way, but Roy Grumman was not interested in just making money. A small engineering company was his ideal: that is why he called it Grumman Aircraft Engineering, not Grumman Aircraft Manufacturing.

His wisdom with the Gulfstream was to go after Fortune 500–sized companies—that was to be our market with what he thought was a good airplane, one that would be successful with big companies with money. I noticed during that meeting that he had a picture of a Gulfstream 1 on the wall, autographed by Walt Disney. Not only did he want to safeguard jobs at Grumman, but he also wanted to retain an experienced team. "I want to try to hold this nucleus together," he told me, "preserve as many jobs as we can. And I think we can really build a fine turboprop airplane using the Rolls Royce Dart engine." So we did. People argue about whether it was a successful program, but it was in the sense that it placed within the commercial world the greatest flying billboard conceivable. Grumman Gulfstream, with the Rolls Royce image added, had the same cachet as Tiffany or the Waldorf Astoria in the executive aircraft world. Flying around in a G-1 or later a Gulfstream 2 or 3 or even now G-4 or G-5, hey, you're up there on the top of the mountain.

Gulfstream 1 was just one airplane type. To tap the commercial aircraft market takes a family. That's how Boeing developed its dominant airline jet transport business: first with the 707 four-engine long-range jet transport and then the 727 three-engine medium-range transport, the 737 short-haul twinjet, the 747 jumbo for international routes, and the 757, 767, and 777 followed. Grumman was aware of commercial families and tried a couple of things. There was a meeting with Olive Ann Beech, Walter Beech's widow who ran Beech Aircraft, which turned out to be at cross-purposes. Grumman had visions of acquiring Beech with its smaller aircraft and Beech wanted to buy the Gulfstream to fill out its twin-engine family with large turbine-powered aircraft. Mrs. Beech and Frank Hedrick, a relative and second in command, flew out to Calverton to see the famous F-14 production line, which I showed her because I was running the operation at the time. Although our Gulfstream and Beech's high-quality smaller airplane family would have made a powerful combination, the deal didn't go through. Clint Towl and Mrs. Beech knew each other socially, and Clint admired her as a widow who was successfully running her husband's legacy. Yet what helped kill any deal was too much negative baggage surrounding the F-14. Eventually Raytheon bought Beech. I remember Frank Hedrick asking me later: "Why did you sell the Gulfstream? Are you crazy?" It used to irk me that people would key on me about Gulfstream when I, too, thought selling was stupid.

Then there was an acquisition of a company called American Aviation. "I'll take a good deal of the blame for that," John Carr recalled many years later. Someone, name forgotten, brought the offering to Carr's attention and he elected to go out to Cleveland, where the company was located, to look the operation over. Russ Meyer, who went on to bigger things, eventually running Cessna, was then the president. "I must say I was smitten," Carr recalls. Jim Bede, a maverick light plane builder, had started the company, and he had completed an interesting design with the company's first airplane, the AA-1, a light single-engine aircraft. "I think he was a poor business-man," Carr said, "and that's why the board decided to take over. Russ Meyer had been their lawyer and they made him the president. He was doing fairly well with the little company." They had just the AA-1 to start with, but they had plans to build the AA-2, which was a pretty good airplane, a light twin.

Grumman was serious enough about acquiring American Aviation that the latter's board was sitting one day expecting an answer from Lew Evans, yes or no. Lew was president at the time, and he was wrapped up in other things, like the F-14. Even so, I kept call-ing Jack Jennings, his aide, telling him, "Look, American Aviation needs to have some answer from you." Lew just never did respond, and that created such a rift that the acquisition lapsed. Except that it resurrected itself a couple of years later. They'd been pretty ticked off with a Grumman they viewed as terribly arrogant and ill-mannered. Nevertheless negotiations were going again despite spin problems with the AA-1, the Yankee, and a deal was pending when Lew died and Jack Bierwirth came in as financial vice president.

Bierwirth had no aviation or defense background, but he under-stood his mandate from Clint Towl, who had then become corporate chairman, to expand the company into commercial areas. Carr took the acquisition to Bierwirth, because he assumed, since it would be a commercial deal, it was something Bierwirth would want to do. Once again Carr went to Cleveland, this time to meet with American Aviation's three director/owners, an Ohio triumvirate that included the owner of the Cleveland Browns. Grumman unfortunately was mired in the escalating F-14 situation, Carr said. "We didn't have any money to buy anybody. That generated the idea of taking the Gulfstream and merging it with American Aviation to create a general aviation company with a broad line of aircraft that would fill in gradually." Lacking cash, Grumman offered, instead of a buy-out a minority interest in what would become a separate company with outside stockholders, which would have tax advantages. For two or three years it was to be 80 percent Grumman, and the American Aviation people would hold a minority in what became Grumman American Aviation. The American Aviation people were to have the option after three years or so to buy another 20 percent, according to an agreed formula. At that time Grumman had been told that the company was just about in the black. We were not told—and I think we could have possibly made a lawsuit out of this—how serious the Yankee's spin problem was and about the ensuing lawsuits.

At any rate, the deal went through, Grumman had a new subsidiary, Grumman American Aviation, and Russ Meyer was the president. Cleveland was not an ideal place for an aviation company, with all the lake effect rain and snow. Instead the company was moved to Savannah, Georgia, where Grumman had transferred Gulfstream production in the late 1960s. By this time the Gulfstream 2, the twin turbojet business aircraft, had come along. Unfortunately this was a large and rather expensive airplane for a corporation, and it was by no means selling like hotcakes. There were three completed airplanes on the line unsold, running up inventory and storage charges.

Also in the mix after a fashion was another innovative Grumman commercial project, the AgCat and Super AgCat, originally designed as agricultural spray planes. Grumman's board refused to countenance its production at Bethpage so manufacturing was subcontracted to the sailplane manufacturer Schweizer in Elmira, New York, which later bought the rights. Russ Meyer moved to Savannah, and with the AgCat the company had a product mix emerging, or so Carr thought. "I was very impressed with Russ Meyer," Carr said, "and I thought, he could make a go of it. The Gulfstream started to sell, and things were going pretty good." Again, so Carr thought, until the morning Russ Meyer walked in and said he was leaving. He'd been offered a chance of a lifetime to go to Cessna, then one of the big three general aviation companies. "We didn't have contracts with our people," Carr recalled with a rueful laugh. "That was a blow." Personalities played some part, particularly when Clint Towl got irritated because Grumman American didn't turn a profit. The light airplanes were still losers because of the lawsuits, but a projected light twin was a big hope. Cheaper than the Cessnas and the Beeches, though with a little less power, it could be a big seller. Because he thought the Gulfstream was making money and the light planes weren't, Clint Towl got fed up and decided he didn't want to invest in the twin. Carr was dismayed.

The Ohio bunch could be delightful, Carr remembers, funny as a crutch. But Clint didn't get along with any of them very well. Because they were building up quite a bit of cash, mainly from Gulfstream sales at one point, Clint elected to declare a substantial dividend, about $7–8 million. They weren't too happy about that because they were only 20 percent owners and their thinking was to reinvest and get 40 percent. It later became a lawsuit. Besides, there was still the need to invest in the light twin.

Clint as Grumman chairman and Russ Meyer as Grumman American president had tangled at board meetings over such matters. There was more bickering about who would replace Russ Meyer when he left. Carr himself left the board, ticked off at what Clint Towl was doing. "I didn't think he was being fair," Carr said, "particularly over refusing to build the light twin. The whole thing didn't make any sense. So I resigned. And that put me in Siberia for a year or two." Jack Bierwirth liked Towl, but Carr considered him pretty icy. "I lost all respect for him, frankly," Carr said, "because he had a place down at Stuart, Florida. The company Gulfstream would make trips ostensibly to visit the Grumman Stuart plant, but really to take Clint to his retreat there. That was at a time when Lew Evans had had a heart attack, and Bill Zarkowsky as president was having health problems. That left Bill Schwendler as the senior person around. And Bill frankly wasn't much help at that point." He was an engineer, not a marketeer or businessman.

"Clint would blithely take off Thursday morning and come back on Tuesday," Carr went on. "Charlie Bluhdorn of Gulf & Western was making a run at us. Critical things were going on, and Clint would be gone. Frankly, I did a lot of things that I shouldn't have, that I had no authority to do. I bought some of Charlie Bluhdorn's stock for the company. Not with my money, but with Grumman's money."

And there was the Russ Meyer succession question. Joe Gavin, who was then president of Grumman Aerospace, favored Corky Meyer, a veteran test pilot who had moved into management. "Corky Meyer could be a difficult guy," Carr recalled. "At any rate, I was hoping that Al Lemlien, who was down there already as essentially

Meyer's number two man, would succeed Russ. But Clint and Jack took Joe Gavin's recommendation to make Corky president."

For a while, the Ohio triumvirate seemed to get along very well with Corky at the Savannah operation. They had built a plant next door to the Gulfstream factory for the light airplanes. Towl had relented and they did go ahead and develop the twin, and a plush version called the Cougar was built. Of course it cost a little bit more than everybody expected and was a little underpowered. Nonetheless it went into production. But they weren't very far along when the board began to lose confidence in the job Corky was doing. A search for a replacement had begun, a search in which Carr participated along with the minority directors and that had generated a couple of pretty good candidates. By then the two fuel price shocks from OPEC in the 1970s had shocked America. And Jack Bierwirth had become chairman of the corporation, and he was emphasizing things that were environmentally correct—such as windmills and solar hot water heaters.

In one of the great cases of the opaque crystal ball, Bierwirth decided that the future of executive aircraft was limited because no company, once fuel became scarce and expensive, would be willing to pay that kind of money. That was common wisdom at the time because corporate profits were under pressure; the banks looked at executive aircraft as perks, not business tools, and stockholders raised Cain at annual meetings. Big corporations that did have corporate aircraft, especially those as large as the Gulfstream, refused to put their company markings on them for fear of hostile reaction from stockholders and a spendthrift image with the public. "Plus," Carr said, "it was becoming apparent that the Gulfstream 2 had just about run through its life." It had old, noisy, and less fuel-efficient turbojet engines, and Carr said it was obvious that Grumman was going to have to modify it. That is, put better engines in it, make it quieter and more modern. Grumman, still digging out from the F-14 financial crisis, didn't have the money. Savannah saw it differently: development could be financed with an initial down payment of several million dollars from potential buyers.

Bethpage was skeptical, and for what turned out to be practical reasons—developing a new engine would cost more than $50 million, not to mention the need for a wing redesign to accommodate the winglets. So Jack Bierwirth, by that time chairman, decided to sell the company. Finally he brought around a very reluctant Joe Gavin, who was by then president of Grumman Corporation. Lew Evans had made, at some point, a semicommitment to Jim Wilmot, who operated an aviation service company at National Airport in Washington, among other enterprises. "Wilmot was politically very well connected," Carr recalled. He was also a Gulfstream distributor, and Lew had promised that if Grumman ever sold Gulfstream American we would give him a chance to buy. Wilmot was connected with Allyn and Company in New York City, then a well-known investment house, and Grumman actually had offered the company to the Wall Street house that was to finance the deal.

"Then we got their proposal," Carr told me, "and to my horror I discovered they were going to buy it with our money, a typical Wall Street deal." (That is, use Grumman's credit to finance the deal.) Grumman turned down the proposal but had no particular target in mind otherwise. "Then," Carr said, "I happened to read that Allen Paulson, who ran a California company that remanufactured airplanes, was going to buy the North American Sabreliner business jet. Why would he buy the Sabreliner, which was an even older aircraft developed originally as an air force utility airplane, if he had a chance to buy the Gulfstream?" Paulson and Grumman shared the same accountant, who agreed to approach Paulson. Paulson recognized the potential that Grumman's top leadership did not.

Paulson's warm interest was enough to start negotiations, not only with him but also with the minority shareholders who had to be part of any deal. "Probably Grumman didn't get enough money," Carr said, "for we sold our interest for something like $40 million, plus the fact that Grumman Aerospace was to be given the contract to develop the Gulfstream 3 for around $50 million." Some Grumman preferred stock retirement was involved, too. Paulson took the whole thing and eventually bought out the minority holders for a proportional amount to what Grumman received. At a time when Grumman was not financially very well off, the fact that it was going to get paid for developing the Gulfstream 3, and get some cash out of the deal to boot, didn't sound that bad to Carr.

Paulson abandoned the light aircraft and just wrote off the investment, but not the AgCat that was sold. Not only was the Gulfstream 3, and later the G-4, a great technical and financial success, but Paulson then sold the company for about $700 million to Lee Iacocca at Chrysler, who may have seen business aircraft as a counterpart to private cars. Learning soon that business aircraft were in fact a much different business from automobiles, Iacocca sold the company back to Paulson, who then sold it to Forstman Little for another $700 million. Eventually General Dynamics bought it and developed the Gulfstream 5. Paulson began to swan around the National Business Aircraft Association annual gathering, the Paris Air Show of business flying, with a second trophy wife, bought a race horse stud farm in Kentucky, acquired a steel company, and in the process bought out his backer. The latter meant a loan that Grumman had to consent to, which is how Carr knew about it. Paulson took the company public at some point, then went private, then public again.

Despite John Carr's explanation of the rationale, many Grummanites think the sale of Grumman American, the Gulfstream, was one of the worst things Jack Bierwirth did. "He did so many bad things," former Grumman attorney Raphael Mur argues. "The Gulfstream, what a gem. But I admit Paulson would do a better job concentrating on it than Grumman ever would." Mur once went to a Harvard Law School reunion in Cleveland. At a Sunday morning cafeteria-style breakfast he sat down with a stranger. The two started talking. It turned out he was a lawyer in Cleveland who had been counsel to American Aviation. As he said, to Mur, "In came the big wheels from the East." And it took a lot to say that about his client, that Grumman bought distressed merchandise at a premium price then sold the whole thing. Mur still fulminates about the decision.

After both Jack Bierwirth and I went separate ways into retirement and hadn't seen each other for years, we sat down together, appropriately, at the Grumman museum at the Bethpage plant. Although we had had our differences, it was a cordial reunion, for I liked Jack as a person. And it gave us a chance to hash over the Gulfstream and the whole diversification saga. As I've said, Jack Bierwirth had started as financial vice president at Grumman in July of 1972 but became president in the fall of 1972, after the unexpected death of Lew Evans. What he didn't know, and it wasn't really understood elsewhere, was that Clint Towl's wife had terminal cancer. So Towl had to find somebody to appoint as both a president and a potential successor. When Towl subsequently stepped down, the board picked Bierwirth to succeed him as chairman and chief executive officer. "I was an outsider," Bierwirth recalled for me. "But I felt there were two things I could do for Grumman. Because I knew people all over the world, I could handle the development of Grumman's international business if we were permitted to sell overseas. The other thing I could do was to take the other parts of Grumman and see what we could build. As it turned out the international sales of Grumman products was much easier than the diversification of the company. When I was hired, Clint Towl charged me with diversifying the company. He didn't know he was also hiring me to get it financially straightened out."

Grumman had no commercial sales side, Bierwirth decided. To sell to the Defense Department is one thing, for it is a very specialized business. Almost nobody was a regular commercial salesman. Technically, Grumman was perfectly capable of inventing an ultrasonic piece of equipment to monitor a person's heartbeat. At that time it would have been a wonderful addition to the medical equipment field. But there wasn't anybody at Grumman who knew how to sell it. To go after that kind of business, Grumman would have to hire somebody that was selling for Johnson & Johnson and wanted the chance to have his own shot. One area, though, that Grumman built up very successfully was the computer world, the software world. If Grumman had seen that as the future, and it should have, that might have been an out instead of the merger that took place.

"Pick up an electronics company?" Bierwirth asked rhetorically. "All those opportunities were there. But the problem was always the same. Grumman was a whole company of aircraft engineers who thought their business was to make airplanes. Everything else was an adjunct. To turn it around and say that the airplane business is going to evaporate and that we are going to be an electronics and software company would have meant convincing everybody else to leave and keeping about 5 percent of the people there to grow. That wasn't acceptable. George, you remember we created an electronics division. From then on the main business for the aircraft engineers was to make sure they weren't forced to buy anything from it. They didn't want the electronics division. It was almost impossible to get them to the point of saying, 'Yeah, this is good. I'd love to have that in an E-2C.' So the electronics folks ended up selling to all of our competitors."

I had another view. "In all fairness," I said to Jack, "we had the same problem with the data people. Aerospace wanted bids for this stuff, open competition because we were being driven by the Navy to get the price down. So if we had an electronics division just as a sole source, that's not real competition on price. That was the thing that was always sticking in the craws of a lot of us in aerospace. But there are pros and cons."

"No question about it," Bierwirth agreed. "The data people said, and it was true, that the negotiations with the aerospace division were the toughest they had all year. It sometimes took six months. If Grumman Data Systems wanted to sell to us, it had to be at a competitive price. Yet there was a dilemma, because we didn't want to have that impact on our total corporate bottom line and profitability."

Diversification for Clint Towl was, in Bierwirth's understanding, a way for Grumman to be independent from the Defense Department. The pullout from Vietnam was knocking a hole in the defense budget. Apollo 17, the last trip to the moon, had flown and the rest of the Apollo landings were canceled. There were possibilities with the shuttle coming along: Grumman did have a lot of company. In the meantime, TRW flirted with modular housing and Vertol, now Boeing Helicopter, built streetcars. But to paraphrase Norm Augustine, the former chairman of Lockheed Martin, aerospace in its attempts at commercial diversification had a record unblemished by success.

Bierwirth contends that was not entirely true for Grumman. He is referring to a business I was involved with early in my career. Grumman had gotten into the aluminum truck body business and done well with the postal trucks. For years Grumman had been in the canoe business,. where it could adapt its aluminum manufacturing expertise. Yet Clint Towl had a jaundiced take on it: "Those businesses were successful as long as you kept the rest of Grumman out of them." When Grumman first made canoes, it couldn't make one that would pass internal inspection. One rivet was always off by a centimeter and had to be fixed. By shipping out of Long Island to Marathon, New York, and employing apple pickers to make canoes in their spare time without so much fussiness, the business turned profitable.

Bierwirth remembers that the truck business was created by a fellow who wanted to sell those Grumman made to his specifications.

"By the time I got involved, the truck division was partly owned by Grumman, not wholly owned. I changed that, made it a wholly-owned subsidiary by getting the minority shareholders to sell to us. There were some people in there who had come at some point from Grumman. But basically they were not in their minds part of Grumman. As a matter of fact, when I went over to visit Grumman Allied at its headquarters in Roosevelt Field, I was the first Grumman officer who had ever been over there. Clint Towl never went there. When they had to talk to Grumman officers, they always came to Bethpage. Nobody ever came to see them."

"One question people always ask me, and have asked you, Jack, in front of company meetings: Why did we sell the Gulfstream when we were trying to diversify in commercial business? The Gulfstream 5 has a $2 billion backlog today. Do you ever have any regrets? Was there a financial reason for doing it, too?"

"No, no," Bierwirth insisted. "The first part of the problem was that Lew Evans and Clint Towl had had the desire to make the Gulfstream business into a full-line commercial aviation business. And that's where the American Aviation deal came from. Evans had it on his desk when he died. And Clint said to me, 'You might take a look at this. Lew was all ready to go with it when he died.' I did, and asked Towl, 'Do you really want to do this?' He said yes. Russ Meyer came with the package, and Lew Evans had thought that Russ Meyer might be good enough to succeed him as president.

"But we got into a period where we had about three Gulfstream orders on the books. We were way down. Then we got an order from Saudi Arabia, from our overseas dealer, Jim Wilmot. His company operated at National Airport in Washington, Page Airways. Wilmot had been appointed Gulfstream agent for the rest of the world. The commission on the Saudi order was going to be about 15 percent, which was high. Then the Saudis added on all sorts of electronic equipment and the price kept going up. Still they wanted to do it. Then a second airplane came along, again all loaded up."

At that point, the Treasury began to investigate Grumman under the Foreign Corrupt Practices Act, while Wilmot repeatedly insisted that there were no problems. Then the government began to go after anyone who had anything to do with international sales in the Gulfstream business and investigated their bank accounts, their personal transactions, and what they'd done in Panama or Colombia, or what not.

Finally Bierwirth put it to Towl, "I think best thing in the world would be if somebody would buy the Gulfstream business from us." It turned out in the end that the CIA had worked this deal out with Wilmot, and a Swiss company had been created as a front just for this transaction. The CIA eventually called off the dogs.

"Did Wilmot get out clean?" I asked Jack. "Absolutely," he answered. "And Lew Evans knew about it, that is, the arrangement between the CIA and Page and Wilmot. But nobody explained it to me, and Clint Towl didn't know. That brush with an overseas payments scandal precipitated the idea for the sale, although business was not good then. We were being put in the position where we could hardly do any more business outside of the country."

An indication of how some top Grumman officials failed to understand the commercial business is evidenced in early Gulfstream service support. Bob Watkins told me a story from his service department days, for field service was involved in support there, too. Unlike supporting the military, the Gulfstream had individual customers throughout the world. "One of the things that my boss Schoney Schonenberg proposed," he said, "was that we stage parts for the Gulfstream all over the world that our dealers would handle. If anybody's airplane went down—and this was important particularly with the first Gulfstream 1 sales—those customers had to have fast support. Clint Towl turned the idea down. 'Grumman isn't going to stage parts around the world,' he said. 'That's up to the dealers. If dealers want to do it, fine, but we, Grumman, are not going to get involved.' About six months ago I was talking to Goldie Glenn in Savannah. Goldie left Grumman to go with Gulfstream and Al Paulson. One of the successes of the Gulfstream operation now is that Goldie staged parts all over the world. To this day if a Gulfstream goes down, there is a parts depot within some reasonable distance."

Another story Bob Watkins tells about the Gulfstream concerns Jack Bierwirth's dealings with Paulson. In their talks, Paulson had boiled over about what he took as Grumman's patronizing attitude. He perceived that Grumman thought of him as a mere junk dealer, the caretaker for the Gulfstream, and that Grumman ultimately was going to get it back. When he told Jack he was pretty sick of that attitude, Jack did call over a group of senior Grumman people and made an articulate, professional presentation. As before, the substance was that we were selling the Gulfstream operation and that, although Grumman had designed and built a very fine airplane, the company didn't know how to market it.

When Bierwirth finished, Bob Watkins's hand shot up. "Jack," he said, "I guess I have a problem understanding why, in lieu of getting rid of the program, we don't find the people who know how to market it?" Bierwirth just walked off the platform. Later, riding down in the elevator, some of the others were chuckling to Watkins, "That is not the smartest thing you ever did." But Watkins survived, although he, too, had his critics inside the Grumman veterans club. Why did Bierwirth think Grumman couldn't market a Gulfstream when it could market a more expensive and complex airplane to the Navy? Most likely, he viewed the Navy as a single, homogenous customer and didn't think we were sophisticated enough to go out and sell airplanes to General Motors and McDonalds or a hundred different other companies. Yet Grumman had the technical people, and, in the final analysis, corporate airplanes are sold through the pilot. If a pilot says this airplane's a dog, it's dead. So those were surface reasons Bierwirth gave us that day.

After Grumman sold all of its shares in Grumman American to Allen Paulson, Bierwirth spent the next six months telling all of Paulson's prospective customers that he was a fine fellow and he would deliver, and that Grumman would make sure he would deliver. Paulson got the Cleveland trio out as fast as he could and ended up owning 100 percent. Paulson then did something that Grumman had never done: he doubled and tripled production. Grumman had limited its sales of the Gulfstream to a certain number per month because Clint Towl's experience had been that whenever Grumman had revved up the manufacturing rate, it exhausted the demand and business slumped. Grumman had always tried, unsuccessfully, to sell Gulfstreams to the military, but, when Paulson got in, the U.S. Air Force bought them for the president's executive fleet and later for utility.

I hadn't been involved much in the Gulfstream early on, but, as I recall, part of deal with Paulson was that Grumman would design, develop, and certify the Gulfstream 3 for about $35 million. Then

Grumman would get a 2 percent commission on two hundred Gulfstreams after that, that is, another $40 million. The Gulfstream sale had its pros and cons, but many of the Grummanites felt that it was a bad mistake. I was part of that group. Not only was it diversification, if that's what Clint Towl wanted, but it also represented the kind of manufacturing Grumman knew. Furthermore, it carried with it opportunities that could have placed us into the regional jet transport business ahead of the crowd. Instead it merely became another stop on the path to an unfulfilled destiny.

10

DIVERSIFICATION ENDS IN FIASCO

GRUMMAN'S MOST AUDACIOUS THRUST AT DIVERSIFICATION, though not the first, came with Jack Bierwirth's accession to the chairmanship of the corporation. Bierwirth, at least in his own mind, considered diversification as his charge from Clint Towl, to expand what was still mostly a navy aircraft builder. This was despite Aerobuilt Bodies (the truck business), forays into space with the Apollo lunar module, air force commissions for the EF-111 electronic version of the TFX, and, of course, the Gulfstream. Diversification was strictly academic, though, until Grumman worked itself out of the F-14 swamp.

One of reasons Bierwirth moved in was because of his Wall Street connections; he was to patch up Grumman's bona fides with banks after the F-14 put the company close to bankruptcy. John Carr passed along a legend as to why Jack Bierwirth was hired. Clint Towl had been looking for a financial vice president for years, and he reasoned that the people who knew all about finance were those who bought Gulfstreams. So Towl would solicit Gulfstream owners for their recommendations. One of the first customers for the Gulfstream 2 was Jack Bierwirth Sr., the chairman of National Distillers, and Towl asked the elder Bierwirth the same question: Do you know somebody with financial smarts? "How about my son, Jack?" came the reply.

146

The son was then with National Distillers and had done extensive international work. His offer may have been Machiavellian because there had been defections at National Distillers, possibly because of the father-son relationship. Many who left National Distillers went mainly because of old Mr. Bierwirth, his son among them. Join a company and one figures that eventually, with promotions, you'll rise to the top. Well old Mr. Bierwirth never retired. At the age of eighty-one he still remained chairman of the board. Young Jack became a Grumman director at first. After Lew had had a series of heart attacks it been settled that Jack Bierwirth, once on Grumman's board, would come in as financial vice president. When Lew had his final heart attack in 1972, the plan accelerated.

Jack Bierwirth agrees with Carr's recollection about Clint Towl combing the list of Gulfstream owners, assuming that these owners would at least know the name Grumman. Roy Grumman's son, David, was on the board then, and the board was looking for someone younger to replace him. Bierwirth was then in his late forties. On top of that, Grumman was seeking somebody with international, financial, and commercial experience, all of which he had. Though he was then with his father's company, Bierwirth had been a commercial banker and a lawyer. In fact, he was the antithesis of the typical Grumman manager, most of whom had come out of engineering or manufacturing. Italian, Irish, or Eastern European names were common, like mine. Typically they were first-generation sons of master craftsmen trained in Europe and whose skill in, say, shaping a cowling to final form, was artistry. Bierwirth was Ivy League, urbane, articulate, socially adept—and inherently suspect to old-time shop-floor Grummanites.

National Distillers bought the first Gulfstream 1 as well as the Gulfstream 2. "In all honesty," Bierwirth told me, "there were about three first Gulfstream 2s." Several customers wanted to be number one, and Grumman managed with sleight of hand to confer that distinction multifariously. When Bierwirth joined the board it used to meet late in the morning, have lunch at one o'clock, and adjourn. "What amazed me once I had been on board for a time," Bierwirth recalled, "is that there were internal boards for the various subsidiaries, but they didn't really discuss the subsidiary's business with the parent board. That's hard to believe now." Bierwirth thinks the original founders sat in on all the subsidiary board meetings and they didn't want to be bothered with the repetition at the corporate board. Besides, Grumman was then a fairly unsophisticated company in the corporate world.

Grumman had only one bank, Bankers Trust, which had since vanished in a merger. When Bankers Trust, after a lifelong relationship, refused to extend any more credit to Grumman in the wake of the F-14 crisis, about the time in 1972 when Grumman was asking Bierwirth to come into the company, the whole credit structure disappeared. All the other banks that did business with Grumman were under a Bankers Trust tent. Lew Evans was on the board of the Travelers Insurance Company, and consequently Grumman did all of its insurance business with Travelers. Clint was on the board of Bankers Trust, and that perforce was Grumman's bank. With small companies in the 1930s that was the way it would be—long relationships and no alternate sources. Besides, until the 1960s, military contractors didn't need or couldn't get much in the way of long-term bank credit. Progress payments from the U.S. government financed much of their inventories and payrolls.

When Clint Towl asked Bierwirth to join Grumman's board, the latter had already decided to leave National Distillers. Then Towl asked Bierwirth if he would consider becoming financial vice president of Grumman. "Clint was a little shy about it," Bierwirth said, "the reason being I was executive vice president of National Distillers, a bigger company than Grumman. So he felt that he was in a way asking me to step down, whereas I was leaving because I wanted something more interesting. I had done everything I wanted to do at National Distillers."

Bierwirth had created the international side at National Distillers. "But I had done as much with the international petrochemical world as I had ambition to do," he related. "Hell, I was only forty-nine, and I figured I had one more good career in me someplace. Anyway, I agreed to come. Lew Evans was out with a heart attack, but I said I'd like to talk with Lew. If Lew Evans didn't agree with the plan, then it wasn't going to work. I had talked with Lew on the phone and he said it's all great, just great." Since Lew was coming back to work about the first of July, Bierwirth suggested dropping in the next day after lunch. Lew begged off because of a heavy schedule, but instead proposed the

Monday after the Fourth of July weekend. He died the day before, so Bierwirth never had the opportunity to discuss the company with him.

Once the F-14 contract and Grumman's credit line was resolved, Bierwirth turned to his charge from Towl: diversification, to make Grumman a fifty-fifty defense-commercial company. Where did Bierwirth's diversification ideas come from? John Carr says that engineers or managers in the company would bring them forward. In several instances, Bierwirth assumed that before these schemes got to him, somebody had screened them, which wasn't always the case. Windmills were one proposal. Joe Gavin was interested in environmental technology, and windmills were a pet project of his. Again, Grumman was not alone, for Boeing got interested, too, and built some for testing as power generators in the West.

Sometimes Jack would try to convince me, "George, aerospace has it easy. Others here are trying to sell solar panels or Dormavac containers or windmills in a commercial market. They really have it tough, and we have to give them good bonuses." My answer was that Grumman prided itself on being an advanced technology company. "Why are we supporting the idea one of your vice presidents sold to you for a coin machine that would dispense French fries in a wax bag. Why is Grumman doing that?" Off he would go: "That's the trouble, all you in aerospace can see is the Navy." He was enamored of a run-flat tire that came out of our space work. Uniroyal was interested, but why was Grumman doing this?

Grumman also branched into modular housing, and later formed what we called Grumman Eco-Systems, which Bill Schwendler's son, William Jr., ran. This led to sewage plant construction, a losing enterprise that we didn't know much about. "One thing we did," John Carr adds, "is that after talking diversification with Dillon Read, we were awed by Ross Perot, who was then getting started in data processing, the kind that made companies hot in the market, selling at fifty times earnings. Grumman was spending millions of dollars developing software programs. Why couldn't we do that? So we formed Grumman Data Systems. I was pretty much the instigator of that. Only the trouble was that what we had developed wasn't really commercial."

At least that was a known technology to build on. In a way, so were windmills, which were rotor aerodynamics, although not something Grumman knew intimately. Dormavacs, cold-storage modules, had a tie in-house as well, but again with large unknowns, through Grumman Allied and truck bodies. "Dormavac didn't look bad on paper," Carr recalled. "The problem was to build the modules right, and if Grumman was going to build it, it was going to build it right."

Auspiciously at first, an order for fifty came in to ship lamb from Australia or New Zealand. A practice run with one Dormavac worked great. Grumman built more Dormavacs, and a whole shipment of them traveled on a freighter coming through the Indian Ocean. "These things were on deck with the sun beating on them," Carr told me. "Even though they were cooled with an internal refrigeration system the meat had all spoiled when it got to the Middle East. We had to give the buyer his money back. They were pretty expensive, too. Furthermore, it was a one-way trip. You'd send beef to some distant destination. But what were they going to take back? Dormavac could do incredible things, keeping flowers fresh for ninety days, things like that. But commercially it wasn't that feasible. Someone else eventually bought the rights."

Raphael Mur, the Grumman lawyer, agreed about what he called the "cryogenic thing"—Dormavac. "Like so many of these things," he said, "the technology was just too expensive. We had the same problem with the hydrofoil boat we built. We had this beautiful Swiss watch that worked fine. When you went to bed, you put the watch on the table. These little elves came in and took your watch off the table and spent all night working on it, returning it just you before get up. Put it back on and it works fine. In other words, a nightmare of maintenance."

Mur had a point, and one day a couple of years ago when I was having coffee with Mike Pelehach at one of the golf clubs on Long Island he echoed such sentiments. Mike had started at Grumman in preliminary design and was the kind of innovator with airplanes for us that Mikoyan was to the Russians or Kelly Johnson was to Lockheed. Later, when he went into international, he got involved with Bierworth's diversification—to his dismay. "But," Mike said, "the biggest culprit in diversification, strangely enough, was Joe Gavin. I say that even though he's a friend and I ski with Joe out in Vail every year." Bierwirth didn't know the airplane business, Mike pointed out. Still, he was looking for help, but he never received the support he should have. "Gavin made all of these decisions to go for the fire hose or for Dormavac, but he was involved in a bunch of other things. We needed somebody to concentrate on the diversification within our capability." To that comment of Mike's, I said, "Amen!" Mike, who experienced the frustration of attempting to sell products like high-tech fire hoses internationally in places like the Philippines, said amen, too.

Aerospace became a big cash cow after Grumman emerged from the F-14 troubles. The money that the aerospace engineers made from their products was skimmed off to the corporation that Joe Gavin and Jack Bierwirth were running. Let's just say it would have been different if somebody else were in there. And Mike added: "I explained to Jack that we are good, but in a certain area. Yet aerospace engineers want to diversify to exercise their technological smarts." So Grumman got involved in buses and windmills, garbage disposal, solar panels, Dormavacs—and then was sued by the town of West Palm Beach because of the waste business.

Then there was the bus, the big loser. That came from an aerospace company, a West Coast subcontractor, Rohr, which built airliner nacelle/engine packages. Rohr owned the bus company, Flxible, which was bringing out a brand-new vehicle to meet Department of Transportation requirements. Flxible received many orders, for it seemed to have the ability to underbid General Motors, the only real competition. Grumman knew General Motors was losing its shirt on the bus program. "Rohr had a clever marketing type who knew what you had to bid to win," said John Carr, who knows the story. "I don't know how he got that information, but they could pretty much get the jobs they wanted. But then a problem with the bus undercarriage reared its head. Testing by driving over two-by-four planks wasn't enough. Allegedly, Flxible had put the bus through complete tests, and allegedly it had passed. Later it turned out that some of the problems in service in New York City did, in fact, show up in testing. Worse, they had not been disclosed before the acquisition. Grumman spent a bundle fixing that bus, tarring its name in its hometown. Mostly, though, the failures were those of New York City maintenance more so than Grumman—particularly after it had made the fixes—because the same buses were driven over the New York City streets by private lines with no problems."

Not the least of the fiascoes was the hydrofoil vessel that Bob Hall, who was chief engineer, a former test pilot, and a sailboat racer, took a shine to. Grumman won a contract to build the Flagstaff, a surface-piercing hydrofoil, for the Navy's Bureau of Ships. I was aerospace president about this time and had begun to worry when Grumman was doing something I didn't think was going anywhere. Boeing was into hydrofoils, too, and both companies bid on a hydrofoil gunboat the Israelis wanted. Although Grumman didn't have a shipyard or naval architects, Bierwirth liked the possibilities. Since I was having a little give and take with him I didn't want to be punching all the time. "Okay boss," I agreed, "we'll do this." So I was suckered into a contract for $33 or $34 million to build two hydrofoil boats for Israel that engineers had told me were just like a Flagstaff, the same size, not new to us.

John O'Brien then ran contracts and administration, and claimed to have all the answers to everything. Jack Bierwirth called, wanting to see the contract royalty terms, fearing the Israelis would re-engineer the boats and sell them to all the littoral countries around the world. "John, go over there and kill this damn thing," I told O'Brien. "Show him it's a fixed-price contract, and I think we are going to lose $10 million." Back he comes about an hour later. "Did you shoot that thing down?" I asked. "Boss," he answered, "I don't think it's that bad. We'll do all right." Did he tell Gavin and Bierwirth I thought we might lose $10 million, although I just pulled a number out of the air? He had, but they thought it would be worth it to get into the business. Out of our own pocket we put in about $65 million, that is, doing a hundred-million-dollar job for thirty-five million bucks. They're in the junkyard now: Grumman delivered them, but we had problems up to our neck. After work started, Larry Mead, who had been A-6 project engineer, came to see me. "Got to tell you something, boss," he said. "The only drawing you can take from the Flagstaff is the flag mast. This boat is not built to commercial specification, but military." Welding alone was a far tougher job than we expected.

At this point costs were running over $40 million or $45 million, and the program was starting to look stinko to me as I went into an aerospace board meeting with Bierwirth, Gavin, and the other directors. After a presentation on where we stood on the hydrofoil, I proclaimed, "I rue the day we got involved with hydrofoils in any way, shape, or form here at Grumman. Especially this boat we're trying to build for the Israelis." Finally, with the meeting over and breaking for lunch, Bierwirth fell in beside me as we walked out the building. "You shouldn't take this too personally, George," he said. "The hydrofoil overrun?" I answered. "Jack, that's happening on my watch. I don't know where this is going to end. Yet I shouldn't take it personally?" He didn't want me to talk that way in front of the board. About a year later, Bierwirth spoke at one of Mike Pelehach's big international love-ins—parties and lunches and dinners and guest speakers for his people. "You wouldn't believe it," exclaimed my staff man, who was there. "Jack Bierwirth told that crowd he believed, notwithstanding what some other people are saying, that the hydrofoil boat program will be the success story of the 1980s." Not to the tune of $65 million it wasn't.

These diversifications weren't research. They weren't strategically integrated with any sensible long-range Grumman growth plan. Somebody would come up with an idea and we'd do it. Tom Jones of Northrop told me at one of the Aerospace Industries Association meetings in Phoenix: "George, don't ever listen to these analysts who will talk you into doing things." Tom went into curtain wall construction, panels for buildings. It was a misfit. Grumman could have saved its money and bought a company, maybe one like E Systems. What were we doing making baseball batting rings? We had engineers who thought they could market anything. But on the other side of the street, why spin off the Gulfstream because we didn't know how to sell it? Why did we think we could sell buses to cities that had multiple requirements, all different? Don't try to make and sell composite shaft golf clubs. Buy a company that makes golf clubs, then invite their designers into the technology arsenal to see what they can find. But let the golf club people run the business. Don't start one inside a company like Grumman. Fundamental! Otherwise it will drive you to drink.

John Carr's lawyerly attitude is, "Let's hear both sides of the diversification story." His remonstrance was a hint at an inside-Grumman paradox: those who grew up in the Grumman family rarely could do wrong in the minds of the veterans; outsiders—as Bierwirth was—rarely could do much right. Still remains the conundrum of trying to diversify an aerospace organization focused on and exquisitely attuned to the government's procurement system. If one tries to adopt aerospace practices, which can run to gold plating a product, the hardware gets pretty expensive. This I discovered with the truck body business. Try to commercialize sophisticated technology and the rubber band won't stretch that far. Hence I still choke on Grumman's frittering away its capital in its later diversification strategy. I wrote a letter to Bob Anderson, who came from Firestone to be the vice president of finance, that stated:

> This will give you an idea of the disastrous nature of the Corporation's hope and pray diversification effort during the period 1971 through 1984. During that time Aerospace was the goose that was laying the golden financial eggs for the company. If we had just socked those eggs away and not gotten into chasing rainbows, I am sure today we would have at least a few billion in the till. The board (and that includes me) really let the shareholders down during those years by allowing the continuation of most of the programs year after year. If Grumman hopes to enter the 21st Century as a solid business company, it has to reinvent itself in the 1990s and cast off the concepts inbred in the corporate culture philosophy of the founding fathers!

A table I put together spelled out the write-offs on eight efforts over ten years that added to $492 million. These included $243.9 million on the buses, $66.3 million on the hydrofoil boats, and $45.1 million on Dormavac. Put it all together and it says Grumman had a lot of nicky-poo hope-and-pray diversification. "That's right," Mike Pelehach agreed, "and it should have been concentrated on aerospace diversification instead, where we had so much capability." If Grumman hadn't sold the Gulfstream he thinks there would have been a Gulfstream 6 or 7. He enthuses about the Pratt & Whitney F119 engine for the Air Force's Lockheed F-22, which, with nozzle changes, could power a supersonic Gulfstream, cruising at Mach 1.6 coast to coast in two hours. A Gulfstream was a couple of million a copy in the beginning. Now, Pelehach said, it's $10 or $20 million. "So when you talk about a $40- or $50-million-dollar Gulfstream Supersonic, it's no big deal."

Bush pilots in Alaska flying corroded survivors of the amphibian family used to ask Grumman when it was going to come out with another Goose, a Super Goose. What they wanted was an inexpensive turboprop they could fit a canoe into. Grumman did that, by building a glass-fiber fuselage mockup in Plant Five, opening up the windshield, and shoving a canoe right down the centerline. "So there were a lot of products that we could have got involved in," Pelehach said, and I had to add: "And more potentially profitable. But, Mike, to make it viable, you'd have to sign up customers for about four hundred airplanes. With the price tag we started to quote, those bush operators weren't quite ready for that." Nevertheless, Pelehach argued: "The point is that there were so many products that we could have got involved in, but we kept screwing around. I love Gavin, he's a brilliant engineer, but you know, we needed somebody who saw the potential. Now, Lew Evans was this kind of guy, but you know, nobody helped him either."

Although Grumman did make connections with NASA, it never really cultivated the other services as McDonnell Douglas or Lockheed Martin did. Roy Grumman was a navy type, who made the military connection to begin with. Grumman was very slow in getting involved with the Air Force. We didn't have any real air force hitters in the company. To my astonishment, Mike Pelehach told me that of the top people, the one who avoided the Air Force the most was Joe Gavin. "Joe was very navy," Mike told me. "He was in the Navy, a navy man who just didn't take to the Air Force. When you sit down and talk to people, you have to leave the impression that you love them." Some of Grumman's top people didn't do that.

Another diversification story Mike told me was one he labeled as very typical. One day he got a call from George Spangenberg, the Navy's Mr. Fighter, whom I've mentioned before. "Mike," he said, "have you been on the army airplane?" "What are you talking about?" Mike asked, and Spangenberg told him: "The Army came to us and they want a new airplane designed from scratch. So, it looks as though the Navy is going to run the competition." The Army wanted something that could take off and land in three hundred feet, have a big bubble canopy so the crew could clearly see the ground, and have Martin Baker ejection seats. The Navy got a bunch of sharp marines to run the program, for affinity with the ground troops. Then Jake Swirbul received a call that mystified him from an admiral offering congratulations. So Swirbul went to Dick Hutton, whom I was working for then, to find out what it was all about. Grumman was one of thirty-five companies that had submitted proposals, and it had won the damn thing! This was the Mohawk, and Grumman built three hundred of them in various versions: the OV-1A photo-reconnaissance aircraft, the OV-1B with a side-looking radar pod, the

OV-1C with two photo- and one infrared-surveillance systems, and
the OV-1D with improved infrared and radar. "We'd go to a design
meeting where there would be about a hundred guys from the Army,
Air Force, the Navy, and the Marines, and there would be three of
us," Pelehach said. "But we managed to get the job, and it turned out
to be a good airplane. The point here is that we had so many things
that we could have done, that had nothing to do with fire hoses or
waste disposal. I would brainwash my people who went to these
meetings where there would be Air Force and Army: 'They are the
top mangers, the top engineers; they know what they want. So don't
get smart and say here's the Navy, and we'll do it the navy way. You
listen to them because they're usually giving you a message.' Never
listen to someone in terms of what he's saying. Ask, 'Why is he saying this? Why is he telling me that?' You'll find out that he was trying
to tell you something. But Joe Gavin was navy all the way."

Much as I disliked diversification into areas Grumman knew
nothing about, Grumman had had fair-to-middling success in some
nonaerospace diversification. I ran one of these programs, and I bring
this up to make it clear I was not antidiversification. This happened in
the 1950s, when I was getting restless about my future and had
dropped the word around about a change. The upshot was that Clint
Towl offered me the job of running Grumman's aluminum truck
business, Aerobuilt Bodies. Towl, the archetypal dry accountant, Old
Frosty himself, used to take notes in pencil at board meetings.
(Interestingly, I found out later that he knew his way well around the
speakeasies of New York during prohibition.)

Towl sat back in his chair that day and announced, "I have a
dream." We were doing about $3 million a year in the truck body
business. This, in the 1950s, was decent. "Let's see if we can't make
this a one-hundred-million-dollar business." Through my head went
the thought, He doesn't know what the hell he's talking about, but
even if he's only half right, that's a challenge. Even to go to $30 mil-
lion, ten times over ten years, would be something. Hell, I'll take this
job. This sounds better than sitting out on the engineering floor.

Grumman had found an old whaleboat factory in Athens, and the
company started to build truck bodies there, in what I called Sleepy
Town, a Rip Van Winkle sort of place near Washington Irving's setting
for the story. Did truck bodies have much in common with aircraft

construction other than just being aluminum? Not much. That, in fact, was one of the things I learned in a hurry and why Grumman moved the factory out of the aerospace environment. More or less on top of stress analysis for the truck bodies was a sharp, old-time stress man, Peter Aranson, who, as a matter of fact, ran the stress department for a long time. Unfortunately, he and his people thought that over-the-road equipment makers should do things the way we did in the aviation business. Aluminum was the core, and we knew about working aluminum, how to make extrusions and such. And we knew about dynamics from airplanes. What we didn't know was how to design our over-the-road equipment for abuse rather than use. When something broke we said, "Well you can't use it that way. That isn't what we designed it for. You can't take that fork lift and have it drop off a lip of a warehouse dock four inches onto the back of a trailer floor! No, you have to put a ramp there." The guys down at the warehouses had a succinct response: "Ah, get the hell outta here!" So, we had to go from an aluminum extruded floor to a wood floor. There was no common philosophy as to how to deal with these commercial people.

Sure, there was lots of talk then and later, especially after Vietnam, about how to take wonderful aerospace structural technology and make lighter truck bodies and lighter cars. It never happened. To design something like a commercial truck body you have to know what the abuse parameters are. Business picked up for the truck business after we learned the language of the truck operators. We used a sledge to demonstrate that aluminum bodies wouldn't dent. They wouldn't rust; they were lighter; and one body could outlast several chassis, so we had an economic story to sell. By the early 1960s, Grumman had become the biggest over-the-road aluminum truck body builder.

If I seem to imply that Grumman should have diversified only in aerospace, I have another admission. Even aerospace diversification had its own pitfalls. Specifically I mean the X-29, the forward-swept-wing experimental airplane that came out of the Defense Advanced Research Projects Agency but was managed by the Air Force. Forward-swept wings had been conceived by the Germans during World War Two, and one German company had actually built a business jet—the Hansa HFB-320—using the concept, which did not ignite the corporate world. Our X-29 was an amalgamation: an F-5 nose, F-16 landing gear, and a General Electric 404 engine. Only the graphite epoxy wings were new. Grumman learned a great deal, I admit, about how to build a composite wing and design it with the unconventional twist it needed, a trick in itself. Subsequently Grumman got a subcontract job on the Israeli Lavi fighter to build a handful of wing sets, based on our X-29 experience.

When the X-29 study work started, I had been president of Grumman Aerospace for a couple of years. Not only was Grumman polishing the rail with four major production lines, but it was also driving to achieve production line efficiency, satisfy the customer, and, not the least, land ground support equipment contracts for these programs, a nice piece of business for us. By the time I finished the golden decade in 1984 and moved over to corporate as president, aerospace had made more damn money for the corporation than it had ever made or would subsequently. My point is that profit came after socking $28 million of our own budget into the X-29 in just one year. Eventually that grew into a $58 million overrun of Grumman's $75 million fixed-price contract. In the end Grumman wrote off its investment. I doubt whether Rockwell or General Dynamics, who also did studies, would have taken a fixed-price contract for this job. Although I had great reservations, I was willing to throw money around on the X-29, which Bierwirth and a few other zealots thought was wonderful. As long as aerospace was making profits like that, I chose not to stand in the way of the flood of enthusiasm in Grumman for the X-29's dramatic configuration, never thinking it would ever run up the kind of excess costs it did. At the beginning, it kept engineers busy, and we proved to ourselves we could predict performance from paper. Two X-29s in two hundred flights at Edwards Air Force Base, California, met or exceeded those estimates.

Why did it cost so much money? Many software difficulties arose from its fly by wire and computer stabilization. Inherently unstable high-performance aircraft were coming into fashion then as a way to reduce drag. Besides, the X-29 had a set of canard surfaces in the nose, which also were sprouting on a lot of airplanes at the time for sensitive control, and they oscillated at about forty cycles a second to keep the airplane in balance. Indeed, I concede it was a great technology demonstrator, but no business came out of it. Bierwirth was enamored because he saw the X-29 as an opening to work more closely with the Air Force, and this was an air force program at DARPA. Furthermore, Bierwirth thought he could identify with X-29 more than with historic Grumman navy relationships or the lunar module, neither of which he had a part in.

Grumman wooed Gen. Larry Skantze, commander of the Air Force Systems Command. I called on Tom Stafford, whom I knew as leader of the Apollo 10 mission and who returned to the Air Force with flag rank as head of air force research and development in the Pentagon. Right off the bat he gave me the bad news: "George that airplane will never get into the air force inventory. We're going to stealth, and the X-29 is the worst stealth configuration anyone could dream up." Despite its maneuverability and successful flight test program, the X-29 was a complete zero as far as any business for us.

Sure, we could have spent our money in wiser ways. Just putting the money into Treasury bonds would at least have provided a return. But Bierwirth and Joe Gavin at headquarters were smitten, and the whole world knew so because the public relations drumbeaters were bringing in writers to talk to our people working on these diversification programs. Not wanting to be viewed as a negative person in this situation, I supported the X-29, but with the feeling it was never going anywhere. Had I suspected what it would cost, the initial justification that we could write off $10 million against independent research wouldn't have helped. Costs grew exorbitantly. Tom Jones at Northrop parlayed DARPA programs for an inside track into stealth, and the B-2 came out of it. All of our test data became public. We had no proprietary advantage over Rockwell or McDonnell Douglas, but no one ever produced a forward-swept-wing airplane anyway.

Concentric diversification was my goal, not disjointed hedge-hopping all over the place. Dormavacs or windmills were not the only problems. Bierwirth got Grumman into gallium arsenide rather than silicon-based chips, an area in which there were a lot of companies more expert than us. We lost about $40 million. Gallium arsenide was touted then as the wave of the future, less heat and more reliability than silicon, and a means toward self-sufficiency in electronics. So, too, was manufacturing in space, which became a hot button in the 1980s, something Bud Evans, Lew's son, was promoting from his headquarters post in NASA. I confess I put $2 million into growing

159

gallium arsenide high-purity crystals in space, for no return. McDonnell Douglas went into GaA development. Where is it today?

Grumman did make progress in ground support equipment cables, and we had the Great River Electronics Test Center make GSE black boxes. This started without any real initiative from Jack—he just appropriated that. Jack did get interested in the John Fluke company, a good aerospace supplier, and tried to buy a position or take Fluke over. But nothing ever materialized. Grumman built aluminum deck chairs for the Grace lines and bought Pearson Yacht in an effort to break into the glass fiber boat business. Selling the Gulfstream on top of that! Awful! Look at Gulfstream or the Canadian Bombardier Challenger or Brazil's Embraer today. Expand and extend the business we knew was my proclaimed goal. I wanted a piece of every major subcontract opportunity in the aerospace industry we could get, which is what I meant by concentric diversification. Although we did go after anything that came up from DoD, NASA, or the commercial sector, and often won, Grumman had one serious shortcoming: the company lacked a long-range, formalized, strategic planning organization.

Great River is a story in itself, for it was one of Grumman's successful commercial diversification efforts. When Renso Caporali shut down the commercial side in 1990 after he became head of the corporation, Great River's business with IBM and other companies was $75 million a year. With its in-house business of $175 million, Great River had grown from $70 million annually in 1976, when Bruno Caputo took it over, to $250 million. "This is nothing more than a feeder plant," Caputo told me when he'd been there about six months. "Electronics is the future and I'd like to move out of the company to independent programs." Go ahead, I told him, "but I ain't giving you a dime." Great River soon landed a $2–3 million contract from IBM, shocking the rest of Grumman. IBM remained a consistent customer, and the biggest coup for Great River was developing an electron beam lithography tool. IBM sold its own lithography equipment, and with four other companies, including Grumman, formed a joint venture for this work with an investment of $10 million each. When Grumman sold its interest, it went for $150 million. Great River went downhill when the commercial business stopped, Caputo said, and Northrop shut it down after the acquisition.

Grumman did have aerospace technology diversification assets, first of all a cadre of bloodied managers who had agonized in pulling the F-14 and the A-6E out of the ditch. Then we had the automatic riveting machines to build F-14 wings that could work just as well for a jet transport. When we did win a contract from Boeing, we took those machines out of Plant Three and put them down in Stuart, where we built a three-million-dollar factory to manufacture 767 wing center sections. Bierwirth thought that was courting disaster, based on his talks with Menasco. A landing gear supplier, Menasco had run into grief with commercial airliner subcontracting share-the-wealth policy. Boeing and McDonnell Douglas wanted participating equity from the supplier—and I don't blame them, and I demanded the same myself later. Initially Bierwirth was right, though. Neither Jack nor I realized that Boeing wrote the contract so that Grumman would absorb a certain number of changes. Here's Boeing, I thought, a high-class outfit, and building a commercial airliner isn't that complicated structurally. Instead Boeing surprised the hell out of all of us, changing stuff left and right while Grumman was stuck with the expense. Soon enough we had another whack at the contract and we squared that away. I wanted to beat LTV's Vought, which Boeing considered its best supplier, on delivery and price and climb out of the subcontractor class to associate contractor. Stuart did fare well with Boeing, judging by the awards we received. Grumman also made a dent in the commercial transport nacelle business. Along with the F-14s going down the line at Calverton, we had CFM-56 nacelles for re-engined DC-8s that the one-time Douglas heavy hitter Jack McGowan's Cammacorp was building. Big business.

Then there were Mike Pelehach's V/STOL A and B concepts that became the frequent subject of presentations to the Navy. But when British Aerospace approached Grumman about teaming on its V/STOL Harrier that the Royal Air Force operated, Grumman passed. Then in the early 1980s, the U.S. Marine Corps bought the Harrier, and McDonnell Douglas secured the long-term production of the modified version, the AV-8B. Again, more of Grumman's unfulfilled destiny. Way back when I was in structural flight test, my boss Walter Scott was pulled off to write a proposal for a missile with the Marquardt ramjet engine, what I think became the Navy's Talos ship defense weapon. With the talent we had, Grumman could have designed a Sidewinder or a Harpoon. Thousands of missiles were built, but Grumman just let the opportunity pass by.

Danny Knowles, who ran personnel for years, had some insights into Jack Bierwirth's uphill slogging to change Grumman. Bierwirth came into a company where he wasn't born, unlike so many Grummanites. He tried to change the culture of the company, but he didn't know how to do it.

Swoose Snead later gave me an insider-outsider, plus-and-minus insight when we had lunch together a couple of years ago. "George," he told me, "you lost communication with Jack Bierwirth, for good and valid reasons I'm sure. But your inability to communicate caused you to fail to convince him or work effectively with him." That was not totally true, but mostly true because Gavin stood in between as president of the corporation. Gavin and I could communicate pretty well. My impression of Jack was of a socialite industrialist who didn't fit in Grumman's nuts-and-bolts culture. "And he knew you thought that," Swoose said. "Bierwirth didn't know anything about building an airplane and resented such a strong team in aerospace making money. Why wasn't he smart enough to accept that, sit back, pull you people in, and ask where you thought the company should go? Of course he didn't have to take your advice, but at least he could have listened to it. George, you were the heart and soul of Grumman, not him, and he knew that, and he resented that." Fair enough, but here was Bierwirth taking all of Grumman Aerospace's hard-earned money and sluicing it away on hope-and-pray diversification. He wasn't listening to me. He resented me. If Jack Bierwirth was chairman and I was president for ten years like Gavin was, we would have had a showdown. But Gavin, the quintessential engineer, was fascinated with expanding technology's horizons.

In fact, Jack and I did have a showdown. One day, four or five years before I retired in 1986, Jack called me up late on a Friday afternoon, about the time he usually went home. "I'm coming over to see you," he said abruptly, and left me wondering what the hell he was stopping over here for and why. There I am, smoking a big cigar, sitting in Lew's old office that we had turned into a conference room. In marches Jack and slams the damn door so hard the walls rattled. All six feet plus of him glared down at me and he said: "I understand you don't like the way I'm running this company." I put my foot up on the

pedestal, nonchalantly, puffed the cigar, and said, "Jack, that's right."
I think he was flabbergasted. Probably he thought I was going to dis-
semble and bluster, "Who said that?" But we began to talk, and we
had at least a half an hour of soul-baring conversation. I finally said,
"Jack, you know, you ought to get out in front of the world and put
your arm around me and say, 'This is my boy,' instead of listening to
all those leading you down the path of jelly beans mixed with
diamonds and solar panels and windmills and garbage and buses.
We're pissing away our future." "George," he answered, "there are all
kinds of things we have to do." When we got through with the conversation, we had buried something. We had what's called a defining
moment. To myself I thought, "I'll never change him. I'll never convince him of my philosophy of what this company ought to be and
become. It's near the tail end of my career. I better not be so damn
dumb as to just go in there and throw bombs at him or pull hand
grenades and roll them down the hall." So I began to work with him
and demonstrate, I would say, extraordinary deference to his position.
If he's the boss, I better salute him. We got very close after a time, and
he was very good to me in my consulting contract, almost unbeliev-
able. But the old Grummanites felt he didn't fit, and the feeling was
showing. Gavin had already warned me, "George, you better take it
easy with Jack." He could have gone to the board with all the outside
directors he picked, pointed out rightly that the clash of personalities
and philosophies was beginning to show among the troops, that it was
not good for the company. Then he would have eased me off to some
nothing job in a little division somewhere.

Okay, I got the message, or more precisely a lot of messages after
I became president of Grumman Aerospace in 1974. That year
Grumman Corporation netted after taxes only about $20 million.
When I moved over to headquarters ten years later, aerospace had a
net of $115 million, or $4.50 a share. Even though I wasn't a financial
type, I used to sit down once or twice a week with Carl Palladino to
keep an eye on the books. If the numbers looked good, I knew, I
looked good, and I was out to win. Aerospace profit margins were
zipping along at 10 percent or 11 percent or more, so over my ten
years in the front office net had grown by almost a factor of six. While
it sounds like I keep beating the same drum, understand how I fumed
when I saw the money come out of aerospace and go over to

headquarters. There it was frittered away on fruitless diversification schemes, such as windmills and solar panels and the other baloney that Gavin and Bierwirth cooked up, trying to build a new nondependent-on-defense Grumman of the future. All just mixing jellybeans with diamonds.

11

COPING WITH CONGRESS AND THE CUSTOMER

GRUMMAN'S LONG RELATIONSHIP OF MUTUAL ADMIRATION WITH the Navy was never really shattered, but it did fade. Despite the recovery of our manufacturing touch with the F-14, the strains of that program knocked the halo askew. I've pounded on the four aces, the F-14, A-6, EA-6B, and E-2C, that kept Grumman busy and profitable through the 1980s, until after I retired. Obviously something had to replace those winners as Ronald Reagan's openhanded defense budgets peaked in 1986.

John Lehman had become Ronald Reagan's secretary of the navy, and in some ways that was a blessing for Grumman. His experience as a naval flight officer in the A-6 made Lehman a protagonist for that family—but only up to a point. Ralph Clark, a Grumman technical rep with the fleet starting in World War Two, had become a pillar of the Washington office in terms of access to his decades-old friends in naval aviation. To John Lehman, he was always welcome. Through Ralph, I got to know John pretty damn well. I had him come into Calverton and collected two thousand people in a hangar just before quitting time and introduced him up on the stage. Stroking him, that is. When I wanted to fly the F-14 off a carrier, he made all of that happen. Friendly, true, but that didn't stop him at one point from telling me, "Grumman is turning into a monopoly around here." Not only did that reflect our four aces programs but also John's obsession with competition.

He was not a ceremonial secretary of the navy. He was a hands-on, fly 'em, spunky little guy. He liked to hand out the awards to aviators at the Tailhook Association meetings until the uproar over the harassment of a woman pilot deep-sixed navy participation for a while. He came around to Grumman looking for a job at Ralph Clark's suggestion after Bush, whom he supported, lost out to Reagan for the 1980 nomination. At that time, when I talked with him, he wanted to be a consultant, which I think he was already with Northrop. Before we could make a decision on him, Ralph tipped me off that Lehman might well be the next secretary of the navy, notwithstanding his brashness, which put off some of the Reagan staff. What surprised me was that John could associate himself so closely and for such a long time with Mel Paisley, his undersecretary, who went to jail because of the Ill Wind investigation into contractor abuses and payoffs to Pentagon officials. Lehman and Paisley were sticky, not just one working for another but maintaining a close social relationship as well.

He had no qualms about personally pushing a contractor. I experienced this on the F-14D/A-6F combined package idea I'll get into later. Then there was a head-knocking incident over the rewinging program the Navy started for the A-6 in the mid-1980s because of structural problems. My letter to Vice Adm. J. B. Busey, commander of the Naval Air Systems Command, in April 1985, lit a fuse:

> Please be advised that as a result of a comprehensive analysis of the Naval Air Systems Command's Invitation for Bid (IFB) dated 29 March, 1985, for A-6 aircraft wings, and careful consideration of the economics involved, the Grumman Aerospace Corp. will not submit a bid. The basis for this decision is primarily those concerns outlined in the corporation's letter of 14 March to the contracting officer and my belief that a lower risk, lower cost approach is more appropriate at this time. In addition, we respectfully advise that the information available to the prospective bidders in the IFB does not completely describe the contemplated task and may lead to substantial contract modification as the full-scale development of the wing progresses.
>
> I am pleased to advise you that Grumman is preparing an unsolicited proposal for retrofitting A-6E wings that will incorporate load alleviation and other fatigue enhancements. It is anticipated that this proposal, when coupled with Grumman's prior offer on the A-6F enhanced wing contained in my 21 December 1984 letter, will

provide an attractive viable alternative for NAVAIR. I anticipate sub-mittal of this proposal to your office on 29 April 1985.

Additionally, an agreement in principle has been reached on a 4,000-hour warranty for the fiscal year 1986 production aircraft wings and we will offer a more extensive warranty with increased hours through use of load alleviation in our proposal of 29 April 1985.

Boeing was awarded the rewinging job, opened a facility in Mississippi to do the work that was to include the A-6F, too, and eventually gave it back to us to redo. I had a fight with NavAir, which pushed us to agree to an unrealistic number. We never did bid it, as the letter says, and Boeing lost about the number we thought it would. No doubt the Navy was sore about our no-bid. In good con-science, though, I couldn't accept a sure loss.

While all this was going on, Jack Bierwirth was basking in the attention from the media, as an article in *Forbes* magazine in April 1986 with the headline "The Resurrection of Grumman" demon-strated. He got the credit for renegotiating the F-14 contract, to the consternation of some old-line Grummanites, but the failures of the company's diversification efforts were no longer a secret. While the diversification versus four aces issue wore on, Bierwirth had made another move that was to have repercussions later on in the endgame for the F/A-18 decision and Grumman's missteps in Congress.

Corporately unsophisticated, one of Jack Bierwirth's labels for Grumman, soon fell particularly on Grumman's public relations department. Jack Rettaliata, a Grumman old-timer who ran those affairs, wanted to or was told to stick with community relations, i.e., the local politicians. Bierwirth brought in Sandy Jones from Xerox. As an outsider, Jones had his teething troubles, especially when he brought in McKinsey, the management consultants who gave Sandy the idea that we had a problem with the Navy. To me it was a lot of nonsense, and consultants conducting interviews around the com-pany were going to make people wonder what the hell was going on. Out came a summary stating that Grumman's reputation with the Navy was bad. I called up Adm. Forrest F. Peterson, who had retired from NavAir, and asked him for his assessment. We weren't 100 per-cent clean, but far from what the consultants made it to be. His letter went over to Jack Bierwirth and Joe Gavin, but I never heard anything back from them.

In particular, Jones tangled with Gordon Ochenrider, who ran Grumman's Washington office. Gordon's was a most sensitive job, for it entailed both cultivating the military customer and lobbying in Congress without irritating one or the other in the process. "I had a very difficult relationship with Gordon Ochenrider," Sandy recalled over coffee one morning on Long Island. "Gordon had a legitimate point of view. Grumman had sent him down there to be—and I take him at his word—a kind of czar of Washington, responsible for all of the company's operations there. I showed up on the scene and said, 'No, wait a minute, press relations is mine.' So we had a territorial dispute. Each of us was right from his point of view. Each of us was sufficiently bullheaded that we were not going to compromise, and we wound up in big arguments. I became convinced that the press relations in Washington were undisciplined and were doing us a disservice. It was hard for me, I felt, to do my job when we had, in my eyes, amateurs doing their own little things with the press down there. I couldn't get Gordon to tie that off. So I developed a kind of device. I persuaded Gavin and Bierwirth that it was time to take a look at us through outside eyes to see how Grumman was perceived on Wall Street or in the New York and Washington press."

Ultimately Grumman hired a big name public relations consulting firm, Earle Newsome, then headed by Craig Lewis, a former editor at *Aviation Week & Space Technology* who knew the industry well. Jones thought he did an excellent job, and, not surprisingly, produced a report that said there was trouble in River City. It was a way for Sandy Jones to escalate his own problems, a device and recognized as such.

Ultimately this brought Grumman general counsel John Carr, who arrived with Ronald Reagan in 1981, down to Washington to take command. Grumman actually had three Washington offices then. One, Grumman Aerospace, was run by Gordon Ochenrider. Flxible and Grumman Data Systems had separate offices, too. Newsome's study indicated that Grumman was not terribly well known outside of naval aviation. Generally speaking, the study found, the press and television didn't know exactly what Grumman was or what it did. Carr recalls that the board was concerned and thought Grumman ought to do something about that.

Vice chairman by this time, Carr was told that it might be a good idea if he went to Washington. He had worked in Washington before, in the Navy Department, liked it, and the company made it worthwhile. "But the big fly in the ointment was Gordon," Carr said. "He was not happy at all about it, and it never really met with his approval. We worked together fairly well through the years, nevertheless."

At that time the lightweight fighter lobbying joust was still going on, even though the issue had been essentially decided. Not only were the contractors involved, but the Navy itself had an F-14 mafia and an F-18 mafia. When the F-18 was going through its navy testing at Patuxent River, it could blow a tire on landing in the morning and the word would be all over Washington before nightfall. Then General Electric, which was building the F/A-18 power plants, got in the act in Massachusetts and went to Rep. Tip O'Neill and Sen. Edward Brooke, who later became a Grumman director, and convinced them that the plane was going to be built in their district, and that, of course, turned the tide.

Despite the F-18 situation, with Reagan coming in, military hardware of all kinds was ordered in great quantities. Shortly after Reagan took over, one of our people ran into Caspar Weinberger, his secretary of defense. "Oh, we're going to be buying lots of your airplanes," Weinberger said. And they did. Such was true, even though some models were supposed to go out of production. Relations were pretty good with the Navy in the early years of the Reagan administration right up to the time I left in 1986. But we lost one competition that left some heartburn. This was the jet trainer. There was to be an initial competition. In the second phase, those on the short list would develop proposals, but not really make a firm proposal. Instead, at the end of Phase Two, the Navy was supposed to pick two and go on to have a major, final competition for the deal.

"I thought we had made a damn good proposal," Carr recalled. "Beech was our partner and was going to do the maintenance. The competition was the British Aerospace Hawk, with McDonnell doing the Americanizing and navalizing. John Lehman decided on his own—maybe because he was an Anglophile to begin with—that it was not possible for a brand-new airplane to be as cheap as the Hawk. He declared the competition over. I happened to see the evaluation of the Grumman proposal, and it was about the worst thing I ever read, really pathetic. Our flight test program ran a little longer than McDonnell's. Of course it cost more on paper. Nevertheless, McDonnell had its problems later, complete with program management changes. Beech made a big difference in the cost of maintenance of our airplane, and I'm convinced to this day we could have built that airplane cheaper."

After Carr and I retired, Grumman's relations with Congress sagged. This was clear from a letter dated October 24, 1989, from Sen. John Warner, who had helped the company out of the F-14 contract imbroglio and liked Grumman. Significantly, the letterhead was from his 1990 campaign fundraising committee and addressed to Gordon Ochenrider.

Dear Gordon:

As a member of the House-Senate conference committee, I must participate in decisions relating to your company programs.

Candidly, I am totally in opposition to the tactics being employed on behalf of your company. They have created the most serious disruption of an armed services committee conference in the eleven years I have been a participant.

The President and the Secretary of Defense made extremely difficult budget decisions. The Senate, in its deliberations on the authorization bill, was supportive of the Administration's goals.

I am returning funds received by my 1990 campaign committee from the Grumman Corporation.

I recognize the need to reach certain compromises in the context of a conference report, but the "gridlock" the Grumman supporters have placed this conference in are [sic] totally unacceptable to me. As I write, this conference report is at risk of not being completed. The Grumman issues are a major factor.

As I said, I had retired by then. But a few people who stayed on told me that Grumman had begun to throw its weight around in Washington. Whether Gus Kinnear was involved in the Warner blowup isn't clear. But a couple of former navy leaders remembered that Gus, a retired four-star admiral and former commander naval air, Atlantic (ComNavAirLant), tangled with people when he went to work for Grumman in Washington in the mid-1980s. Grumman being Grumman, with its doubled-edged informality, didn't know what was going on at first, and it took a while before realization sunk in. "Gus was a good guy," Adm. Dutch Schoultz recalls, "but he was very ambitious and pushed himself very hard, and in a less than genteel way." The problem seemed to be that he pushed others, in the military and on the Hill, the same way. A former principal deputy to the assistant secretary of the navy for research, engineering, and systems, Richard L. Rumpf, remembers some of the same problems. Later president of Rumpf Associates International in Alexandria, Virginia, Dick Rumpf said that Gus Kinnear was one of the Grumman people who put the company crossways with several members of Congress, but not necessarily John Warner. Renso Caporali later had his own go-arounds with the Navy, too, as head of the company. For perspective, the idea of defense contractors and the military as a holy alliance exists mostly in the press. This kind of head-butting is reality, and the contractor has to walk a narrow line between good customer relations and good business sense.

What happened did have something to do with the F-14D. Since I stayed on as a consultant for three years or so, I did know about the F-14A, -A+, and -D and about zero 8, zero 12, and zero 18. To explain a complex history, the F-14 was designated originally as the F-14A with the existing TF30 engines and existing radars. There was to be an F-14B that was going to be re-engined with the never-developed Pratt & Whitney 401. Then there was an F-14C that was going to have new avionics. None of these ever came to fruition. A decade after introduction of the airplane to the Navy, there was a lot of discussion about re-engining with the General Electric F110 engine powering the Air Force's B-1, creating an F-14D that would have all-new avionics as well. Lehman and Grumman wound up signing a fixed-price development contract for the F-14D and the A-6F concurrently, waiving the profit. Grumman accepted the risk inherent in that, predominantly because we believed the Navy would buy more than 300 new F-14D aircraft and at least 150 or so A-6Fs.

Under development in the 1980s and re-engined with the F-18's General Electric 404 engine, but without an afterburner, the A-6F could have been a big enough program to carry along an unmerged Grumman. Yet Pete Oram, a veteran program manager who ran Grumman International at one point and succeeded me as president of aerospace, had doubts about the airplane. He tried very hard to convince the Navy to increase the wing size on the A-6 by seventy square feet, and managed to voice his concerns to the then deputy defense secretary, Paul Thayer. "John Lehman was insisting that we make it out of plastic, quote unquote, but keep it the same inner and outer aircraft," Oram said. "That's like building a house inside out. Tactical airplanes grow a pound a day. The A-6 had the same wing but they kept stuffing gear in. As a result, the airplane was just too close to the margins, even though John Lehman thought the Navy could save money by not having to redo a lot of flight tests, which a new wing would have brought. While the Navy was unhappy with Grumman's no-bid, you can't in good conscience give the company assets away."

About three quarters of the way through development, right after I retired, the Navy broke the bad news. What it really wanted to do was remanufacture four hundred F-14s into an F-14D configuration using existing airframes. Then the Navy would buy new airplanes at twelve a year for ten years—120 new airplanes—and shut the line down. The Navy turned the screw one more time and added that it would also compete the remanufacturing between Grumman and the naval aviation depots. On top of this, the Navy terminated the A-6F program.

Grumman begged Adm. Bill Bowes, the Navy's F-14 program manager at time, not to have the F-14D production line run out at twelve a year for ten years. Because the unit costs of the airplane would be so high, the production line would not survive. Better to buy thirty-six a year for three years and shut the line down. Admiral Bowes pointed out that he would then show an excess aircraft inventory—and that he couldn't sell. Grumman completed the development and began production of the F-14D. Because the engine had been ready earlier, Grumman had also built a bunch of F-14A+s, which had GE engines in them. (They are now called F-14Bs.) When Dick Cheney, from the House, became secretary of defense in the Bush Administration he made three major decisions in the first two months of his stewardship. He killed the V-22 Osprey (which lived again to enter service with the Marines) and the Lockheed Martin P-7 that was to replace the P-3 Orion patrol aircraft. And he terminated new production of F-14Ds. Here was Grumman with a remanufacturing program only competing against a government depot with differing ways to measure costs and overhead.

John O'Brien was the new president of the corporation then, having succeeded Jack Bierwirth, who had also retired. O'Brien's career tumbled into disaster later, but he was riding high then and launched an aggressive, intensive congressional campaign to try to save some of the new production F-14Ds. Grumman narrowly won approval of the House Armed Services Committee to fund twelve new airplanes. As is procedure in Congress, the different House and Senate authorization bills went to a combined conference committee to work out any differences. In the appropriations cycle, the same procedure is followed. When the bills left the Senate Armed Services Committee, there were no new-production F-14D airplanes. But the House had plussed up the F-14 by twelve. The way the conference normally works, with numbers like twelve and zero, if you're lucky you get twelve. Often as not they split the difference and you get six. Grumman's marketing philosophy at time was to take the six and live to fight another day. Instead, to Grumman's astonishment, out of the authorization conference came eighteen airplanes. Hence the 6, 12, and 18 codes.

As a result, there was a series of communications from high-level senators to the company expressing outrage at Grumman's aggressive lobbying. John Warner's letter was one, sending back his political action committee check. Good authority has it that not only had John O'Brien worked hard on the New York congressional delegation, but he had also leaned on his friend Tip O'Neill as speaker to warn Rep. Les Aspin that he could lose his chairmanship of the House Armed Services Committee if Aspin didn't go along with adding the F-14Ds.

Politics, before I retired in 1986, gave me qualms. The Warner letter is the kind of thing I worried about, and there seem to have been others I never saw. Our troops would go down to Washington when we were fighting for our fair share, and some went too far. Bob Watkins, my longtime assistant, made a good point to me. "Grumman's strength was in its informality," he said. "The weakness of Grumman was its informality." To balance them was the trick. For instance, the Gulfstream went to Washington on Tuesdays and Thursdays. One of the problems with this situation, because of our informality, was that the Gulfstream carried F-14 marketing people, A-6 marketing people, program people, you name it. They flooded

Washington. You could only get to see that particular admiral or congressman for an hour. First through the door would be an F-14 type, and, after the first hour, the next in the door would be the A-6 representative. Much as we, or especially Tom Kane, tried to control who went down on the airplane and who they saw, there would still be people with five different programs getting out of that Gulfstream, jumping in taxis, and tearing all over Washington. In the process, someone or something clearly annoyed the Navy or Congress.

Washington and politics are an unpleasant fact of life for a defense contractor, and my misgivings were shared by other contractors. Grumman had to stroke the politicians, although I leaned toward Grumman's old-time attitude to let politics take care of itself and concentrate instead on the operations level—and especially field support.

* * *

When I became president of Grumman Aerospace in 1974, I happened to play golf with a visiting rear admiral from NavAir, Bud Eakas. My style, developed at the Cape on the lunar module program, was to mix with the customer and ask for suggestions or ideas on what we should be doing. So I asked Bud Eakas what the Navy thought of Grumman. His reply was a lesson and a challenge, for he told me that McDonnell Douglas was number one in the navy's book and Grumman's reputation had fallen behind. No basking for me under the stars when I got production rolling again on the F-14, the A-6E, and the EA-6B. Instead, I realized, I'm going to have to drive this company, polish the rail, force the learning curves down, and, not the least, emphasize field support to the user. Out of the latter came my decision to have the field service department report directly to me as president, which it hadn't before. My troops heard the Bud Eakas story over and over. Field service became a mantra to improve relations with the navy customer.

Grumman had a big annual dinner for its field service top guns, and I told them first off that they were my eyes and ears. Tell your interfaces in the officers' clubs and the squadron offices that you have a direct pipeline to an operational type from flight test, that you work directly for the president of Grumman Aerospace, who will crack the whip and get results in a hurry. "And," I added, even with the necessity for frugality, "when you fly around the country, fly first class. You never know who you might sit next to." That brought a big hurrah and the whole idea worked.

"When I came up to Calverton with George on the F-14," Bob Watkins, who grew up in service and support, recalled in a later interview, "one of the first things I did was to go out on the assembly line and, literally, put my left hand on the side of an F-14. With my right hand I reached behind me. To the shop foreman I then said: 'When your hand comes back like this, I want to put there whatever it is that you need—a part, a piece of paper, a person, a tool, whatever. That's my job. Now you and I have to work together to make that happen because I don't have eighty-eight jillion dollars.'"

Field service is where Grumman established part of its reputation with the Navy and later with NASA. Roger Wolfe Kahn, who fathered Grumman's field-service mindset, was a hands-on guy, in the same tradition young engineers absorbed on the shop floor. Roger used to fly his own red F8F all over the country. His troops knew his airplane had better be supported, and they had a set of circular zones and rules to track him everywhere, sometimes dispatching two service representatives there within twenty-four hours, sometimes, in the red zone, a service rep within four hours. His F8F ultimately became a flight test bed at Cornell's aeronautical laboratory. Roger preached one thing: Support the product out in the field. Back in those days, Grumman's relationship with the Navy was a lot less formal than it is now. So we could even entertain, whereas now we can't even buy the military customer a drink.

"Roger would bring back the people from the field at least once, more often twice a year," Watkins recalled, "for a briefing on what was going on in the company. More important from their standpoint was to learn what problems the airplane and the customer had. Everybody loved to work for Roger because he was such a kind man in many different ways—financially and from a career standpoint. His philosophy was that for someone to operate effectively inside the service department it was necessary to know how Grumman operated. When I went to work after getting out of the Navy in 1954, the very first thing he did was use me as a prototype for an idea, for sending newcomers on a two-month tour of Grumman, initially to the service change group writing all our tech bulletins. Roger didn't want service types to sit in an office and make telephone calls raising hell with engineering or manufacturing. Deal face-to-face to develop a relationship. You knew him, and he would know who you were and would recognize your problem. Inherently the service department was always bringing in problems. Obviously one of the ways not to solve these problems is to alienate people. Sit down with them instead."

Initially field service representatives were tech reps, dealing with engines, airframes, and, to some degree, electronics. The original cadre came out of Plant Four, Grumman's flight operations facility then. By and large they were plane captains, jacks of all trades who knew the whole airplane, not engineers. As the airplane became more of a platform for electronics, though, they had to evolve into avionic reps or airframe or engine specialists. Logistic supply reps also became a necessity to deal with the centralized Aviation Supply Office in Philadelphia. Service became compartmentalized. Then the program manager system came along, and the program manager reeled in everything. Program managers had all the disciplines. Service did the same thing. When the program manager roll-up happened, it created part of the problem Grumman ultimately ran into. Program managers were vice presidents with all-encompassing organizations. But that complicated the materiel world because the same type of hardware might be used across the spectrum of, say, five programs.

"Until 1974," Watkins said, "when George became president and I pushed and prodded to set up a materiel management department that would be a core organization supporting all the programs, we ended up with a humongous inventory in Grumman. Every program vice president said, 'I want mine.' Remember we were a matrix organization—so we had the three elements: programs, functional departments, and geographic locations. What I did was to take the organization charts from all three elements and color coded what was a materiel type of function as I saw it. When I looked at that, I realized materiel basically came from four different sources: parts we made ourselves, purchased parts from vendors, government furnished equipment (GFE), and miscellaneous, which meant the parts could have been borrowed from somewhere. Instead I wanted one master department in control but not tied to any of the four, neither prejudiced against nor leaning toward any of them. Thanks to George's backing, they let me do it."

Dealing with vendors and GFE as well as manufacturing internally could become an exercise in how and where to push. Back in those days, there was no Japanese approach to just-in-time inventory. Grumman or the Navy had the materiel physically. In the case of GFE, if an airplane was down in Japan, for example, the navy supply system would work its way into getting that part. If Grumman's rep in Japan started screaming because of no delivery, we would have enough GFE in house for production airplanes, and service would cajole to borrow from production stock. This was especially true early in the F-14 program because of a dearth of GFE in the electronic world.

Several different navies were out there. Pilots, the air boss, and the skipper of the boat were not tolerant of an airplane on the deck. But to the supply world, spares were just a bunch of numbers. Field service was emotionally involved in supporting Grumman's airplanes on the production line and out in the field. The Aviation Supply Office wasn't emotionally involved. The air boss and the CO were emotionally involved, but people in the middle quite often were not. Going aboard both the *Enterprise* for the first deployment of the F-14 in the Pacific Fleet and the *Kennedy* for the first deployment of the F-14 in the Atlantic Fleet, as Bob Watkins and I did, they found that the Navy had tremendous problems supporting airplanes on board. Memos that I still have detail how the Navy never even provisioned some of the items. Because they had no navy stock number, it was impossible to have these on the boat. Here they had six or eight very sophisticated airplanes in the F-14 with growing pains in its weapons systems and engine. The navy supply system was not in a position to have spared the airplane the way it should have, for it didn't have the money or the knowledge that came with time. They didn't know where the weak spots were, whether in the airframe, power plant, avionics, or ordnance. The parts just weren't there.

Commercial airlines will estimate what they think they will need and use in percentages. The Aviation Supply Office laboriously reviewed each drawing; buying one of those, one of these. Most times the navy lists were based on Grumman drawings and technical manuals that the company knew far better than the Navy did. Watkins recalls me convincing Rear Adm. Phil Crosby, who arrived from the West Coast to take over the Aviation Supply Office, to stop by Grumman. One remark he made caused chins to drop but it summed up the situation. Crosby said, to paraphrase, "I'm a realist. I'm going to go back down to Philadelphia as the boss of the Aviation Supply Office." He held up his thumb and forefinger, maybe an inch apart. "If I can make that much of a change, that will be tremendous." Grumman was trying to make changes internally a foot long, but the admiral was indeed a realist. The Navy was faced with development problems as the money was coming down. Money first had to buy the airplane.

Sometimes a support orientation helped, sometimes not. Aboard the *Enterprise* and *Midway* in the Pacific, Bob Watkins and I found airplanes down all over the place. On the way back we stopped at Pearl Harbor to see Adm. Maurice F. Weisner, who was CincPac, a purple suiter at a joint command. Admiral Weisner had asked me what I thought about navy support. "Admiral," Watkins recalls me answering, "the way you're supporting the carriers out there, I don't know if they can last." That started a huge uproar with the Navy. "But," Watkins continued, "we had analyzed what happened on *Enterprise* and *Midway* and asked why. That's when we learned the Navy had not provisioned the items, that they had no federal stock numbers, so there was no way spares could be on board. Or if they did provision, they did it in onesies and twosies and they were using up two squadrons' worth. On the lunar module we did the provisioning using a maintenance analysis group whose job it was to take all the drawings, all the tech manuals and analyze them for potential consumption. If there was a question, they would call the cognizant engineer. The Navy had none of that. The Navy simply took the Grumman drawings and some kid in ASO who didn't know zilch would look at them. If there was something like a part he knew on the F-4 he would think the Navy better buy a couple. So it wasn't until that growing pain phase, which takes place with all airplanes, that the shortages surfaced. As airplanes got bigger and more complex and nineteen-year-old kids still manned the flight deck, there was a problem. Does a nineteen-year-old kid know how to handle a radar in an F-14 or an AWG-9? Nope. In passing George mentioned an A-7 that had been a hangar queen on the *Midway* for six to eight weeks. Weisner took umbrage, to the effect that someone better not come out here and tell him what's wrong with his airplanes. Weisner insisted that Grumman analyze its own support." Watkins took the results back out to Pearl Harbor for a briefing with, as he remembers, seven admirals in the room. "Fortunately," he added, "we were in pretty good shape and the briefing went fine."

Roger Kahn died at the age of fifty-five from emphysema—he was a heavy smoker—in 1962. Tom Connor who was Grumman area rep on the West Coast replaced him but soon demonstrated Roger's wisdom of sitting down with the engineer, or the tool guy, or whoever, and finding a solution, thus avoiding an adversarial relationship. Tom had experienced out in the field the problems everyone always had with airplanes. When one of us would go in to tell him about one, he would immediately pick up the phone, call headquarters, and raise hell. That lasted for a time until they said, wait a minute, this isn't what we want. Eventually I put Watkins in charge until a rear admiral succeeded him. Service, as I said, had to report to the president of the company to get the attention of all the supporting elements. Roger Kahn, having grown up with Jake Swirbul and Roy Grumman and being the kind of guy he was, built a whole organization of people whose mentality was the same: keep the product flying. Let engineering design them and manufacturing build them. Service makes sure they work. People don't buy another car from a dealer with a lousy service department.

Adm. Dutch Schoultz favored the F/A-18 but agrees with Grumman's service reputation and the Roger Wolfe Kahn legacy. When he was ComNavAirPac on the West Coast in the 1980s he used Grumman as an example for McDonnell Douglas when introducing the F/A-18 to the Navy. "I called the people back in St. Louis, and said, 'I don't know who the hell is doing your customer relations, but you guys have to talk to Grumman and find out how to do it. We're putting new airplanes in, and I can't even find who to talk to at McDonnell.' In the next couple of days I met a whole lot of new people!" Grumman's field service people made sure that the Navy was always up to speed on what Grumman was doing, which was really an advantage.

Grumman favored prevention in service. For Apollo at Cape Canaveral we had parts trailers at the base of the pad. At Calverton we put up what was called the airlock, right next to the production line on the north side of the building because the warehouse per se was far back on the other end of the production line. Naturally the operators used to take their time coming down off the work stand, sauntering over to the warehouse, getting parts, sauntering back. With the airlock parts and the engines right next to the production line, the property north of that at Calverton was declared as inviolate.

A pivotal—for future fighter tactics and weapons—and some-times controversial air intercept missile and air combat evaluation (AIMVAL/ACEVAL) in the late 1970s at Nellis Air Force Base became, in passing, an F-14 versus F-15 contest. To keep F-14s flying, Grumman used a wagon train system, based on what it did at Cape Canaveral and Calverton, of putting all the spare parts it might need at the site. Everything known to mankind was stored out there, in trailers at Grumman's expense. This was a twenty-four-hour-a-day support concept, using Grumman's own Gulfstream to fly out spares. To elaborate on Bob's thought, the word got around that I was the godfather of the support world. And I did support field service mightily. Joe Rees, a former navy captain and Mike Pelehach's assistant program director on the F-14, the same Joe Rees who waved a red flag in front of me when he said there was no way to get the fifty-fourth F-14 out by the end of 1973, felt something of the same about the wagon train. Do that, he warned, and the Navy will want everything. "They're throwing money out the window around here on all this diversification baloney," I answered. "I'll throw some out the window, too, and it will be better invested than what headquarters is doing." In any event, the F-14 looked like the most available airplane in the world out there in the desert.

12

A MISSED OPPORTUNITY?

Grumman's last chance to knock off a program with the scale of an F-14 or an A-6 came with the Navy's foray into stealth technology in a new attack aircraft—later designated the A-12. Not that we had any way of knowing this at the time. The whole story started, though, with an abortive—and ill-considered—F-14 and A-6 amalgamation. John Lehman, the navy secretary, had grown enamored with what was called the Super Tomcat, the F-14D Grumman had been trying to sell all along and that eventually was produced. His idea was to meld assembly with the improved A-6F. Fine, except that he called me one day and announced he was going to shut down the F-14 production line for a year and a half during the cutover to the improved airplane. "You can't do that," I protested. "You don't understand what that means." He insisted, so I flew down to Washington in a hurry to remonstrate with him and his deputy, Mel Paisley, and explain: "Shutting down the line would cost a billion dollars. What are the suppliers going to do for a year and a half? What are the people going to do?"

Although they argued with some of Grumman's numbers, reason prevailed. Nevertheless, they wanted to move forward with a combined A-6F/F-14D assembly. Commonality was a buzzword then. Paisley and Lehman thought they could achieve this by having two airplanes with a common AYK-14 computer from the EA-6B, digitizing the F-14, and co-locating engineers to support both airplanes as well. Lehman and Paisley double-teamed me even though I had quoted to them in the Pentagon what I thought was a rock-bottom price of $1.2 billion. I remember the arm-twisting. "We can't afford the $1.2 billion you want, George, for the development," Lehman argued, and I'm thinking, "Maybe I'll take it down $100 million to $1.1 billion." Then he turns to Paisley and says, "Mel, what is the number we really have to get out of George here?" We had already had two luncheons over a two-week period to talk about this stuff. "We're going to need this and that and something for Patuxent," Mel said. "Make it $1.05 billion." After I checked with my staff, they got their $1.05 billion. Grumman wouldn't make any money, maybe a 1 percent profit margin at most, but it would keep the lines open. Although it could have been another F-14 disaster, the A-6F later was canceled. Paul Thayer, who had left LTV to become deputy secretary of defense, didn't believe Lehman could get the job done for that, and, with some skepticism, called me to check. "We did give him that number," I said defensively, "and that's what we think we can do."

Dutch Schoultz, then OP 05, recalls John Lehman was convinced that Grumman was making too much money on its airplanes and should be able to cut costs. Lehman thought Grumman had had an easy ride because nobody had ever squeezed, leaving an inefficient organization. "I used to fight like hell with him to get upgrades in airplanes," Admiral Schoultz said, "and Lehman would argue that contractors ought to pay for them. But he was after Grumman in particular because he thought the company needed to modernize and that it was making too much money. He was adamant."

Anyway Dutch called me at some point with a change of mind on Lehman's part, though we had started work on the combined program. The A-6F was falling out of the tree, and I found out why when I persuaded Lehman to stop by Bethpage on his way to Nantucket for the weekend. Stealth technology had started to come out of the black a little bit by 1980, and I had a couple of our hotshots brief John on what we called the "whale." Using balsa wood to show fairing modifications, and putting a mock-up of a one-piece canopy on a real A-6, Grumman pitched a modestly stealthified version. "You're interested in the A-12 concept," I told him, "but we had a cheaper solution in the whale. "For $600 million, we can do a hell of a job on the A-6 with a new engine and stealthy features. Why go for a brand-new airplane?"

"I hear you talking, George," Lehman answered, "but you don't know what's going on. The state of the art has really moved along." Grumman could tinker around with the A-6, I insisted, but he was adamant about going ahead with the A-12. When I took him out to his airplane, on his way to Cape Cod, he told me more. "The Navy is going to have a competition to replace the A-6 plus the F-111. So the Air Force is going to be part of the program. If I were you, I'd take a good hard look at Northrop." He and Tom Jones were pretty close, for one thing.

When the competition came alive officially, it was convoluted. Contractors were told they were going to have to get a dancing partner. Whoever won the competition would have a joint development program with their partner. Once the development program was over, the Navy would break the teams apart and recompete the program on a yearly basis. To contractors and to some Pentagon troops there was a question whether the Navy was trying to develop an airplane or a competition.

I went down again to see Lehman and Paisley to tell them I thought it was ridiculous. "We're doing it already," they answered, "with Bell and in some engine procurement." "This will never work," I scoffed. "Oh yes it will," they insisted. Lehman, and others in DoD, had fallen madly in love with competition as a solution to all acquisition shortcomings, much in the mold of Dave Packard's fly-before-buy. Whatever I thought, the Navy had the helm. There was more pirouetting around and telephoning than the month before the senior prom, except this was serious business. I was getting phone calls from Northrop and Lockheed and General Dynamics, though nothing from McDonnell Douglas. As a dancing partner, they wanted us for solid background with the Navy, plus experience with carrier suitability. When I insisted my team needed to see some of the stealth work at Northrop and Lockheed to understand what was going on, Lehman balked. "I don't know anything about stealth," I argued with John and Paisley, "and I needed it to join any team. "I can't pick a dancing partner unless I know something about what's going on." "Don't worry about that, George," Paisley replied. "John picked it up right away and so can you." Although I did get one of those top-level clearances from the Pentagon needed at the time for access to stealth technology, none of the rest of my team ever did.

Renso (Cappy) Caporali, then one of our top technical guys, Tom Kane, and some other technical and staff people flew out to the West Coast with me. When we drove up at Lockheed's former Burbank headquarters, I was stunned at the top people who lined up on the drive: Roy Anderson, the chairman, and executives like Larry Kitchen, Bob Ormsby, and Bob Fuhrman—it was a state visit. My next shock came in the conference room when I saw the funny-looking models on table. Dick Heppe, a technical guru at Lockheed, equivalent to our Mike Pelehach, took me into a hangar. There I first saw the F-117, which blew my mind. And it was on the production line! One further shock was to see how far Grumman was behind. I sat in cockpit and tried to comprehend all those angles. "This thing won't fly, will it?" I asked Heppe. Yes it will, he assured me. Weapons bays in the belly had doors that snapped open and snapped closed again after a quick launch so as not to lose stealth. The Air Force only built about a hundred, but projected attrition rates would be so low with stealth that not many F-117s would be needed.

The next day was the visit to the Northrop facility at Pico Rivera. With Tom Jones away in Korea, Kent Kresa, later to head the company, escorted me as host. Kent took me down corridors lined with offices with combination locks on every door—Northrop had seven thousand employees there with special clearances—to the display hangar balcony with the B-2, like a bat sitting there on floor, black composite, serrated joints, bonded structure, and all. Again, it was mind-blowing, especially in those days when both programs were deep in the black world. When I sat in the cockpit, Kent offered to put me in the simulator if I'd like to fly it. I made three takeoffs and landings, easy. Again I thought: Where the hell is Grumman? This is what John Lehman is talking about. Before the next stop, Ollie Boileau called from General Dynamics and said not to bother to come there. "We're going with MacDac," he said, "I can't wait around any longer, and I don't want to be left out."

At the hotel room that night, I made up my mind that Grumman ought to go with Northrop. "They'll be leader," I proposed, "and we'll be the follower." Everybody agreed. I called Lockheed and asked to meet again, for about an hour, just to hear its pitch once more.

Another top-drawer briefing followed, and I promised a decision the following week. Flying back in our Gulfstream 2 over the Grand Canyon, I called everybody to the back of airplane and said, "We're over the big ditch," which we were in more ways than geographically. "One more time, what say you?" All of them agreed, "Let's stay with Northrop."

Jack Bierwirth had reservations about Tom Jones, whom he considered a slick article because of his overseas payments troubles, and so did Joe Gavin. Whether the decision was right or wrong is academic because General Dynamics and McDonnell Douglas won. Subsequently Welko Gasich of Northrop told me, "If we had it to do all over again, we would have had you as leaders. Grumman sent a real good team out." After I turned into a consultant, Kent Kresa agreed with the leader-follower thought, and he was mad. "I'm going to fire ten guys," and he ranted about their not knowing what they were talking about. Neither was he completely happy with Grumman, which he thought had submitted a logistics plan that was just an A-6 rehash. Furthermore, Northrop was stretched thin at the time, not with just the B-2, but also in a competition with Lockheed for what would eventually become the F-22, which it also lost. Kresa was not the only one who was unhappy. Later I found out that none of our master technicians, such as Grant Hedrick, had been asked to look at this thing.

Tom Kane has his own insight into the A-12 unraveling. He told me much later: "A friend of mine, when the Navy was just finishing the evaluation, called with a message: 'I'll be coming in from Washington on the three PM shuttle. Meet me.' I did, and he told me, 'Let's ride around. I don't want to go to Bethpage.' Then he laid on the bad news. 'They don't understand your inlet. The bomb bay is a mess, because there had to be a different hanging fixture for every weapon. And on terms and conditions, you have to bend more. We'll argue about the price later.'" Kane recognized this for what it was, a warning and an advisory from a well-placed friend as to how to salvage the Northrop-Grumman team's bid. Tom went to a pay phone and called Northrop. "I'll be there on the late flight tonight," he said, "and I'll see you guys at seven in the morning over at the plant." Tom laid the whole thing out to them there: "You'll be asked to resubmit your design in about two weeks. Explain the inlet, work

on the damn bomb bay, and do something on terms and conditions."
In two weeks he went back and they hadn't really done anything. To
the bomb rack the only change was dropping two weapons from the
maximum 24 to 22 it could carry. They hadn't talked terms and conditions because nobody had spoken to Tom Jones at Northrop or
John O'Brien at Grumman about it. They thought that what they had
designed was so beautiful they didn't have to change anything.

Terms and conditions problems had to do with what Mel Paisley
had laid on the contractors in his fixed-price development mode.
There were arcane incentive or penalty fees, as Kane said, the "stuff
any sane business man wouldn't buy." McDonnell can't stand them
either, Kane argued, but McDonnell is going to fight, eventually
agree, and then negotiate later. And that's exactly what they did and
they made money—up to a point. But that came only after they sued
when Dick Cheney, who was secretary of defense in the first Bush
administration, canceled the program after the airplane ran over
weight and over cost. Lockheed, with the most stealth experience, got
nothing. McDonnell, which Kane said had the least, won, and that
may have explained where the program went adrift. In any event, the
government appealed the decision to pay the contractors the $2 bil-
lion they claimed in termination costs. By the time the judgment was
reversed and sent back for a new trial in which the contractors lost
both aircraft segments of the winners had been absorbed into Boeing
or Lockheed Martin.

Why was the A-6F canceled? Dick Rumpf, who was navy R&D in
the Pentagon then, thinks it just got caught up in the budget struggle
with the A-12. Compared with the A-12, had it been built, even the
modified A-6F was not a very survivable airplane. As Rumpf points
out: "Why continue to put a whole lot of money into an airplane to
improve its survivability incrementally when the Navy could make a
quantum leap with the A-12?" Grumman ran out of programs for
analogous reasons to its informality. In Rumpf's view, Grumman was
a little too arrogant—or perhaps insular is a better word—to team
early with other people. "It was that family dominance," he said, "the
Grumman family. The first time I ever went there a driver picked us
up at Bethpage. 'How long have you been at Grumman?' I asked the
driver. 'Thirty years driving,' he said, 'and my father was here before
me.' As I understood those people more and more, they really were a

family organization. In one sense that was the strength of the organization: loyalty, good products. But Grumman's inbreeding didn't leave it open for the infusion of new technology it should have had."

That's an issue I wrestled with for years. When Jack Bierwirth first came on board, I was very enthused. Coming from the outside, he, I thought, would move us away from the Grumman traditional conservatism and make changes. Then I began to realize that maybe he was miscast in the aerospace industry. Charming, courtly, well over six feet tall, and a good conversationalist, Jack favored sports coats with an Ivy League look at work. Yet he was shrewd and would have been a good diplomat. At one Aerospace Industries Association meeting at Williamsburg, sitting with maybe ten aerospace heavies, he held forth on the correct way to eat a lobster. My upbringing never even included eating a lobster, which was probably true for most of my peers. Jack did bring to Grumman an awareness and an education in how to work internationally. This was especially true of cultural nuances, which are very important in the Orient. Yet he had nothing to do with convincing the Iranians to buy the F-14 or selling the E-2C to Israel or Japan, for example. But he was very good at showing us how to drink tea the Asian way out of a cup with a cap on it, which I couldn't master. Unlike other Grumman offices, there were no pictures of airplanes in his, just plants and abstract art. He was running an aerospace company, but not worshiping the industry. As time went on, I suspected Jack was not the outsider that we needed, not a Lew Evans, who also was an outsider. Clint Towl had similar feelings. I couldn't understand people who claimed he was a financial expert. Once Jack called the Wall Street security analysts in for a plant tour followed by a briefing on diversification and lunch. Coffee time came. "As you can see, we're involved in a lot of things," Jack said when he stood up. "I don't know if we'll ever make any money with them, but we're sure going have a lot of fun trying." Next to me was an analyst from Wertheimer, who asked, stunned: "What was that?" Within three weeks Wertheimer sold off about 250,000 shares of Grumman. Work ought to be fun was a theme of Jack's, and he would ask people why they were working so late or say that if they had to come in on Saturdays they were not really budgeting their time. He had no use for strategic planning. That didn't stop me from drafting a plan, which I handed over to him sometime in 1983. Later, I'll never forget, I went to an operating plan meeting in the boardroom. At the end of discussion I asked Jack whether he had had a chance to read the strategic plan. "Yeah," he said, "and I don't think much of it. A strategic plan locks in everybody and there's no creativity." With that he picked it up and sailed it across the table to me like a paper airplane. Nothing said, like "George, let's talk about this." Inside I was seething, for those of us in aerospace were busting our chops making money for the company and he was fostering forays like the bus company's daisy path into a humongous loss and all other kinds of embarrassment. Yet he didn't want a strategic plan.

I haven't talked much yet about how I became president of Grumman Aerospace. It's worth going into here, though it happened years before, because one of the contenders at the time, John O'Brien, played a crucial role in the fate of the company later on, and possibly even hastened the eventual merger. O'Brien was one of five or six possible choices when Joe Gavin flew out to Calverton and told me that I was the winner of a competition I didn't know I was in. Mike Pelehach was one candidate, and so were Ed Dalva and Corky Meyer as well as Grant Hedrick, and, on the outside, Ross Mickey. I wasn't licking my lips to be president. My family was still down in Florida because Calverton could have been a geographic waypoint in an evolving career. But things had gone well at Calverton, I liked it there, and now I was getting ready to close on a house in eastern Long Island. With the F–14 back on track, I wanted to be vice president and general manager there. Another family disruption wasn't all that much of a thrill. Gavin didn't put it as a choice, though. I was chosen as president of Grumman Aerospace. That was that.

Word had got out that Towl was going to retire. Jack Bierwirth would move up to the chairmanship of the corporation from president and Joe Gavin was to transition to headquarters and take his place as president of Grumman Corporation, reporting to Jack. Other hopefuls were doing flip-flops up and down the hall at headquarters, trying to shine. Bethpage was awash in speculation. It turned out that Bill Schwendler and Towl as well as Joe Gavin and Jack wanted an operational kind of guy with a proven record of running a major success. So my tour at the Cape on the LM was the kind of high profile they wanted, with the Calverton miracle as even stronger medicine. When I took over I knew there were some broken hearts. Plus the contenders or would-be contenders were obviously looking at one another, each thinking he was the best man. And they all thought they were better then a troll from the wilds of Calverton to sit on top in aerospace.

That had to be met face to face. I called them all into the aerospace boardroom and sat them down around its long table. "Gentlemen," I addressed the group, "I want you to know my name isn't George Grumman, that I didn't marry Roy Grumman's daughter. For some reason the board saw fit to ask me to take this job and I'm humbled at the choice. I know the job ahead of us is formidable, and I have a lot to learn. Fortunately, there are people sitting around this table that are as good as any group of aerospace executives in the business. I can't do it alone. It has to be done with your help. But let me tell you something. If anybody in this room thinks he is going to mickey mouse me, doing things not to my liking, he'll be in trouble, deep trouble." I stared at each one around table. "We have a great company. The experience assembled in this room is a tremendous asset to Grumman. I think we will make a hell of a good team if we pull together, if we continue the heritage of Grumman in design integrity. That's all I have to say now. There will be some changes, but nothing drastic. I'm standing by to talk with each one of you over the next several weeks."

Everybody shook hands with me and offered congratulations. Some had to have been disappointed, but that was that. In retrospect, guys like Mike Pelehach, Corky Meyer, and John O'Brien probably could have picked up their marbles and left. They had talent and reputations. Quickly I went ahead and made four senior vice presidents: Pelehach, O'Brien, Dalva, and Meyer, hoping to ease the pain. At that time, we didn't have any senior vice presidents. Later I made O'Brien and Pelehach executive vice presidents, a new title, what we called the Double X.

All of them were poker-faced through the meeting, no facial contortions or body language. They just looked at me. As I said, I did make it clear that I felt these were not ordinary guys. They were not plotters, but they could have been tempted to ease me out of the way. Gavin was still chairman of aerospace, but, as I said, the news was out shortly that Towl would stand down and Gavin would go to the corporation. Some began to say that I would move into the chairmanship, which I did eventually, and the presidency of aerospace would open up, which it didn't. Clint Towl indeed had pressed me to give up the presidency and become chairman. But I was an operating man, trying to move aerospace into bigger and better things, in terms of both its reputation and its bottom line. I wrote a memo to the effect that I understood how he felt, but that I'd like my turn at bat and wanted to wear two hats for the time being.

Frankly, I was pleased with myself, to get tossed into that crowd, the management circle, and find I could control those high rollers so that none left the company. I didn't have any trouble with O'Brien. Still, he was the Cassius type, and I never really trusted him, which cast a shadow over the future. Mike Pelehach was a different sort. He would come in, vent about how much he had to do, and try to talk about promotion, but he was not a manipulator. Jack Bierwirth told me he would not put either Mike or John O'Brien into the presidency or aerospace, but he named Mike head of international for the corporation. Then, to my astonishment after what he had told me, he brought O'Brien over to the corporation as president and then named him as his successor as chairman.

Warnings about O'Brien came early on. In fact, I had called him in and warned him that stories were beginning to circulate about his friendship with Jim Kane (no relation to Tom Kane, Grumman's longtime marketing vice president). Kane was a Long Island businessman who owned two companies that sold corrugated cardboard boxing and crates to Grumman. By the book, Grumman company policy, this should have been on a competitive bid basis from the procurement department. It emerged later that Grumman procurement workers were creating phony, higher bids so that Kane would be the only real player in the game.

This was not exactly their idea. John O'Brien, according to the documents in a federal investigation, had done more than suggest the business go to Kane's companies. Kane had long floated around the Grumman plants as if he were a badged employee, contrary to security policies. I noticed Kane marching down the corridor to O'Brien's office once and called the head of security to find out what was going on. The casual visits stopped—for a time.

Kane, for unclear reasons, developed a pronounced interest in politics. He took it on himself, possibly with O'Brien's blessing, to act as an unpaid interceder for Grumman with congressmen and Capitol Hill staffers, whom he had managed to strike up acquaintances with through the most elemental and effective modus: fundraising and contributions. He busied himself in the affairs of Grumman's political action committee and, more lethally, with the Long Island Aerospace Political Action Committee (Aeropac). Its members were Grumman suppliers and subcontractors, some who willingly coughed up the money and some who did so only under duress.

One startling incident occurred on a company Gulfstream when Grumman's procurement vice president, Robert Simon, was riding back to New York with O'Brien. O'Brien, as Simon testified later, began to badger him about tightening the screws on Grumman suppliers who were balking. Finally O'Brien reached out, grabbed Simon's tie, and pulled him nose-to-nose to make it very clear how essential it was for Simon's future career at Grumman to get the vendors in line. Simon was already in fear for his job. Almost to the day that he moved into the corporate hierarchy, O'Brien had summoned the procurement director to his office. Thinking O'Brien wanted a briefing on the company's procurement operations, Simon took time to round up his charts and data to bring along. O'Brien wanted nothing of the sort. Again, as Simon testified, O'Brien began to shout and pound on the table, demanding that Simon sharpen his political sensitivity and see that Grumman suppliers did the same. Grumman employees were "persuaded" to contribute to the Grumman PAC, though some preferred not to. Vendors who dropped out of Aeropac were advised by Simon or others to mend their ways or find Grumman's doors closed to them.

Long Island's influential newspaper *Newsday* received word that something was going on—it was at the time of the government's Ill Wind investigation of Pentagon payoffs that sent Paisley, Lehman's deputy, to prison—and all defense contractors were becoming suspect. Justice Department and navy investigators tapped Kane's telephone. When the subject of loans from Kane to O'Brien turned up, the government searched Kane's office. There they found notes that confirmed that Kane had loaned in the aggregate more than $600,000 to O'Brien to buy houses for two of his children and for himself. The loans were interest only, and Kane had begun to write them down himself so that annual interest charges were dropping and the loans themselves would have been paid off in a few years. Adding to the mess was the fact that Thomas Guarino, executive vice president of another Long Island aerospace company, Republic Aviation, which was later taken over by Fairchild, was also the recipient of some Kane real estate largesse. Republic shut down, and Guarino then went to work for Grumman as president of its electronic division.

Kane died of cancer in the middle of the investigation. Ultimately, the government, with a potential key witness gone, was able to charge O'Brien with only two counts of filing false mortgage applications. He had signed affidavits that he had financed mortgage down payments with his own funds when in reality they had been borrowed from Kane. O'Brien did plead guilty to the charges but did not go to prison. As the presentencing report from the government pointed out, however, O'Brien had (1) lied to the Grumman board when they called him in to answer the allegations; (2) lied to Grumman's public relations director when asked whether the loan charges were true, causing the director to deny them to *Newsday*; and (3) lied to Grumman's law firm, whose members also had met with him to discuss the case. All were violations of Grumman policy. O'Brien was fired. Ironically, when O'Brien had moved into the chairmanship, he had issued a finely worded code of ethics and had copies embossed in colorful plastic for display in company offices.

"I liked him," Danny Knowles said of O'Brien, and he wasn't alone. "He had a wonderful Irish wit." John O'Brien had a couple of other character traits. He was a rough guy, to the point of bullying subordinates. Knowles was the vice president of personnel so he had occasion to meet with, banter with, argue with, and negotiate with a massive slice of the Grumman work force. Accordingly, he was able to encapsulate the core of a public image disaster for Grumman in a sentence: "John was a guy who liked to live close to the edge."

O'Brien and Knowles had been very close. "But, when he got into that job," Knowles went on, "all the bad parts that we all have came out, because he had no one to answer to. He was always very tough dealing with people. As I said, he had a natural Irish wit, that if he had used it more often he could have gotten anything done. He didn't have to go around scaring people. Unfortunately, that was his modus operandi. John was a guy who loved to walk on the hairy edge of life. He thought he was impregnable. The first thing he said to me after he became chairman was, 'If they think I'm going to put up with that board of directors. . . . I'm going to get rid of them.' You know, you don't say that your first day you're in the job. When he became chairman he couldn't handle the company being his Jimminy Cricket."

While I was disturbed by some of the things I saw going on around O'Brien, nothing overt transpired before I left. Bob Watkins tells me the same thing. Not only was he my assistant at the Cape, at Calverton, and then in Plant Five, when I was president and chairman, but he also ran the Grumman Political Action Committee. When political action committees became legal in 1976, the then head of personnel fell heir to that operation. Watkins was asked to be the deputy and then ran it as a three-legged stool—along with Tom Kane as head of marketing and Gordon Ochenrider as head of the Washington office. Watkins was the proselytizer throughout the company and all over the United States, wherever Grumman had a facility.

"My father was a Hoover vacuum cleaner salesman," Watkins said, "and I remember his philosophy: you had to believe in Hoover vacuums to sell them. After I took on the PAC, not that I wanted to, I decided we don't have an inferior mousetrap. We are selling the world's best mousetrap, the F-14, EA-6B, and the rest. I'll be damned if I'm going to be out-politicked by Texas and California. If it's going be a political game, then we were going to play the political game and win. Grumman came out of the chocks running, and before long we were collecting $250,000 a year in our PAC coffers. Back in 1976, looking at who had the big PACs, little old Grumman on Long Island was way out in front. Then big guys came along and just wiped us out, put us down in the noise level."

Grumman's integrity in its PAC dealings was never questioned in the investigations later. Jack Bierwirth liked the PAC, because it opened doors and elbow-rubbed for him in Washington. With a $5,000 limitation per primary and general election, Grumman would give $5,000 to each candidate, concentrating on the local politicians, no matter which party. All funds were hand delivered, because it gave a Grumman representative, be it someone from the Washington office or New York, the opportunity go in, deliver the contribution in person, and in the process extol the virtues of, say, the F-14.

Tom Downey was a Democrat congressman from Long Island then and outspokenly antidefense. But Bob Watkins gives him high marks: "He was one who called me at least six times during votes and said, 'Bob, I'm going to vote against you, or look out for so and so, or send this guy money.' He wasn't the only congressman or senator who would tell me, or Gordon, who got calls more often like this: 'I'm going to vote against you on the next one because I owe the guy from California something. But I took a poll and you're okay. The F-14 money is back in there again even though I may show up as voting against it.' They always wanted to make sure they covered their six, by letting us know that in advance. Downey sometimes got his legs pulled out from underneath him by his colleagues, though, because they thought he could be pretty two-faced." Tom Kane and Gordon Ochenrider were excellent at sensing what contribution would be an advantage to Grumman. Looking long term was important. If we saw a senator gaining seniority on a committee important to Grumman, a senator who was going to become chairman three years hence because we knew senator so and so was going to retire, we started taking care of him early. Early money counts critically in the political process.

Because Grumman was so successful internally with the PAC, there came along a Chamber of Commerce–like organization on Long Island called the Long Island Association, with about fifteen hundred members. A great social group, great lunches, and all that, yet what it did for the benefit of Long Island is hard to say. Nevertheless Grumman was up against Texas and California, and their politically expert corporations. In New York Sen. Daniel Patrick Moynihan and those folks weren't in our orbit. Touring plants of members of the association, Watkins found out they really weren't enamored with a PAC because interests were just too diverse. Grumman was Grumman über alles, but the others didn't want Grumman dictating where their money went. Out of that, nevertheless, came a group of small businesses in the area, strong Grumman and Republic Aviation suppliers, who thought it was a nifty idea. So they founded the Long Island Aeropac. Here is where Jim Kane entered the picture, as one of the heads of the organization.

"When it started out," Watkins said, "it was a plain-vanilla type of operation, very straightforward, to react to more air force–

oriented Republic and Grumman requirements. Then I got called to a breakfast with Kane and some others, like Phil Vassallo, who was our vice president of procurement, to tell me that Aeropac was breaking up. Two of the key players were dropping out because they felt the thing was getting way too political—Potomac fever to the nth degree. Hand-holding with House Speaker Tip O'Neill of Massachusetts was getting way out of our league, which was simply working with our New York congressmen and senators. At that higher level, they were frightened."

Kane was a close, longtime friend of John O'Brien's, two good old Long Island Irishmen with an affinity for each other and for an Irishman who was speaker of the House. Typically O'Brien's motto was, "Have no fear, John O'Brien is here, I've got things under control." Not inclined to listen to anyone in Washington, John was going to go where he wanted to go when he wanted to and say what he wanted.

Why did Bierwirth then pick O'Brien as his successor? He was probably the best choice of the options Bierwirth had at the time. Bierwirth had pulled O'Brien out of aerospace into the corporation, even though, when I talked with Bierwirth during my exit interview he had some doubts about what John was telling him. So I asked Bierwirth later how come John became chairman. "Well," he answered, "he had me over the barrel." I think Tip O'Neill and Jimmy Kane put the pressure on Bierwirth. John had also said to him, "When Skurla's gone and then you get ready to leave, if you don't knight me I'm leaving, too."

As to what O'Brien and Kane were doing, Bob Watkins tells the story of Tip O'Neill and the Gulfstream. "When I was running the PAC," Bob related, "I got a call from the speaker's administrative assistant. 'The speaker is not feeling very well,' he told me, 'and for the next few weekends would it be possible to get the Gulfstream to fly him from Washington to Hyannisport on Cape Cod? Otherwise he has to take the shuttle from Washington to Logan Airport in Boston and then take a DC-3 the rest of the way. His health isn't that good.' Jack Bierwirth said, okay, but using our ground rules: One, it had to be a regularly scheduled business flight, and, two, Grumman had to charge the elected official the equivalent commercial air fare. 'You, Bob Watkins, will fly that airplane Friday nights from Bethpage to Washington,' Bierwirth said, 'pick up the speaker, fly him up.

Monday morning you get on the airplane and fly up to Hyannisport and reverse the procedure. And you'll charge him.' Back then the shuttle fare was $69 maybe. It cost about $1,800 an hour to fly the Gulfstream but we just charged him the $69."

On the airplane at the beginning of the assignment, Watkins decided not to talk airplanes right away. If O'Neill felt bad, he didn't want some marketing guy coming on board with a pitch. Four seats were in the back of the Gulfstream, a G-1 tail number 754. O'Neill would sit in one, take off his loafers, and put his feet up on the opposite seat. His wife sat in the third and Watkins in the fourth. Just social chitchat and jokes were exchanged at first.

"Finally," Watkins recalled, "the fourth and last weekend came around. Bierwirth told me to take Dave Walsh with me. Walsh had succeeded Tom Kane in running marketing and Jack wanted to put the arm on O'Neill then. On our approach to Hyannisport, Dave says to O'Neill per script, 'I see we're coming in over the Lynn plant in Massachusetts, which is where the GE engine is made.' O'Neill had just been quoted in the *New York Times* as saying, 'I don't know the back end of an airplane from the front end, but I want the engines built in Lynn, Massachusetts.' So Dave says to him that Grumman's upgraded F-14 and the A-6F were going to have the GE 404 engine. Tip looked at Dave and said, 'That's great, you'll have it in your F-14, your A-6, and your F-18.' To this day, I don't know whether he was totally ignorant that McDonnell built the F-18 or whether he was just pulling our chain. I was at a loss for words and my chin dropped. Dave mumbled something to rescue the mission. About a year or so later I was flying to Washington on the shuttle, first class, as corporate officers could. The flight attendant told me that the only seat open is next to the speaker. O'Neill was very affable, but he didn't recognize me. If he said that it was a nice day, I was going to tell him I worked for Grumman, and I did. The very first words out of his mouth were, 'Grumman? And how's my friend John O'Brien?'"

My own experience was that John O'Brien's friendship with Tip O'Neill, and with his sons, stemmed from Jim Kane. One day Jack Bierwirth called and told me, "George, you and I and Joe Gavin are going down to Washington for a little affair for Tip O'Neill at the Mayflower Hotel." We arrived at the Mayflower and a bunch of people were drinking cocktails. Jim Kane was there in the white sneakers he always wore, even if he had a tuxedo on. I look around and there was John O'Brien, who was then one of my two executive vice presidents. "What the hell is he doing here?" I thought, a bit surprised. Tip's wife and son were there, too. After dinner and coffee, O'Neill got up and mentioned that he and Joe Gavin came from the same Irish part of Boston and bantered about that. Then, I'll never forget what he said next. "And to Jimmy Boy and John Boy, (Kane and O'Brien) I have a debt of gratitude that I can never repay." Later I got hold of Dave Walsh, who was working with him on the PAC, and asked: "What the hell is this? How sticky are we with this guy? Are we getting carried away?" Walsh professed not to know. O'Brien was on the board of a little pewter company that Tip O'Neill's son Tom owned. Then his company's little pewter knickknacks showed up in the flight shop in the plant. Besides that, there was talk about a new building for Grumman Data Systems that purportedly O'Neill, the Kennedys, and Kane were going to fund and Grumman would lease back. That fell through because people began to get nervous. Bob Watkins remembers that Tom O'Neill, who also worked in insurance, was going to get a piece of Grumman's pension business. Though I was gone, I got the impression it was beginning to smell too much for straitlaced Grumman.

Watkins, when he left, picked Dave Walsh to succeed him in running the political action committee. Obviously the chief salesman for the company could benefit from the background. But then, Watkins said, some PAC money went to Tom O'Neill's run for governor of Massachusetts. "Were I running the PAC," Bob told me, "I would have stopped that immediately. That was not why I was taking money from employees to give to the son of somebody who was running for governor of a state that had nothing to do with us. Granted, you could understand why you'd want to please the speaker of the house. I have to say, though, when I got on the shuttle and he didn't recognize me, I took that as an affront. Didn't he remember I was the guy who flew him to Hyannisport for four weekends?"

During the Ill Wind investigation, Bob Watkins was questioned by the U.S. attorney in Brooklyn, who had agents from Naval Intelligence and the Federal Bureau of Investigation with him. Soon enough it became clear to Bob that the thrust was all about Aeropac and John O'Brien, as the indictment later confirmed, not about the

Grumman PAC. In fact, despite his apprehension, he thought the investigators were almost complimentary about the way the Grumman PAC was run. And Bob didn't know much about O'Brien or Aeropac to relate. At the very end of the session, the U.S. attorney asked whether Watkins had a closing statement. He did, and he said, "I believe that a lot of very bright guys did a lot of very dumb things, not malicious or criminal but dumb. Knowing John O'Brien as I did, sitting in an office next to him for ten years and having talked to him frequently, I felt his arrogance got in the way of common sense. John O'Brien to this day, with some exceptions, doesn't think he did anything wrong. What John thinks he did wrong was that he got caught."

Whatever the judgment on John O'Brien, his fall was a sobering prelude for the wrenching defense companies went through in the 1990s—and of harder times to come for Grumman. While it may not have had any direct effect on Grumman's fate, it couldn't have come at a worse time, a time when the company needed inspired leadership and supersensitive insight.

13

THE M WORD AGAIN

JUNE IN THE SUMMER OF 1985 AS USUAL WAS SPAWNING VISIONS OF cool, country glades among those crowding Wall Street's narrow downtown streets whose width dated from the era of the horse car, not the jet airplane. Archie Albright as an outside Grumman director was restless for another reason, and he decided to vent his feelings on paper. As a symbol of Jack Bierwirth's choice to shift the Grumman Corporation's board of directors from insider weighted to outsider weighted, Albright was a former vice president of a famed and now-vanished Wall Street investment house, Drexel, Burnham, Lambert. He possessed something of the traditional investment community skepticism still alive then that perceived the aviation or space business as a coven of visionaries who could build exotic contraptions but would never make money. These were the pre-dot.com days when prudence and risk premium were still principles in the investment fraternity.

So, to his friend Bierwirth, Albright wrote a "Dear Jack" letter:

The recent flurry of speculation in the newspapers with respect to Grumman's potential status as a takeover candidate has moved me to set forth the following thoughts, which have been on my mind for sometime.

My view of corporate America today is that it is basically divided into two classes of corporations: the expanding acquirers and the quiescent takeover candidates. The corporations that are standing still or retrenching end up sooner or later on somebody's "takeover" list.

On the other hand, the corporations that are growing, expanding, and acquiring are rarely challenged. Can you imagine anyone targeting Ed Hennessey and Allied as a takeover candidate—or Harry Gray and United Technologies?

Grumman has gone through four or five years of pruning to eliminate some of its earlier misadventures—solid waste disposal, solar panels, and the bus business, most notably. In the meantime, there has been no significant effort to "grow" the corporation, except as a beneficiary of Reagan's expanded military budget.

It was over three years ago that a management team targeted the electronics industry as the #1 priority for a major diversification by Grumman. As far as I am aware, there is no immediate prospect that a major—or even minor—electronics acquisition will be made in 1985.

Right or wrong, much of the outside world clearly views Grumman as stagnating, with relatively flat earnings projections. In my opinion, this impression will continue to place Grumman on potential takeover lists, in spite of our previous success in fending off the LTV takeover. I strongly urge the management and the Board to reexamine Grumman's long-range planning and diversification strategy, in an effort to recreate both the image and reality of a vigorous growth company.

If any one event could be called a tocsin for Grumman's future for its second fifty years, Albright's letter was it. Not that it was a panicked call to battle stations. Two programs for the A-6 and the F-14 were in gestation to carry the company into the 1990s, even though neither would fully replace the cash generation of the four aces in the golden ten years before. Nonetheless, events were marshalling elsewhere. The next year would see the peak of the Reagan defense buildup, the high point in procurement that began to slide as Secretary of Defense Caspar Weinberger tried to cut a deal with an increasingly hostile Congress on the dimensions of future defense spending. The wheezing Soviet economy had begun to stagger under the pressure of the Reagan defense spending challenge and its own internal strains and popular disaffection. Whether anyone then could foresee the suddenness of the collapse of the Soviet Union was doubtful, but Albright's incredulity about Allied Signal was right at the time, although a merger with Honeywell at the end of the century obfuscated matters. Nevertheless, his questions were prescient in the light of the consolidation of the defense industry that followed in the 1990s.

Bierwirth wrote a "Dear Archie" reply to Albright within a week and promised to pass his letter along to other members of the board. But Bierwirth was cool to his idea and did not hesitate to disagree explicitly with one of his director-bosses:

I have got to admit that you sound more influenced by your days in Wall Street than your days at Stauffer Chemical. I realize that in Wall Street corporations are divided into those who acquire and those who are acquired. But I would put to you the proposition that there is still a place for those who work hard to develop products and grow through the productivity of their own operations. Making deals is not really what business is all about.

You can see that you and I have a real philosophical difference. At the same time, we have been prepared to acquire companies that wanted to be acquired and fitted into our growth pattern. As you know, this has tended to be smaller companies, most in the data processing areas. Interest in our electronic side is beginning to grow now that we have a separate Electronic Systems Division, but there is no way I can promise you that we will succeed in a major merger in that area.

I would also agree with you that the standard Wall Street view of Grumman is that we are stagnating. A large portion of Wall Street can only measure a company by its announced earnings per share. Buying in one's own shares and thereby increasing the earnings per share is viewed as growth by those people. Spending development money and reducing one's earnings per share is viewed by them as decline or stagnation. Happily for Grumman, we are attracting more and more investors who are concerned about real growth and the opportunities that are open to Grumman. Whether there are enough of them to make a difference in the price of our stock remains to be seen.

I can say this to you, however: only once before in my business experience have I seen an organization with as great an opportunity for growth, development and diversification as is now the case for Grumman. The major contracts on which we have the best chance of winning as against all of our competitors would alone tend to reshape this company if we were successful in all of them. The other major contracts where I am unable to gage the odds on Grumman's success could be of equal importance in the long run.

These opportunities come very rarely. Total success would strain our financial capabilities, but is of course unlikely. I can say in all honesty that a reasonable percentage of success in these efforts would bring far greater benefits to Grumman than the acquisition of a company which in all likelihood will have prospects far poorer than Grumman. We do not have the financial or human resources to win and to acquire.

Those two letters, among other things, clearly stated the conflicting views of Wall Street and companies on a host of issues, not just acquisitions. Industry was and still is uncomfortable with what managers consider Wall Street's excessive preoccupation with quarterly earnings and the short term. Bierwirth shared this view that such preoccupation inhibited industry investment in research and development. Albright, for his part, was hardly alone in thinking about merger as a way of building muscle for survival. I was on his side, and had been.

A month later Bierwirth wrote a memo about mergers to the top officers at Grumman, including me, Joe Gavin, and John F. Carr, then general counsel. "At any given time," it said, "Grumman, at some level, is in conversation with as many as half a dozen companies or their representatives exploring possible mergers. Many of these are small private concerns seeking a buyer, but some may be publicly held." That is, some could be sizable. The point of the memo was to tell everybody to clam up, because of a then new Securities and Exchange Commission warning about special risks in making any public comment on mergers. As Bierwirth pointed out, merger activity at the time and merger rumors about Grumman in particular had affected trading in Grumman's stock. Insider trading for a quick killing, though not likely, was always a danger to the company and its reputation. Paul Thayer, who later made a run on Grumman, was involved in just such a situation when he headed LTV, helping out friends.

Nevertheless, Bierwirth was consistent on mergers. Before he retired, he told an interviewer for *Financial World* in 1987 that the company was looking for joint ventures to use its electronics capabilities, which went back to the formation of Grumman Data Systems. At that time, Grumman had just established a subsidiary in New Jersey called Tachonics to produce integrated circuits. These were based on the latest technological buzzword at the time, gallium arsenide. In fact, Bierwirth predicted that Grumman would team with a major commercial aircraft or computer manufacturer in a joint venture or ventures, as opposed to expanding its military business. That was simply bowing to reality in that Grumman's bread-and-butter programs, like the A-6 and F-14, were running down, as was its cash flow, and only the JointSTARS surveillance and tracking system, one of the few air force programs the company had won, had a chance to grow. Those joint venture plans, Bierwirth said, "should scotch all rumors that Grumman is going to be bought up by another company." Boeing was the rumored candidate for a combination at that time.

Eight months after the Albright letter the alarm rang again. Grumman had put to bed its 1986 operating and financial plan when it became obvious that there was no way to meet the profit target. Early that year, now over in corporate, I sent a take-action memo to my top aides. Both upgrade programs for two of Grumman's core programs were in place then, a re-engined modified F-14D that survived and a re-engined version of the old faithful attack aircraft, designated the A-6F, that didn't. At the same time the E-2C early warning aircraft was selling overseas as a lower-cost version of the Air Force's E-3 AWACS airborne warning and control aircraft. Even so, the implication was growing that if Grumman couldn't find its own new programs to generate the revenue it needed to support a major defense contractor's payroll and overhead, it would have to buy them.

Lew Evans, whose expansionist ideas infected me, would have walked the acquisition trail, and I was convinced he was in this mode when I moved up from the Cape to run product engineering. I began to make noises about buying Northrop and was told that, in my position, I should shut up. After I became president of aerospace, one of the first ideas I launched at Gavin was that Grumman ought to take over or at least try to get in bed with Charlie Kaman. Kaman designed and produced its own helicopters near Hartford, just across Long Island Sound, but it also built the tail feathers on the A-6 and the F-14. Diversification galore there, for Kaman, a fine musician, designed and built the Ovation guitar, and manufactured ball bearings along with a rotary wing. Williams International was another appealing company to take over, and Joe Gavin knew its founder, Sam Williams. But Sam Williams was pretty independent, and his company at Wall Lake, Michigan, that built small jet engines soon hit it big with cruise missile power plants. Raytheon wasn't that enormous in those days and could have been another opportunity. Gavin also knew Brainerd Holmes, one of Raytheon's senior officers running Apollo at NASA, where Brainerd made his name. Joe Shea had moved up to Raytheon from NASA as well. Raytheon was in Boston; we were just down on Long Island. Both were high-integrity, high-tech companies and we had interfaces. In my castle I dreamt of Grumman starting an acquisition program: Kaman, Williams, Raytheon, then later going after Northrop, then Hughes. Grumman could have parlayed itself into an aerospace conglomerate as big as Lockheed Martin. None of these merger proposals, and they were more than just "what-ifs," ever went beyond Jack Bierwirth's desk to the board.

No question, this was an inexperienced entrepreneur feeling his way along, a neophyte, a homegrown variety of manager. That's where Grumman had a weakness. Most of us had grown up in the family-oriented Grumman, a good company, but no fabulous salaries and for years very few vice presidents. McDonnell had a dozen or two dozen when we had five or six. Offices were bland; there were no bonuses for many years, no stock options for the rank and file. Other companies were outstripping us on all these perks. Archie Albright used to question me, though Jack always thought he was finagling around. "You're an outside director," I would answer. "You should ask these questions of someone else." Nevertheless I did suggest to Archie that the directors form a committee to review some of the proposals inside the company that Jack was buying. That is, a business development committee to look at windmills and solar panels and all that. Archie made it happen, and I was on the committee for about two meetings. Then Jack just removed me without explanation and put me on the international committee instead. I always felt he didn't want me to pollute other minds.

With Paul Thayer and his LTV attempt, Bierwirth had had a brush with a takeover threat after he came aboard, which could have spooked him about mergers. Paul picked his timing, Bierwirth said, for Bierwirth and his wife, Marian, were on the *Delta Queen* on the Mississippi when Thayer made his announcement. "At the time," he recalled, "I was the only one who really had any Wall Street experience. With me not here, I'd say Grumman was more vulnerable than it would have been otherwise. LTV, which had paid a dividend just before the announcement and pumped up the books of the company, bid about twice Grumman's market price. We had enough money in our pension fund so that if LTV could have got control of Grumman, it could have unlocked the pension fund. It was legal at that time to dissolve the pension fund and Thayer could have used its cash to pay for the acquisition and to pay all its other debts."

LTV itself was a candidate for bankruptcy, but the battle was a tough one because of the price offered. Yet Grumman didn't have to give up anything or find a white knight to buy in and fend off the outsider. Grumman's biggest risk was allowing the pension fund to buy some of the Grumman stock, which got the trustees into legal trouble. LTV folded first, into bankruptcy.

"One of the most interesting things," Bierwirth added, "was that a lot of the employees came around to see me to ask how to keep something like this from happening again. I would say, 'Well, if you own more than half the stock, they have to come in the front door and ask you on bended knee. They can't nail you in the alley.' For the next three years, the retirees and the employees really didn't sell any stock at all. When I arrived and we were going bankrupt, or could have, we stopped giving people raises but they could set aside part of their salary in a savings plan. Grumman, for every dollar the employees saved up to 6 percent of their salary, would pay 25 percent in Grumman stock. I went to the board and said these people aren't getting raises. You ought to change that 25 percent to 50 percent, and the board bought it. Obviously if you have a stock very deeply depressed and have an employee force saving everything they possibly can, the amount of stock that would be eaten up would be huge. At the time, the total market value of Grumman stock was $52 million. So at a very rapid pace, employee ownership got up pretty close to 30 percent. If you take the retiree ownership, it grew into the 40 percent range. When I left, it was about 55 percent. It never occurred to me we would have to resist a takeover attempt, but the effect made a big difference."

Bierwirth was eight years gone when the Northrop acquisition came along. His view now is that the price was such that the retirees were all going to be made rich and consequently the management recommended it. So there was no battle. Considering the conditions at the time, there wasn't that much fight left in Grumman about it. "A lot of the airplane contracts were running out," he said, "and the company was cashing itself in at a very rapid rate." If he were still on the bridge, would he have fought the Northrop or Martin bids? No. Could he have bootstrapped the company into an electronics house? "With hindsight," he said, "you can be a lot smarter than you were at the time. Grumman when I left had, in its data processing division, a company doing roughly $800 million a year. It was much bigger than

Cisco or all these other hotshot companies you read about in the papers now. And Grumman had the know-how, thanks to the moon program originally."

That's unfulfilled destiny. Grumman had a huge reservoir of technology. If somebody had said, We have $800 million, and instead of paying off all of our bond and bank debts, let's use some to acquire companies, we could have turned it into quite an electronics company. Bierwirth contends that doing so would have been a problem among the people who thought they were aircraft engineers. But I argued that Northrop had already made the transition from its origins as primarily a tin-knocking outfit. Not only did it buy what was once Westinghouse's defense electronics business, but it also acquired Logicon, which is doing great. Bierwirth agreed: "Grumman could have done it."

Traumatic as the final takeover might have been, Grumman had plenty of experience with mergers over the years. Grumman wasn't always the target either. Right after the World War Two, Boeing was in trouble, notwithstanding its success and long production run for the famous B-17 Flying Fortress and the B-29 that dropped the atom bombs on Japan. Bill Zarkowsky, then a rising engineer, and Jake Swirbul went out to Seattle many times. Boeing could no longer obtain financing, and the government wanted Grumman to take a look. Swirbul wanted to enlarge the company. Roy Grumman wanted to keep it small and under control. But Swirbul and his associates had bought a lot of Boeing stock and sent several teams to Boeing, as well as lawyers and accountants. "We had reached the stage where one of the conferences was to define the name of the two companies," Zarkowsky said. "We did not have a controlling interest at that point, but it was pretty close. However, the bankers of Seattle finally realized they better back Boeing to keep ownership at home." And they did. Boeing went under the control of the banks in Seattle and stayed independent.

"Boeing and Grumman were a good match," Zarkowsky thought. "The basic Boeing company back in those days was very much like the Grumman company. Very intimate. I don't think it was unionized then, which was one of things Roy Grumman was sensitive to."

Zarkowsky said he and Thornton (T.) Wilson, who later became chairman and CEO of Boeing, grew up in the industry together. Both were in their respective aerodynamics departments and they related to each other. Both changed career paths from technicians to management for the same reason and rose to the top. Zarkowsky was frustrated that he couldn't sell his ideas, so he thought he better understand the other half of the business—hence his case that Boeing and Grumman would have been a good match.

To make the point again, Grumman was no stranger to merger approaches. Charlie Bluhdorn's run, I mentioned before, happened when the F-14 competition came along. Bluhdorn suspected Grumman was the favorite and began buying Grumman stock, accumulating just under 10 percent, the point at which he would have to disclose his buying publicly, thus ratcheting up the price. Grumman knew somebody was buying but not that it was Bluhdorn specifically. John Carr as general counsel was following the saga and eventually verified that Bluhdorn was the mastermind, buying in different names. Although he had a reputation as a raider, Bluhdorn, says Carr, was a very patriotic guy. He wanted to be in the defense business, for patriotic reasons as much as anything. And he had a retired admiral on his board encouraging him. Bluhdorn and his president visited Grumman and proceeded to cite all the acquisitions in which people had opposed him and how they had come to a bad end. He claimed that he just wanted to make an investment, that he wasn't interested in acquiring the company. Well, maybe later on. Charlie Bluhdorn had a simple strategy: just playing conglomerates, buying up random companies.

Then Bluhdorn cooled off, when, coincidentally, the Navy called him and "hinted around" that it didn't want Gulf & Western taking over one of its major contractors. As Bluhdorn started selling some of the stock, Grumman was getting tips from a friend at one of the brokerage firms when a block was on the market. Since Clint Towl was spending a lot of his time shuttling back and forth to Florida no one at the top was around. Carr on his own began buying the stock with Grumman's money and employees also were buying. Grumman holdouts against mergers were counting on the same fact that had blocked earlier takeovers by LTV and by Gulf & Western: more than half of Grumman's stock was held by employees or relatives and the company's investment plan.

About this time Grumman went through an insider-outsider phase. Joe Gavin picked up a bug that what we needed was someone who could do what Northrop's Tom Jones could: get into the secretary of defense's office. "Tom Jones is beating us to the punch," Gavin complained as he called me over to his office when I was running aerospace. "George, I want us to hire a headhunter." Not that I knew what he meant by someone who goes in and out of the SecDef's office. Okay, Joe. In comes the headhunter with three or four names and we hired one, Danny Huebner, from General Electric and an aeronautical engineering graduate from Minnesota. Danny was a picture, smoking a pipe, dressing meticulously, always giving a good impression. Jack Bierwirth could hardly wait to get him into the boardroom to make a pitch.

In the interim, I called in Renso Caporali and Tom Kane and told them we had a gaping hole while we looked for somebody outside. "Hold hands and run this operation in the meantime," and they did, until Huebner came in to sit on top of them as senior vice president. Then Cappy went on to run the technical department and Jack Bierwirth went on a binge naming vice chairmen. As Jack put it to me once, "We can make a bag full of vice chairmen." Cappy moved up to vice chairman of technology, John Carr vice chairman of the Washington office, and I think Huebner became a vice chairman as well. All of this was short-lived. Danny Huebner had talent, but he was not accepted by either Cappy or John O'Brien, and O'Brien finally chased Huebner out of the company with a package that sent him home happy. Bierwirth left six or nine months early. When O'Brien's troubles followed the search committee talked to a big-name outsider at United Airlines. The league was too much for us. The committee decided to stay in house and promoted Cappy. Bob Anderson, a former financial head at Ford Aerospace, came in wielding a hatchet and began to tell the board that Grumman ought to merge. As he told me at one of our luncheons when I was consultant, "George, Grumman can't go on like this, carrying these expensive engineers with no new programs coming." Handwriting on the wall time, it was.

Although I had misgivings when I retired from Grumman in 1986, I had no way of knowing that the world would turn upside down by the next decade, not just for my company but for the whole defense industry. The Berlin Wall started coming down in 1989 and East and West Germany reunified the following year. Defense procurement funding, after a bubble during the Gulf War, went over a cliff, falling by half toward the end of the 1990s. Bush lost to Bill Clinton in 1992, and Clinton brought William J. Perry into the Defense Department to become deputy secretary of defense and then successor to Les Aspin, whom the president fired. Perry's famous dinner with an invited group of defense industry leaders gave them a shock. Not enough money was going to come out of DoD, he said, to keep all their companies in business. Consolidate, he said, and in effect, don't worry about antitrust. Norm Augustine, the witty author of Augustine's Laws, which chronicled the aberrations of the defense business by following a hypothetical program through its development disasters, and eventual chairman of the merged Lockheed Martin colossus, called it "the last supper."

Before I left, there were two turning points. One had come with Northrop and the A-12 that I talked about. The other was Grumman's winning bid, to much astonishment in the electronics community, of the air force–army JointSTARS program for airborne battle management. Reminiscing with me in his office in 1999, Marty Dandridge told me that JointSTARS—and to a lesser degree the E-2C—was the jewel that brought Northrop into the bidding for Grumman after a deal had already been sealed with Martin Marietta. Marty, at the time of our discussion, was then general manager at Northrop Grumman's Melbourne, Florida, facility where the electronics fitting out of refurbished 707s is done to make up what became the E-8C.

JointSTARS began before I left, with a call from Newton Spiess probably in 1983. "Go out to Calverton," he said. "There's something there I think Grumman ought to put a little money into." I did go, and at the west end of Plant Seven was a short, portly engineer with hair down to here named Gerald McNiff. What he had was a synthetic aperture interferometric radar. A good 50 percent of its technology went right over my head, but it had application for finding and tracking ground targets that moved. I did try to interest the Navy in a radar-guided weapon system for the A-6, specifically at the next semiannual contractor gathering where the leadership talked about the five-year defense plan and budgets. Adm. Tom Hayward, who was chief of naval operations then, told the team that had been sent down to brief him that it sounded great but the Navy didn't have any more money to put into the A-6. Eventually Grumman got a small contract for the RGWS, radar-guided weapon system.

Then the Pave Mover radar program came along. "We're not going to do this with all of our independent research money," I said. "Get this new guy from Norden, Peter Scott." Scott I remember as a cigar-smoking entrepreneur who started Scott's Electronics before he went with United Technologies. Newt Spiess and Grant Hedrick brought him down to Bethpage. "Grumman is going to put a couple of million dollars into this thing to go after Pave Mover," I told him, "and I want you to match that." Scott groaned: "I'm a new guy on job. Harry Gray will kill me." Harry was still chairman of United then. "No free rides here," I answered. "We're going to win this thing, and you think you're just going to build all the radars? Baloney. You're going to have to match." Scott was puffing away on his cigar and dragging his feet. "Go home and tell them that this is the deal," I said. He was a big boating man, and he finally called me from the Fort Lauderdale yacht basin to say all right. But he warned me his tail was on the line. Pave Mover turned out very well. Grumman beat out Hughes and put a twelve-foot radar on an F-111, essentially a half scale to what the JointSTARS radar is today. Pave Mover, Marty Dandridge says, is what is referred to around the Melbourne JointSTARS facility as the enabling technology for JointSTARS. The Air Force paid a lot of attention to that.

Then came the competition for JointSTARS, which meant a lot of haggling back and forth over what airplane would carry the electronics system. Because the Army was involved with its own ideas, it wanted a helicopter-borne system. A key House Armed Services Committee staffer, Tony Battista, wanted to put it in a U-2. Eventually the Air Force got the 707 commercial airliner it wanted, which could house eighteen consoles with displays plus all the data processing and cooling systems to go with them. "Grumman's technology and concepts were the driver," Marty related. "We were told later on that, although we also were the low bidder, if we had been the high bidder we would have been chosen anyway. That didn't make anybody feel too good, because this was a fixed-price development contract, worth $657 million." The government was hooked on fixed-price development then. "Either you took them or you got nothing,"

When the word became imminent about the JointSTARS award in October 1985, I was sitting in my office on an edgy morning while Hurricane Gloria blew through the place sending most people home. Lt. Gen. Melvin F. (Nick) Chubb Jr., commanding the electronics center at Hanscom Air Force Base in Massachusetts, where the competition was run, called me at around eleven o'clock. "You guys won this thing," he told me, "but don't you dare let anybody know about it." It was a Friday, and I had to keep quiet until the formal announcement came after the stock market closed. That meant fending off the local congressman when the word began to leak. It was a big surprise on Wall Street that Grumman had run against Westinghouse and Hughes, the big radar bananas, and won it all.

Before the award we had to go through the BAFO process contractors despised, the best and final offer with the last pitch on the numbers. Even before we won the contract, there erupted the first of many crises that stressed the program into the next decade. General Chubb came down for a reliability review in Plant Five. It was a long drawn-out thing, with big presentations, and I didn't sit through it all. That gave the general a chance to ask to see me privately, and we sat down in the boardroom where Lew Evans used to operate. "I'm worried about something," the general said. "Grumman has in its proposal that you're going to do this down in Florida." Indeed the plan was to move the work off Long Island, isolate it from the rest of the Grumman world, and focus on it in a much smaller center. "How," Chubb then asked, "are you going to get guys to move, like that young kid McNiff?" This was a shock because Grumman had already cut some good deals with Melbourne for the facility we were to build at the Melbourne airport, which was an F6F operational training base in World War Two.

"General, we can do it," I argued, citing the lunar module program at the Cape nearby as an example of what a big team of two thousand people had eventually started from zero. "I lived and worked down there five years so I think I have a pretty good idea of what's involved in getting the site activated and off and running. In fact they'll report directly to the president." He demurred, still dubious whether Grumman could get the talent down there, especially the software developers. His reluctance hit me with the thought, "Oh, god. Are we going to be aced out because we picked Florida?" The last thing he did was to urge me to talk to Abe Goo, who then ran Boeing Wichita. "He tried to do something like that," Chubb said, "and it didn't work out." I called Abe Goo and then pulled Albert Verderosa, Marty Dandridge's boss, from the reliability meeting. He left that night for Wichita. What he found out was that Boeing's situation was totally different and we stated as much in an explanatory letter. Eventually, years later and after a lot of strain, Chubb decided that JointSTARS was an example of how to run a program. Marty Dandridge agreed with that, "He loved us after a while."

While the Melbourne facility was being built controversy flowed over when to move the team from New York. "This engineer, that engineer doesn't want to go," Marty recalled. "Frank Milordi [who is] running engineering management and still does in Melbourne, wouldn't come." October then November of 1986 rolled around, and the building was getting ready in Melbourne, where we had sent teams to work with the contractor. "Finally I went over to see Verderosa, whom I worked for," Dandridge recalled, and he told him: "Al, we've got to go." "Maybe we ought to wait until critical design review," he answered. "No, we either fish or cut bait. As far as I'm concerned, we're going over Christmas. We're leaving, getting out of New York. If someone doesn't want to come we'll replace him. We have to go. We're foundering here, screwing around." Al agreed finally.

Still there were holdouts, including McNiff, always the bright guy, but who didn't like to manage, and a few other smart people. "McNiff has got to come," Dandridge told Verderosa. "I don't care what you do, bribe him, whatever, he has to come. He's the ringleader. For the rest, if someone has a personal problem, we'll keep a small place in New York and get a secure telephone line." A bunch of system and software developers did stay there for a while. Verderosa convinced me that we needed to make McNiff a vice president, just one of many kinds of things we had to do. Eventually he gave in. "Within about two years, everybody who wouldn't come, came,"

Dandridge said. "These were all tried-and-true New Yorkers who just were not going to leave Long Island, where they grew up. Well, they're all here today, all happy they did come."

JointSTARS pricing was predicated on modifying used 707s, not buying new ones, which the original program envisioned. General Chubb in fact bought one of the last new ones on the phone in the Melbourne facility. He made a deal with Boeing and the Navy to take a TACAMO, 707-based E-6A submarine communications aircraft, No. 10, and divert it to the Air Force for JointSTARS and to pay the replacement costs at the end of the line for airplane No. 15. Within about six months, Boeing, squeezed at its Renton plant for space to build commercial 737s, decided to shut down the 707 line there. If the Air Force wanted any more new 707s, it would have to pay $500–800 million to reestablish the line at Boeing Wichita. Not only did the Air Force not have the money for a new 707 line, but it also turned down Boeing's fervent pitch to put JointSTARS either on a new 757 or 767, which was going to be a lot of money. For that matter, the Air Force decided not to use the new TACAMO airplane, which had the newer CFM 56 engines. Though much better than a used 707, there were extensive costs for modifying it from the used-707 baseline design.

Boeing, Grumman chairman John O'Brien, and John Betti, the Pentagon acquisition czar then, had a defense acquisition board review in a vault in the Pentagon, Dandridge recalled. Grumman proposed to continue production with used 707s to avoid buying new $150 million 757 or 767 transports. After selling the idea to the Air Force, Grumman sent a team around the world to find every one it could. Primarily Grumman did so because it believed that if it couldn't convince the government to go forward with used 707s, the program wouldn't go forward at all. "Plenty of 707s are out there selling for $3–4 million," he said, "often good ones. But some of the early ones Grumman bought were dogs and brought thousands of extra man-hours later in refurbishment."

Next came a dispute with Boeing. "Boeing was a subcontractor for the 707 to make the modifications," Dandridge recalled. "Boeing was a good subcontractor, but had an approach that this was just like a little flight test modification. Our specification required this airplane to be production configured. We had a lot of good aircraft

engineers, and they saw Boeing wasn't going to modify the environmental control system right. Rather Boeing just wanted to hot-rod up
the old system to run at about 150 percent of its design. This wasn't
going to be enough, and if we didn't keep the electronics cool, we
were not going to meet our specifications. Then we'd be redesigning
all these boxes."

Grumman directed Boeing in how to modify the ECS. Boeing
then sent Grumman a bill for $150 million, a claim. So Grumman put
together a counterclaim of $150 million. The two companies duked it
out for a time but eventually settled. Grumman agreed to do
aerostructures work for Boeing on other programs at a little less profit
for a few years. Out of it Grumman got a licensing agreement for the
707, what Dandridge said was the only licensing agreement ever issued
to anybody for Boeing's designs and drawings. Boeing decided it didn't
want to build 707s anymore. As a consequence, Grumman used the
license agreement and overhauled the 707s at Lake Charles, Louisiana.

What was the reasoning in going to Lake Charles, I asked Marty.
Grumman had completed the architectural and engineering work to
build enough hangar space in Melbourne to hold eight 707s. One
hangar today holds two, and there were to be three more modules,
but for the electronic and radome modifications. Corrosion and
structural refurbishment were going to be subcontracted someplace
else. Then a letter from then Democratic senator from Louisiana J.
Bennett Johnston went to Renso Caporali, who, as I said before, had
become chairman. The senator knew Grumman had JointSTARS,
and he suggested the facility at Lake Charles that Boeing had been
using. To the Melbourne troops the package looked like an action
item from the chairman. Two Melbourne people went over and came
back impressed. Lake Charles is a big facility and can hold twenty-two
707s at one time. It's the old Chenault Air Force Base, but the buildings were all new, built by the airport authority for Boeing.

Boeing's experience, part of Abe Goo's Wichita expansion, was an
omen for Grumman. Boeing had a five-year lease there, doing
modification on KC-135 tankers. Stabilizing the work force was
difficult, and Boeing eventually went out of that business. Another
Boeing facility in Mississippi, where it was going to manufacture the
A-6 composite wing that Grumman declined to bid on, ran into a
similar predicament. Grumman had already sunk $7–8 million to

finish the Melbourne architectural and engineering work, but Lake Charles not only was a nice facility, big and empty, but it was already constructed. "I went back out to meet with the airport authority," Marty said, and he made it clear: "There's going to have to be a compelling reason for us to change our mind." "Compelling reason? What's a compelling reason?" the director of the airport asked. "It's going to have to come down to money," Dandridge answered. They came back with a proposal to lease the facility for about seventy-six cents a square foot per year, for the first five years. Essentially free. For about 1.2 or 1.3 million square feet, the lease was a million dollars a year or $5 million over the term. So we took it. The Melbourne buildings would have been a $30 million capital investment.

"Lake Charles has been a real struggle," Marty went on, "for one thing because you can't get anybody to go there to live. While the people who do live there are good hard workers, it's a petrochemical town, not an aircraft town. Winter is cold, and it's hot as hell in summer—literally 120 degrees in the hangars. In the wintertime we have to heat them. Even with the heaters running, it's cold, and the airplane gets cold-soaked and hard to work on. Nevertheless Grumman built two airplanes there and delivered them on time to the Air Force. Then along came the Northrop merger."

Northrop split up what had been called Grumman Melbourne Systems, that is Melbourne and Lake Charles. "The George M. Skurla plant is really what it was," Dandridge said. Northrop had its California aircraft people take over the Louisiana operation, on which they made no profit and thus it failed to excite much interest for them. Gen. Lawrence Skantze, who retired as head of the former Air Force Systems Command, later wrote a report for the Defense Department on the grief that ensued. Refurbishing of the 707s was supposed to take fifty thousand man-hours and the first test airplane met that figure, General Skantze said. Then the Air Force re-equipped a batch of KC-135s with JT3D first-generation turbofan engines and sopped up used 707s on the market to extract their power plants. By the time JointSTARS was ready to buy, used 707s were no longer a buyer's market and the supply of good ones dried up for a while. Even the second JointSTARS 707 stayed on the man-hour target. But when the high-time 707s the Air Force had to buy came into the program, the hours bounced up to more like 350,000. The

Air Force had to put $900 million more into its budget to cover the cost growth.

Burdened by refurbishment and the organizational disconnect, deliveries stalled and the situation deteriorated to the point where the Air Force warned that it was going to have to issue a show cause to Northrop Grumman on why it shouldn't terminate JointSTARS production. The program had hit bottom, but Northrop's now retired CEO Kent Kresa simply asked Marty what he had to do to fix the program even though three different teams over three years hadn't made a dent. Total immersion was the answer, work it from the inside out. Kresa put Lake Charles back under Dandridge, and Dandridge's team worked for a year getting the program straightened out. By the following year, three airplanes came out of Lake Charles, and the first was two months ahead of schedule.

Grumman had hoped to sell thirty JointSTARS, but the requirement stayed at nineteen. Funding of $113 million for the seventeenth aircraft was released in 2003, but the Air Force is starting a new program called the multisensor command and control aircraft (MC2A) using a bigger Boeing 767-400 for the platform and fitted with a new radar. Northrop Grumman's Integrated System sector in California is heading a team which won a $112-million contract to adapt the company's multiplatform plus radar technology for the advanced system, called the airborne ground surveillance/cruise missile defense. All nineteen JointSTARS might eventually be funded, given the lead time to design new electronics and the intelligence-collecting performance in real time of the JSTARS in Kosovo, Afghanistan, and Iraq.

JointSTARS is making money now for Northrop Grumman after the long grind to integrate the program. Indeed the JointSTARS technology fits into Northrop's strategy, revised after its merger with Lockheed Martin was turned down, to deemphasize the airplane business and push deeper into electronics and surveillance. Whether the JointSTARS program will in fact work out as a crown jewel for Northrop is yet to be seen, but the billings at around $700 million a year were expected to drift up to $800 million with two new contracts. One is a radar improvement effort and the other is an indefinite delivery/indefinite quantity (ID/IQ) program for support. These are $1.2–1.3 billion contracts over their life. But as I pointed out to

Marty, a $1.2 billion program over five years is about $250 million a year. Burn time at those rates is too long for a big company.

Burn rate is important because it reflects costs for producing low-rate-production defense hardware, and costs had much to do with forcing the eventual merger with Northrop. As I've said before, the Navy and DoD criticized Grumman about its costs over the years and the last time I remember dealing with it was with John Lehman. When we partitioned the company into eight or nine separate operations with a president for each, Jack Bierwirth and I went down to explain to John how the efficiency gained would benefit the customer. In fact in one of his books Lehman makes the point that he whipped Bierwirth and me into line—and Sandy McDonnell, too—on holding down expenses. Congress and the services had a legitimate perspective in looking at all these individual companies trying to build airplanes and recognizing that each had an overhead to cover. Bill Perry wasn't the only one who wanted to see the mergers. When I did tell Bierwirth we ought to merge or marry and get into the twenty-first century, he astounded me with his answer—that I didn't understand the company. There I was sitting at the tail end of forty-three years of working my way through the shop up to the top, and he had been there about twelve years. "Oh, I don't?" I said, and just kind of smiled. At that moment a call came in from the Navy and I never picked up on that thought. Jack didn't want any outside merger, I think, because, lacking much aerospace history, his future at Grumman with any kind of an amalgamation could have vanished.

Export sales might have helped tide Grumman over. But the A-6 never got any overseas interest because of its old J52 engine. The E-2C was a small but steady seller to other countries, but just enough to keep the program alive. While Iran was the only export customer to buy the F-14, Pete Oram, who ran Grumman International in the 1970s, said there was other interest from Canada and from Australia. But the F-14 was expensive, in two ways. A two-man crew doubled people costs, and it was a relatively expensive and complicated investment from a maintenance standpoint. "The Aussies didn't have any money," Oram said. "They had vintage French Mirages, and U.S. F-111s were a maintenance headache. For the Canadians, two engines were an advantage over the Arctic regions. What Australia really wanted was an E-2C for customs. But the F-14 never got much serious consideration after Iran. One of the things you can't convince people is that the Canadians probably could have bought the F-14 in the quantities we're talking about for the same as they paid for F-18. Just one of those things."

Oram came back from International as senior vice president in Aerospace for aircraft and marine programs in the 1980s. When Caporali moved over as vice chairman for technology, he became president of the aircraft group. When he retired in late 1992 the merger pot was just beginning to bubble. Nothing had been discussed officially before he left, but Oram added: "What really was happening, to be honest, was that I was one of the ones pushing Cappy and his team to consider selling the company. We didn't have enough work going through. That was true even though the continuing E-2C and the EA-6B were not airplane but electronic programs. Airplanes sell for about $200 a pound, electronics for about $2,500 a pound."

If the Navy had bought the A-6F that could have carried the company along in hope something else would turn up. What had to happen then, and JointSTARS was part of it, is that Grumman needed to redirect what it was doing. Grumman had some absolutely fabulous systems people who had taken a lot of years to mature. But see how few airplanes people are building today. As for manufacturing, one of the big plants at Grumman, Plant Three, which made detail parts as well as massive wing skins, at the end was costing $10 million a year to maintain, operate, and produce $3 million worth of business. You can't stay around very long doing that. We needed to do what Kent Kresa has done. Say, "I'm not an airplane company, I'm a systems company." Northrop has done very well with that. McDonnell's acquisition by Boeing was a wallop, though. It had the world by the tail. What it says is that it takes stupendous amounts of capital to tide over a big defense company through the hiatuses in programs in the post–Cold War era. When Pete Oram went to work for Grumman in its salad days, between Grumman and Republic, there were seventy-two thousand people on Long Island involved in the aerospace business. There are six hundred now. And the few employees left at Bethpage fear the whole New York operation will close down eventually. Others, on the other hand, see a reprieve in the Joint Strike Fighter subcontract award possibilities.

Cappy, as the Grummanites called Renso Caporali, started running the company after John O'Brien's fall from grace. Though he sold the company, he has more admirers among the alumni than Jack Bierwirth and his ill-fated pro-diversification, antiacquisition strategy. Caporali brought in Bob Anderson as chief financial officer to package up the company for sale. From the day he came in, Stephen Wienberg as contracts manager could not get any more equity funding from the corporation to go after new commercial work. And in the commercial business everything had to be financed, or share the wealth as it's called. "So we were just dead," he said. "I never put two and two together until the merger happened. Now I know why. They were just trying to get the books balanced, the debt down, the profits up, the return on equity up."

Dick Dunne, who spent so many years at Grumman in public relations and on the line, was philosophic about the cuts prior to the merger in 1994. "Costs had to be cut," he told me after the merger. "Anderson, the chief financial officer at the corporate level, was ordered to get this company shipshape, and he did it. Emotions were out of the place, and all those things the Grumman people had learned to love and to have as a birthright were disappearing. Of course the finality was that the company was eventually going to be sold to somebody. Northrop was blamed for all the cutbacks, but, believe me, it got blamed for something it didn't do. The cost picture was already set."

In a sense the final merger was anticlimactic. Caporali cut a deal with Norm Augustine at Martin to buy Grumman at $55 a share. He considered that a good match, a navy airframe company with good electronics capability married with an information systems company with a good army and air force background. Northrop came in and raised it to $60. Bob Anderson ran a Chinese auction, giving each bidder two or three weeks for a best and final offer. Norm Augustine said flatly and publicly he would not play that game, refusing to get into a bidding contest. Northrop won, much to Caporali's dismay and distaste, and Caporali left Grumman to join Raytheon after Northrop took over.

Tom Kane, before he retired as marketing chief, was still around when the Northrop acquisition took place. But he calls it an occupation, not a merger. "When you had the Tom Jones approach to things," he said, "Northrop was a hell of a good company to work with. But under Kent Kresa they were a bunch of old ladies." Tom Jones, in Kane's view, was technically competent, and Kane had a lot of respect for him, especially his political astuteness. "I retired as a result of the acquisition," Kane said. "Kresa called me in and asked when I wanted to go to Los Angeles. 'I don't,' I answered, and then he said, 'You can consult then.' 'I don't want to do that either.' 'What do you want to do then?' I said, 'I want to go home.'" In other words, Kane was saying he didn't want to work for Northrop.

Grumman had agreed to a $55 a share offer from Norm Augustine at Martin Marietta, but earlier Kresa had called Cappy and said, "Let's get together." Cappy declined. Then Northrop came at it at $62 a share. Augustine just dropped out, and Grumman had to pay Martin $50 million bucks in penalties for failing to go through with the agreement. A Martin Grumman deal would have been good for Grumman, bringing more diversity. I saw Norm Augustine down in Florida at the Florida Institute of Technology where he was a guest speaker, and Norm repeated to me, "George, I'm not getting into any auction, that's it." Later Kresa complained bitterly to me that he had overpaid. Much as the old-time Grummanites disliked it, the extra $7 a share put a lot of money in their pockets. I think Cappy played the hand as best he could. When the higher offer came in, he was in a bind with the shareholders if he did anything else but agree. "I know Cappy personally would have preferred Martin," Kane said. "Among other things, he was a good friend of Augustine. Too bad Grumman didn't know how to be the aggressor."

That, to George, summed up the anticlimactic end of Grumman after all its glory days as the backbone of naval aviation: unfulfilled promise. To his last days, George was convinced that the new company could have been Grumman Northrop, creating another Lockhead Martin.

INDEX

Missileer, 47–48, 55, 62. *See also* Eagle
Mohawk, army aircraft project, 47, 155–56
Mur, Raphael, 49–50, 57, 93, 139, 150

NASA spaceflight: commercializing, 159;
early Apollo efforts, 83; Echo satellite,
81; Gemini, 9, 87–89; Mercury, 9, 40,
80–81, 87–89, 91; Orbiting
Astronomical Observatory (OAO), 81;
shuttle competition, 93–94; support,
86–87, 175. *See also* lunar module
Naval Air Combat Fighter concept, 70–72
Navy: A-12 stealth program, 182–83,
185–86; attitude toward Grumman, 6,
15, 20, 40, 42, 46, 75–77, 98–99, 104,
107, 118, 126, 174; Bureau of
Aeronautics, 38, 46; buying aircraft, 38,
49–50, 51–53; F6F, 5 (*see also Grumman
aircraft*); F-14 contract settlement, 108,
110–14; F-14X concept, 70; F-15
proposals, 62; foreign military sales
support, 126; Grumman dependence
on, 9, 45, 146, 149, 155; internal
arguments over F-14, 75–76;
lightweight fighter, 63, 70, 72 (*see also*
F/A-18); NASA work objections, 81;
quantity plans for F-14, 55, 60–61;
reaction to floats, 13; TBF, 7; V-5
program, 3
Nicoli, Reno, 20–21
Norden, 210
North American Aviation (later
Rockwell), 3, 16, 53–54, 90; AJ-Savage,
51; FJ-4B, 34, 50; F-86, 34; Sabreliner,
138
Northrop: A-12 partnering, 183–86; B-2,
159, 184–85; JointSTARS, 215–17;
merger with Grumman, 5, 10, 19,
24–25, 45, 160, 204–6, 209, 218–20;
offer to Skurla, 101–2; VAX, 50; YF-17,
68–71;

Ochenrider, Gordon, 168–69, 193–94; and
Warner letter, 170
Oram, Pete, 117, 171–72, 217–18
Orbiting Astronomical Observatory
(OAO), 81–82. *See also* space programs
OV-1: competition for, 155; versions,
155–56. *See also* Mohawk

Packard, David, 58–60, 69; and fly-before-
buy, 183

Paisley, Mel: and A-12 recompetition, 183;
fixed price development, 183, 186; Ill
Wind investigation, 166, 191; line
shutdown idea, 181–82
Palladino, Carl, 21, 163; F-14 losses,
108–10
Paulson, Allen, 138–39, 143–44
Pelehach, Mike, 97, 184, 188–90; Air
Force relations, 156; diversification,
150, 153–56, 161; F-14 design, 54, 103,
180; F-111B, 54; Gulfstream, 131–32,
156; Grumman international, 190
Petrone, Rocco, 85–86; lunar module
criticism, 89
Phoenix missile, 53–55, 59–61, 64, 70, 72,
111, 129
politics, 74, 173–74; political action
committees (Aeropac), 191–97
Pratt & Whitney. *See* engines

research and development, project startup
funding, 51–52
Rettaliata, Jack, 44, 167
Romano, Dennis, and Iranian flyoff,
114–17, 129
Rumpf, Richard L.: and A-6F cancellation,
186; Grumman/Navy relations, 171

Schoultz, Robert F. (Dutch): and EA-6B,
36–37; F/A-18 rationale, 66–68;
Grumman problems, 171, 179, 182
Schwendler, William, 11–13, 17–18, 20, 27,
29, 101, 188; and diversification, 149;
F8F design, 31, Gulfstream role, 136
Scott, Peter, 210
Scott, Walter, 80, 161
Sewell, Chuck, 115,
Simon, Robert, 191
Skantze, Lawrence, 159, 215
Skurla, George: as apprentice engineer, 1;
and diversification, 141, 152–53,
160–61, 163–64; diversification losses,
154, 159; expansionist ideas of, 203–4,
206; flight test engineering, 3, 40,
82–83; F6F line, 5–6; F-14 production
fixes, 103–6; Gulfstream sale regrets,
145; JointSTARS/Pave Mover role,
209–12; lunar module management
issues, 84–88; lunar module delivery
problems, 89–90; Navy fever, 2;
Northrop job offer, 101–2; product
engineering, 97–98; stress analysis, 13,
27, 29–33; structural flight research,
41, 82; truck bodies, 156–57; wife
Marie, 84, 103

ABOUT THE AUTHORS

George M. Skurla joined Grumman Aircraft Engineering Corporation in 1944 where he remained until his retirement in 1986. After his dream of being a naval aviator was frustrated by a back injury when he was still an aeronautical engineering student at the University of Michigan during World War Two, Skurla was hired as an apprentice engineer on Grumman's F6F Hellcat production line. He worked in stress analysis and flight test engineering before turning to operations. By 1974 he was president and chief operating officer of Grumman Aerospace Corporation. Two years later he was elected chairman of the board and chief executive officer, and a year before he retired he was named president of the division's parent, Grumman Corporation, and a member of the corporate executive committee. He died of pneumonia in September 2001.

William H. Gregory served in the U.S. Navy as an aviator in World War Two, flying Grumman F4F and FM-2 fighters off escort carriers in the Pacific. A graduate of Creighton University in Omaha, Nebraska, he worked as a reporter and copy editor at several midwestern newspapers, including the Kansas City *Star*, until joining *Aviation Week and Space Technology* in 1956, eventually becoming editor in chief in Washington in 1979. Gregory has written frequently on airline economics and operations, regulatory issues, technology policy, and lunar science. Currently editor at large for Armed Forces Journal International, he is the author of two other books, *The Defense Procurement Mess* and *The Price of Peace*.

The Naval Institute Press is the book-publishing arm of the U.S. Naval Institute, a private, nonprofit, membership society for sea service professionals and others who share an interest in naval and maritime affairs. Established in 1873 at the U.S. Naval Academy in Annapolis, Maryland, where its offices remain today, the Naval Institute has members worldwide.

Members of the Naval Institute support the education programs of the society and receive the influential monthly magazine *Proceedings* and discounts on fine nautical prints and on ship and aircraft photos. They also have access to the transcripts of the Institute's Oral History Program and get discounted admission to any of the Institute-sponsored seminars offered around the country.

The Naval Institute also publishes *Naval History* magazine. This colorful bimonthly is filled with entertaining and thought-provoking articles, first-person reminiscences, and dramatic art and photography. Members receive a discount on *Naval History* subscriptions.

The Naval Institute's book-publishing program, begun in 1898 with basic guides to naval practices, has broadened its scope to include books of more general interest. Now the Naval Institute Press publishes about one hundred titles each year, ranging from how-to books on boating and navigation to battle histories, biographies, ship and aircraft guides, and novels. Institute members receive significant discounts on the Press's more than eight hundred books in print.

Full-time students are eligible for special half-price membership rates. Life memberships are also available.

For a free catalog describing Naval Institute Press books currently available, and for further information about subscribing to *Naval History* magazine or about joining the U.S. Naval Institute, please write to:

Membership Department
U.S. Naval Institute
291 Wood Road
Annapolis, MD 21402-5034
Telephone: (800) 233-8764
Fax: (410) 269-7940
Web address: www.navalinstitute.org